WILLIAM SHAKESPEARE

William James
Remembered

Linda Simon

William James Remembered

University of Nebraska Press

Lincoln and London

Acknowledgments for materials in collections and previously published materials appear on pp. xxxi–xxxiii, which constitutes an extension of the copyright page. Manufactured in the United States of America. ♾ The paper in this book meets the minimum requirements of American National Standard for Information Sciences—Permanence of Paper for Printed Library Materials, ANSI Z39.48-1984. Library of Congress Cataloging-in-Publication Data. William James remembered / [compiled by] Linda Simon. p. cm. Includes bibliographical references and index. ISBN 0-8032-4248-4 (cloth : alk. paper) 1. James, William, 1842–1910. 2. Philosophers—United States—Biography.
3. Psychologists—United States—Biography. I. Simon, Linda, 1946–
B945.J24W475 1996 191–dc20 [B]
95-34521CIP

For Thilo Ullmann

CONTENTS

INTRODUCTION

In his own time, William James was the foremost philosopher and psychologist in America. His *Principles of Psychology, Varieties of Religious Experience,* and *Pragmatism* established him as an innovator who was creating, almost single-handedly, an original American philosophy for a democratic and culturally diverse community. James's articles in popular journals and his frequent lectures brought his ideas, rendered easily intelligible through lively anecdotes and wit, to a wide audience of ordinary men and women throughout America and Europe.

But it is not only his ideas that attract our attention and attracted the interest of his contemporaries. James energized the men and women who knew him. His contemporaries responded not only to what he said and wrote but to his charm and warmth. 'He was in a marked degree unpretending, unconventional, human and direct,' wrote Dickinson Miller, one of James's students at Harvard. At just over five foot eight inches, trim and spry, with lively blue eyes, James, even in old age, seemed spirited and vigorous. Wearing his favorite Norfolk jacket, red and black checked trousers, and one or another of his vibrantly colored ties, there was, his dour colleagues thought, an air of Bohemia about him.

This anthology brings together twenty-five memoirs by individuals who knew James in a variety of contexts: as a father, brother, friend, colleague, mentor. The writers testify to James's kindness and understanding, to his sprightly irreverence, to his unpretentious friendliness. 'Properly speaking,' James wrote in *The Principles of Psychology*, '*a man has as many social selves as there are individuals who recognize him* and carry an image of him in their mind.'[1] *William James Remembered* reveals many of James's social selves. But the writers here note with frequency certain recurring traits: James's enthusiasm for new ideas and new experiences, his optimistic support of his friends, his compassion, his energy.

William James was born in New York City on 11 January 1842, the first child of Henry James and his wife, Mary. Although there would be three other sons and one daughter in the James family, William, the first-born male, had a special role. He was his father's chosen son, the child bright enough and aggressive enough to fulfill his father's dream of success.

That dream is not easily understood. Henry Sr., liberated from the need to earn a living by an inheritance from his wealthy father, devoted himself to a quest for truth and enlightenment. Like his contemporaries Ralph Waldo Emerson and Bronson Alcott, Henry James was a lecturer and writer—but he never achieved Emerson's or Alcott's fame, and he suffered in their shadow. His writings on religion, marriage, education, and social issues reveal a man trying to reconcile the contradictions between his intellectual constructions and his visceral responses. He preached tolerance but could be remarkably insensitive to the feelings of others; he wrote that human beings were essentially good, but felt that self-love would interfere with one's belief in the goodness of God; he wrote that children should be free to discover their own identities but exerted overwhelming control within his own family. In his essays, he took on the voice of a benevolent man who had found peace through his special vision of the relationship between humans and their God; in his letters, he sometimes revealed a desperate, depressed, pessimistic misanthropist. 'My besetting sin is anxiety,' he wrote to a friend; 'and no sooner does any occasion for it arise, *ab extra,* than the whole "clanging rookery" of hell comes darkening the air, and settling down in my devoted bosom as if it were their undisputed nest.'[2]

He was, in short, a difficult man to have as a father, and he caused his children considerable distress. Even before the children could understand the ideas their father professed, they knew that he had the power to interpret reality and manipulate their lives. William, his brothers Henry, Garth Wilkinson, and Robertson, and their sister Alice did not go to school like other young children but were taught at home by a succession of tutors with whom their father, sooner or later, became dissatisfied. Nor did they grow up with a firm sense of home and community. Instead, they moved from New York to Europe, to Newport, Rhode Island, to Massachusetts, shuttling back and forth across the Atlantic in an attempt to find a place where their father felt fulfilled and productive. When they moved throughout Europe to England, Switzerland, Germany, and France, they made few friends. On a visit to Geneva as an adult, William recalled that at his last visit—when he was an adolescent—he had not seen the inside of any Swiss home.

Even before the children could read the essays and books that Henry Sr. published or could attend his lectures, they responded in confusion to his insistence that their identities be separate from anything they decided to do with their lives. Henry would not allow William to go to college, although he ardently desired to do so. Henry Sr. seemed to exalt the role of the artist, yet he discouraged William's interest in art, instead urging William to study science. Faced with William's unyielding desire to be an artist, he brought the family from Europe to Newport, Rhode Island, where William could study drawing and painting; when that enterprise failed—William felt he would be at best a second-rate painter—he permitted William to enroll in the Lawrence Scientific School. But suddenly Henry Sr.'s admiration of science lessened, and he insisted that William was training to become a technician rather than a philosopher. Since William did not publish any of his important works until after his father died, one may speculate that his intellectual career required a sense of liberation from his father's control.

After leaving the Lawrence Scientific School, William enrolled in the Harvard Medical School and graduated with a medical degree in 1869. He did not want to practice, however, and in a well-known letter to his friend Henry Bowditch, a fellow medical student, James proposed what he saw as an ideal partnership: 'you to run around and attend to the patients while I will stay at home and, reading everything imaginable in English, German, and French, distil it in a concentrated form into your mind.'[3] Although reading everything imaginable and distilling it for others eventually would become his career, James, then in his twenties, had no clear idea of his future. After graduating from medical school he spent the next few years in states of mind that ranged from lassitude to despondency. Although his friends were all training for medicine or the law, he was living at home with his parents, reading. 'I feel melancholy as a whip-poor-will,' he wrote to his brother Henry, who himself had escaped the nest by traveling in Europe.[4] Beset by many ailments—bad back, bad eyes, recurrent depression, digestive problems, and insomnia—he believed himself to be a sick man facing a dismal future.

In 1872, however, his life took an unexpected turn. His friend Henry Bowditch, seeking a replacement teacher for his course in anatomy and physiology, recommended James to Harvard's president Charles William Eliot. Eliot, in the third year of his presidency, wanted to expand Harvard's faculty. Because he did not want to increase costs for the college, however, he preferred to recruit young instructors who could perform competently for little remuneration—men of independent means especially attracted him—and his friends and neighbors offered a likely pool of candidates. Remembering James as his bright young chemistry student, and persuaded by Mary James that her son would benefit from a job, Eliot offered William a chance to teach anatomy and physiology.

When the offer came, James was in a state of depression alternating with anxiety. 'The fits of languor have become somewhat rarer,' he wrote to Henry, 'but what were the healthy intervals have been assuming . . . more and more of a morbid character, namely just the opposite, nervousness, wakefulness, uneasiness.' Although he seemed not to consider the possibility of making teaching his career, he saw the opportunity to offer some courses as possibly therapeutic. 'The appointment to teach physiology is a perfect godsend to me just now,' he wrote to Henry. 'An external motive to work, which yet does not strain me—a dealing with men instead of my own mind, & a diversion from those introspective studies which had bred a sort of philosophical hypochondria in me of late & which it will certainly do me good to drop for a year.'[5]

James's first course at Harvard, begun in January 1873, was Natural History 3: Comparative Anatomy and Physiology. James taught the material on physiology; his colleague Timothy Dwight, who shared the course, taught anatomy. After a month, James confided his reactions to Henry.

> I find the work very interesting and stimulating. It presents two problems, the intellectual one—how best to state your matter to them, and the practical one, how to govern them, stir them up, not bore them, yet make them work &c. I should think it not unpleasant as a permanent thing. The authority is at first rather flattering to one. So far, I seem to have succeeded in interesting them, for they are admirably attentive, and I hear an expression of satisfaction on their part. Whether it will go on next year cant [*sic*] at this hour, for many reasons, be decided.[6]

Eliot did offer James another year of teaching, but James vacillated before deciding. In May he accepted, but at the end of August suddenly changed his mind, deeming another year of teaching too tiring for his delicate disposition; instead, he would go to Europe. But this trip, like others before, did not result in an epiphany. He returned with the same doubts about his future but was willing to try his hand at teaching again. For the 1874–75 academic year he taught Natural History 3; the following year he added a graduate course on the relationship between physiology and psychology. The year after that he added Natural History 2: Physiological Psychology, using Herbert Spencer's *Principles of Psychology* as the textbook.

As he moved gradually from physiology to psychology to philosophy, James became a figure of power and authority at Harvard, taking part in the enormous changes that the college was undergoing at the turn of the century. When James began his teaching career Harvard had just over thirty faculty members for some six hundred students. The philosophy department, where James spent most of his career, offered a mere five courses taught by a staff of three: Francis Bowen, a long-time faculty member and staunch anti-Darwinist; Andrew Preston Peabody, a Unitarian minister who taught ethics; and George Herbert Palmer, President Eliot's new appointment. By the time James retired in 1907, the department had grown substantially: George Santayana, Hugo Münsterberg, Ralph Barton Perry, and Josiah Royce brought their diverse philosophical perspectives and teaching styles to the faculty. Dozens of courses were offered, including many in psychology; graduate level courses prepared Harvard doctoral graduates for positions at other major universities.

James took an active role in the development of the department. His correspondence with Charles Eliot reveals his recommendations of many men for full- or part-time teaching positions. Despite his notorious dislike of laboratory work, he recognized the importance of setting up adequate facilities for psychology experiments and planned and organized Harvard's new psychology laboratory—which, with great relief, he eventually handed over to Hugo Münsterberg to direct.

Many of the memoirs included in this collection were written by James's colleagues and students at Harvard. To many of his colleagues, James had the reputation for being an iconoclast, whose opinions sometimes seemed radical. The endeavor of philosophy seemed to mean something different to James than it did to them. 'He once said to me,' writes George Santayana, '"what a curse philosophy would be if we couldn't forget all about it!"' James's philosophical interests were shaped by his personality and background, and his philosophical wanderings were not systematic and rigorous but passionate and idiosyncratic. 'His excursions into philosophy,' reports Santayana, 'were accordingly in the nature of raids.' George Herbert Palmer notes that James's sympathies 'toward the under-dog' sometimes led James to support causes—and philosophers—that did not meet the approval of his colleagues. In the essays by Palmer, Santayana, and Perry, one can sense an undercurrent of irritation with James's unconventional enthusiasms.

Sometimes, too, apparent praise masked a hidden rivalry or subtle reproach. Hugo Münsterberg, for example, writes warmly of James's contributions to psychology, but nevertheless reveals implicit criticism by pointing out James's lack of interest in laboratory experiments and rigorous research. While Münsterberg praises James for 'the vividness and freshness with which he brings to life the most manifold inner experiences,' he is quick to remind us that 'such delightful intimacy and warmth may sometimes antagonize the bloodless abstract theories toward which each science after all must tend.' James may be popular with students, Münsterberg notes, but *real* psychologists prefer 'to overcome the capriciousness of life by stiff consistent principles.'

Yet James's students were not disturbed by his capriciousness, and they praised his ability to root himself in the concrete. Gertrude Stein, for example, who had adored James when she took his classes at Radcliffe, once exclaimed, 'Is life worth living? Yes, a thousand times yes when the world still holds such spirits as Prof. James. He is truly a man among men; . . . a scientist of force and originality embodying all that is strongest and worthiest in the scientific spirit; . . . a metaphysician skilled in abstract thought, clear and vigorous and yet too great to worship logic as his God, and narrow himself to a belief merely in the reason of man.'[7]

Although Stein did not write a memoir of her esteemed professor, other students offer ample testimony to James's quirky, exciting teaching style; his sincere interest in his students; and, despite his protestations to the contrary, his deep engagement with teaching. James urged his students to remain open to new ideas, new ways of thinking, new perspectives; he urged them to invent ways to complicate their lives. 'We are all to some degree oppressed, unfree,' he wrote in his essay 'The Energies of Men.' 'The threshold must be made to shift. Then many of us find that an eccentric activity—a "spree" say—relieves. There is no doubt that to some men sprees and excesses of almost any kind are medicinal, temporarily at any rate, in spite of what the moralists and doctors say.'[8] He encouraged his students, his audiences at lectures, and his children and friends to take action to effect change in their own lives.

His students' memoirs include George Angier Gordon's portrait of James at the beginning of his teaching career; an extensive, anecdotal essay by John Elof Boodin, who later taught at UCLA; praise of James's open-mindedness from noted political journalist Walter Lippmann; Dickinson Miller's testimony that James was not the 'impulsive and hasty thinker' that his critics charged; recollections by Edmund Delabarre, Roswell Angier, and Edwin Starbuck, who attended Harvard around the turn of the century.

James's reflections on education help us understand why he was such a beloved teacher. James believed that only an educated populace could achieve the highest ideal of democracy. In a community—Harvard—that saw itself as intellectually elite, and in a society that still debated the necessity for a privileged class, James's unwavering celebration of democracy was not always popular. One can imagine, then, James's applause for Walter Lippmann when the young man dared to criticize *The Privileged Class,* a reproach of the poor and laboring classes by James's colleague, English Professor Barrett Wendell. James believed that an educated populace would, and should, push to the vanguard its most worthy and moral leaders—and he believed that institutions of higher learning needed to serve this cause. A college education, he wrote, 'should *help you to know a good man when you see him.*'[9] A liberal education, James argued, must generate 'a lasting relish for the better kind of man, a loss of appetite for mediocrities, and a disgust for cheapjacks.'[10] This ability to discern gold from dross, so to speak, could happen only if students were taught to think for themselves, not through their indoctrination with any one philosophic system.

Indeed, James held a somewhat utopian ideal of the university as a community that tolerates all manner of thinkers, however unpopular their ideas. He confessed that because he never attended Harvard as an undergraduate he sometimes felt as if he were an outsider, but during his long career there he found many kindred spirits among both faculty and students. James was attracted to independent thinkers, to those who came to Harvard because 'they have heard of her persistently atomistic constitution, of her tolerance of exceptionality and eccentricity, of her devotion to the principles of individual vocation and choice.'[11] Certainly he welcomed such thinkers into the philosophy department, as colleagues and students.

James believed that philosophy should make students aware of spiritual and intellectual problems, not present them with a system of answers. 'What doctrines students take from their teachers,' he wrote early in his teaching career, 'are of little consequence provided they catch them from the living, philosophic attitude of mind, the independent, personal look at all the data of life, and the eagerness to harmonize them.'[12] For James this 'philosophic attitude of mind' meant 'the habit of always seeing an alternative, of not taking the usual for granted, of making conventionalities fluid again, of imagining foreign states of mind.'[13] He encouraged his students' quirky responses to class readings and life experiences; he wanted to know about them and eagerly questioned them about their backgrounds, families, hopes, and aspirations. Memoirs by such students as Dickinson Miller, Edwin Starbuck, and Roswell Angier attest to the sincerity of James's interest, his ability to make them feel valued and affirmed.

As soon as he firmly decided on teaching as a career, James realized that his credibility as a scholar—and marketability as a teacher—would be based in large measure on his publications. His letters, beginning in 1878, reflect the urgency he felt about making his name known in his field. Yet, though he published many book reviews and a few articles before his father died in 1882, James's first book, *The Literary Remains of the Late Henry James* (1884), was an edition of Henry Sr.'s writings that was a memorial to his father and an attempt by James to explicate for himself and readers the essence of his father's ideas. That task recurred throughout his career, as he addressed the same questions of religion, morality, and identity with which his father had struggled.

While James worked on *The Literary Remains,* he also began a major undertaking, *The Principles of Psychology,* which he contracted to write for his friend, the publisher Henry Holt, in 1878. *The Principles* turned into a twelve-year project that resulted in one of the most important psychology textbooks of the time.

James Rowland Angell helps us understand why readers responded to the book with such enthusiasm. 'Who does not remember the sense of glowing delight with which we first read the pages of the big, cumbrous, ill-bound and rather ill-printed volumes,' Angell recalls. Finally students had a textbook that insisted on psychology as a discipline separate from philosophy, and one that drew upon the most recent scientific research. As much as James complained about working in a laboratory, he recognized that the future of psychology depended on its being validated as a science. 'Physical science,' he wrote as early as 1876, 'is becoming so speculative and audacious in its constructions, and at the same time so authoritative, that all doctrines find themselves, willy-nilly, compelled to settle their accounts and make new treaties with it.'[14]

James's treaty was not a capitulation to scientific method or goals. James roundly opposed both reductionism (which explained mental processes by reducing thought to interactions of atoms within molecules) and the quest for a unifying theory to explain thought and feeling. When James first began teaching psychology he had used Herbert Spencer's *Principles of Psychology* as a text. But he soon discovered that he disagreed intensely with Spencer's application of Darwin's theory of evolution to the development of human personality. He argued against Spencer's portrayal of personality as 'absolutely passive clay, upon which "experience" rains down. The clay will be impressed most deeply where the drops fall thickest, and so the final shape of the mind is moulded.'[15] He also argued against Thomas Huxley's materialist view that feelings are the result of nervous processes, 'juxtaposed . . . without mutual cohesion, because the nerve-processes to which they severally respond awaken each other in that order.'[16] Instead, he offered his own definition of personal consciousness that rooted the self in experience: an individual experiences thoughts, perceptions, and feelings; the memory of these mental processes give the individual a sense of self.

James was impatient with scientists who based their theories solely on experimental data, as if they themselves, and their own senses of self, were not factors in creating those theories. 'The desire on the part of men educated in laboratories not to have their physical reasonings mixed up with such incommensurable factors as feelings is certainly very strong,' he wrote.[17] In *The Principles,* James presented a wide range of possible ways of thinking and feeling. The book might well be called *Varieties of Psychological Experience,* since James included many examples of abnormal psychological behavior, aberrations, and pathology. Angell remarked on James's use 'of materials drawn from the pathological side of mental life. This was in part no doubt a reflex of his medical training, in part was due to his intrinsic interest in the unusual.' Certainly James included such examples to persuade his readers that they needed to question generalizations about psychology; he wanted to remind them that exceptions abounded. And, most important, he wanted them to test psychological theories against their own experiences.

The Principles of Psychology earned James the acclaim that he hoped for and insured his place in the field of psychology. Perhaps the most enduring concept presented in *The Principles* was James's notion of the stream of consciousness, a metaphor that eventually made its way into modernist literary criticism.[18] But it was not in psychology that he established his most lasting reputation. As he knew, eminence in the field required that he conduct psychological experiments or amass clinical data, and he was not interested in doing either. What did interest him was formulating philosophical ideas that would be useful for productive, intelligent members of a thriving democracy. He wanted to give individuals, and himself, a philosophical perspective that would affirm personal authority. These ideas were integrated into his many writings and lectures on pragmatism and pluralism. John Boodin, F. C. S. Schiller, Ralph Barton Perry, Horace Kallen, Arthur Lovejoy, George Santayana, and G. K. Chesterton offer their differing perspectives on these concepts.

Perry was not alone in trying to offer succinct and useful definitions of the terms. Pluralism, he wrote, was generated from James's rejection of any theory that posited the idea of an Absolute: James demanded recognition of a multiplicity of experiences and perspectives. Pragmatism, Perry suggested, 'consists essentially in the doctrine that knowledge is a natural process through which experience shapes and orders itself consistently with practical needs. Truth is in the making. Experience is both plastic, in that it lends itself to knowledge; active in that it knows and directs itself, and progressive in that its most orderly systematizations tend to survive and cohere.' James Putnam put it more concretely. James, he wrote, 'insisted on making "experience" the touchstone for determining the value or the truth of a belief. . . . If a man could truly say that his life was made richer in any important respect by the acceptance of a given doctrine, vision, or intuition, then, in so far, the doctrine should count as true for him.' Schiller tells us that for James pragmatism was 'a revolt against a number of pernicious abstractions which had long blocked the path of philosophic progress. . . . Pragmatism reinstated *life in its integrity* as the supreme aim of philosophic thought.'

Yet precisely because pragmatism was rooted in the concrete and connected truth with individual perception, the concept had many critics. Santayana, for example, was uncomfortable with the idea that anyone's interpretation of reality would be as valid as anyone else's—and he doubted that James really believed in such intellectual relativism. But James, he thought, 'was respectful and pitiful to the trustfulness of others. Doubtless they were wrong, but who were we to say so?' Santayana saw James as an agnostic and compassionate romantic who allowed his sentimental feelings to dominate his philosophy. 'I trusted his heart,' Santayana wrote in his autobiography, 'but I didn't respect his judgment.'[19]

Arthur Lovejoy also suggested that James's philosophy reflected his personal temperament: Generous by nature, hearty in his admiration of ingenuity, and deeply committed to the ideals of democracy, James did not want to create a philosophical system that incorporated within it any kind of exclusion. He wanted to give each human being the right to live according to his own sense of reality. But James's generosity, according to Lovejoy, made him resistant to 'those intellectual processes of classification and generalization in which, in one form or another, scientific philosophical reasoning largely consist.'

G. K. Chesterton was no defender of classification and generalization, but even he saw that James's conflation of usefulness and truthfulness contained inherent problems. Pragmatism, Chesterton wrote, 'asks how ordinary people do actually use and feel ideas. Now ordinary people do actually feel the notion of truth and the notion of utility as utterly separate.' But James's pragmatism, as Chesterton understood it, 'substantially means that the sun being useful is the same thing as the sun being there.' According to Chesterton, James, although personally charming, had little to offer in the way of philosophical theory. 'It was his glory that he popularised philosophy,' Chesterton wrote. 'It was his destruction that he popularised his own philosophy.'

Boodin, Schiller, and Kallen are more generous in their evaluation of pluralism and pragmatism, as were many of James's readers. But among his colleagues, James found that his credibility was undermined not only by his refusal to create a rigorous philosphical system but also by his unflagging interest in psychical research. Palmer, Delabarre, and Angell each refer to James's involvement in spiritualism, including his attendance at seances with the medium Leonora Piper, about whom James wrote extensively. This involvement was not transitory: Palmer mentions 'cabinet seances' held every Saturday during one winter, and James, along with colleagues, his wife, and other members of his family, met frequently with Mrs. Piper and other mediums. James was an active member of the London Society for Psychical Research, serving as its president for two years; he helped found the American Society for Psychical Research; and he published often in the *Proceedings of the Society for Psychical Research*. Even some of James's defenders, such as James Angell, seem embarrassed by this intense interest, explaining it as just one more example of James's 'honest independence' but failing to understand its importance in James's intellectual life.

James believed that the enterprise of philosophy could only be strengthened by paying attention 'to facts of the sort dear to mystics, while reflecting upon them in academic-scientific ways.'[20] He realized that many ordinary men and women believed without doubt in supernormal and paranormal phenomena. If psychology, philosophy, and medicine chose to ignore hallucinations, telepathy, apparitions, haunted houses, multiple personalities, mediums, and clairvoyants, James and his colleagues in the London and American Societies for Psychical Research were committed to examining these phenomena systematically and objectively.

His motivation was not entirely professional. Experimenting with hallucinogenic drugs, self-hypnosis, and automatic writing convinced James that there were alternative states of being that might help us define the self and understand the workings of the mind. He was interested in what he called 'hidden selves' and layered states of consciousness, found not only in mentally ill patients but in normal, functioning men and women such as James himself. Perhaps the most poignant motivation for James's questions about the possibility of transcendent states of being was the death of his young son, Herman. Their correspondence suggests that in many seances, he and Alice hoped for some message from or about the child, any proof that he was not forever lost to them.

James spent his days among friends and colleagues. He might walk to campus with his neighbor, Josiah Royce; meet Santayana or Palmer before his classes; or bring Walter Lippmann or Edwin Delabarre home for lunch. On any evening he and Alice might dine with Elizabeth Glendower Evans, with George Gordon and his wife, or with James Putnam and his wife. And even when he retreated to his country home in Chocorua, New Hampshire, or went hiking in the Adirondack Mountains, James surrounded himself with colleagues, students, and friends. He was a member of many clubs and professional associations, some informal—like the various philosophical discussion clubs that met during his early days as a faculty member at Harvard; and some formal—such as the American Psychological Association, for which he served as president, or the Tavern Club, a men's dinner club that included prominent lawyers, writers, physicians, and businessmen.

Even when he was alone, whether at home or traveling, James spent hours each day corresponding with his friends all over the world. When he and Alice were apart, frequent mail deliveries made it possible for them to write to one another several times a day. His letters, and the memoirs in this volume, attest to the variety of his relationships. James counted some great intellectuals among his friends, but he also cherished his relationships with men and women who made no lasting contribution to psychology or philosophy but who were warm and stimulating companions. His social world was not limited to colleagues and students. Friends such as Elizabeth Glendower Evans and the Goldmark sisters brought James into a community of eminent social reformers. His frequent travels, lectures, and attendance at international conferences widened his community.

The men and women who peopled James's world directly inspired his work: he spoke to them and for them. In understanding his relationships, we can come to understand the context for his thoughts. Among James's 'social selves' that are revealed in this anthology, we see the intellectual rebel, the idealist, the artist, the romantic, the protector, the liberator. He had the rare ability to make people believe that they could find within themselves lush new corners in the gardens of their own spirits. He was loving and beloved, powerful and compelling. 'And yet,' John Chapman reminds us, 'it is hard to state what it was in him that gave him either his charm or his power, what it was that penetrated and influenced us.' The writers of these memoirs all try, as Chapman does, to respond to that challenge: to help us to sense the vitality of James's personality, the freshness and excitement of his ideas, and the buoyancy of his spirit.

*

The following memoirs were not included in this volume because of space limitations:

Kaltenborn, Hans von. 'William James at Harvard,' *Harvard Illustrated Magazine* February 1907. Kaltenborn, a print and radio journalist, remembers being a student when James last taught Philosophy D.

Lovett, Sidney. 'A Boy's Recollections of William James,' *Yale Review* Winter 1987, 246–55. Lovett, a friend of James's son Alexander, recalls anecdotes of family life at the Jameses' homes in Cambridge, Massachusetts, and Chocorua, New Hampshire, beginning in 1904.

Neilson, William Allan. 'William James as Lecturer and Writer,' *Harvard Illustrated Magazine* February 1907. Neilson, a member of the English Department at Harvard, comments about James's lively style.

Orcutt, William Dana. From *In Quest of the Perfect Book,* pp.90–93. Boston: Little, Brown, 1926. Orcutt—novelist, essayist, and editor—writes of James's close attention to the details of publishing.

Raymond, Mary. 'Memories of William James,' *New England Quarterly* September 1937, 419–29. Raymond, a student of James's at Radcliffe, shares anecdotes about his teaching and includes letters from James dating from 1895 to 1908.

The editor has provided endnotes for introductory material. All footnotes are part of the original selections.

NOTES

1. William James, *The Principles of Psychology* (Cambridge: Harvard University Press, 1981), 281–82.
2. Henry James Sr. to Julia Kellogg, 31 July [1869]. Houghton.
3. WJ to Henry Bowditch. *Letters* 1:123 (12 December 1867).
4. WJ to Henry James. *Correspondence* 1:157 (7 May 1870).
5. WJ to Henry James. *Correspondence* 1:167 (24 August 1872).
6. WJ to Henry James. *Correspondence* 1:191 (13 February 1873).
7. Quoted in Rosalind Miller, *Gertrude Stein: Form and Intelligibility* (Jericho NY: Exposition Press, 1949), 146.
8. WJ, 'The Energies of Men,' *Essays in Religion and Morality,* 136.
9. WJ, 'The Social Value of the College-Bred,' *Memories and Studies* (New York: Greenwood, 1968 [1911]), 309. James was quick to add that he included women in this statement.
10. WJ, 'The Social Value of the College-Bred,' 315.
11. WJ, 'The True Harvard,' *Memories and Studies,* 353.
12. WJ, 'The Teaching of Philosophy in Our Colleges,' *Essays in Philosophy,* 5. Originally published in *The Nation* 21 September 1876.
13. WJ, 'The Teaching of Philosophy in Our Colleges,' 4.
14. WJ, 'The Teaching of Philosophy in Our Colleges,' 5.
15. WJ, 'Brute and Human Intellect,' *Essays in Psychology,* 18–19.
16. WJ, 'Are We Automata?' *Essays in Psychology,* 38.
17. WJ, 'Are We Automata?' 39.
18. James had explained this term earlier in the 1884 essay 'On Some Omissions of Introspective Psychology,' *Essays in Psychology,* which became part of chapter 9 of *The Principles.*

19. George Santayana, *Persons and Places: The Middle Span* (New York: Scribner's, 1945), 166.

20. WJ, 'What Psychical Research Has Accomplished,' *William James on Psychical Research,* ed. Gardner Murphy and Robert Ballou (London: Chatto and Windus, 1961), 28. The statement also appears in 'The Hidden Self,' *Essays in Psychology* (Cambridge: Harvard University Press, 1983), 249.

CHRONOLOGY

1842 11 January. William James born in New York City.
1843 15 April. Henry James Jr. born in New York City.
1843–44 Family travels in Europe.
1845 21 July. Garth Wilkinson James born in New York City.
1846 29 August. Robertson James born in Albany, New York.
1848 7 August. Alice James born in New York City.
1855–58 Family travels in Europe.
1858–59 Family lives in Newport, Rhode Island.
1859–60 Family travels in Switzerland and Germany.
1860–61 Studies painting with William Morris Hunt, Newport.
1861 Enters Lawrence Scientific School, Harvard.
1864 Family moves from Newport to Boston.
1864 Enters Harvard Medical School.
1865–66 Joins Louis Agassiz on expedition in Brazil.
1866 Family moves to Cambridge.
1869 Graduates with medical degree.
1873 Becomes instructor in anatomy and physiology, Harvard.
1875 Begins teaching psychology.
1876 Named assistant professor of physiology. Meets Alice Howe Gibbens.
1878 February. Lectures at Johns Hopkins University.
10 May. Announces engagement to Alice Gibbens.
June. Agrees to contract with Holt for *Principles of Psychology*.
10 July. Marries Alice Gibbens.
1879 Begins teaching philosophy, Harvard
18 May. Henry (Harry) James (son) born.

1880	Appointed assistant professor of philosophy, Harvard.
1882	29 January. Mary James (mother) dies.
	17 June. William (Billy) James (son) born.
	18 December. Henry James Sr. dies.
1883	15 November. Garth Wilkins James (brother) dies.
1884	31 January. Herman James (son) born.
	The Literary Remains of the Late Henry James published. WJ helps found the American Society for Psychical Research.
1885	Appointed professor of philosophy, Harvard. Meets Leonora Piper, a medium living in Arlington, Massachusetts.
	9 July. Herman dies.
1886	Buys country home in Chocorua, New Hampshire. Publishes account of seances with Mrs. Piper in *Proceedings of the American Society for Psychical Research.*
1887	24 March. Margaret Mary (Peggy) James (daughter) born.
1889	Moves to 95 Irving Street, Cambridge.
	August. Attends First International Congress of Experimental Psychology, Paris.
1890	*Principles of Psychology* published.
	22 December. Alexander Robertson (Tweedy, Aleck) James (son) born.
1892	6 March. Alice James (sister) dies.
1894	Serves as President of the American Psychological Association.
1894–96	Serves as President of the London Society for Psychical Research.
1897	*The Will to Believe, and Other Essays in Popular Psychology* published.
1898	*Human Immortality: Two Supposed Objections to the Doctrine* published.
1899	*Talks to Teachers on Psychology: and to Students on Some of Life's Ideals* published.
1901–2	Presents Gifford Lectures, Edinburgh.
1902	*Varieties of Religious Experience* published.
1906	Named visiting professor for spring semester, Stanford University.
	6 April. San Francisco earthquake.
1907	*Pragmatism* published.

1907	Resigns from Harvard.
1908–9	Presents Hibbert Lectures at Oxford.
1909	*A Pluralistic Universe* and *The Meaning of Truth: A Sequel to 'Pragmatism'* published.
1910	26 August. Dies, Chocorua.

SOURCES

Harvard University Press has published annotated editions of the following works of William James. All references to James's works in the text are to these editions, unless otherwise noted.

Essays, Comments, and Reviews. Introduction by Ignas K. Skrupskelis, 1987.
Essays in Philosophy. Introduction by John J. McDermott, 1978.
Essays in Psychical Research. Introduction by Robert A. McDermott, 1986.
Essays in Psychology. Introduction by William R. Woodward, 1983.
Essays in Radical Empiricism. Introduction by John J. McDermott, 1976.
Essays in Religion and Morality. Introduction by John J. McDermott, 1982.
Manuscript Essays and Notes. Introduction by Ignas K. Skrupskelis, 1988.
Manuscript Lectures. Introduction by Ignas K. Skrupskelis, 1988.
A Pluralistic Universe. Introduction by Richard J. Bernstein, 1977.
Pragmatism and The Meaning of Truth. Introduction by H. S. Thayer, 1978.
The Principles of Psychology. 3 vols. Introductions by Gerald E. Myers and Rand B. Evans, 1983.
Psychology: Briefer Course. Introduction by Michael M. Sokal, 1984.
Some Problems of Philosophy. Introduction by Peter H. Hare, 1979.
Talks to Teachers on Psychology: And to Students on Some of Life's Ideals. Introduction by Gerald E. Myers, 1983.
The Varieties of Religious Experience. Introduction by John E. Smith, 1985.
The Will to Believe. Introduction by Edward H. Madden, 1979.

MANUSCRIPT SOURCES

HOUGHTON: James's papers are housed at the Houghton Library, Harvard University.

ADDITIONAL WORKS

All references are fully annotated in endnotes, except for the following works, which are referred to in short form:

Letters	*The Letters of William James,* ed. Henry James III. 2 vols. Boston: Atlantic Monthly Press, 1920.
Correspondence	*The Correspondence of William James,* ed. Ignas K. Skrupskelis. Vols.1–4. Charlottesville: University of Virginia Press, 1992–1994. Additional volumes are forthcoming.
Perry	*The Thought and Character of William James,* ed. Ralph Barton Perry. 2 vols. Boston: Little, Brown, 1935.
Scott	*William James: Selected Unpublished Correspondence, 1885–1910,* ed. Frederick J. D. Scott. Columbus: Ohio State University Press, 1986.

ACKNOWLEDGMENTS

Excerpts in the introduction from letters of William James published by permission of Alexander James Jr.

James Rowland Angell, 'William James,' was originally published in the January 1911 issue of *Psychological Review.*

Roswell Parker Angier, 'Another Student's Impressions of James at the Turn of the Century,' was originally published in the January 1943 issue of *Psychological Review.*

John Elof Boodin, 'William James as I Knew Him,' was originally published in *Personalist* 23 (1942). Reprinted with permission.

John Jay Chapman, 'William James: A Portrait,' is reprinted from *Selected Writings of John Jay Chapman,* ed. Jacques Barzun (New York: Farrar, Straus, 1957).

Gilbert Keith Chesterton, 'The Philosophy of William James,' was previously published as 'William James' in *The Collected Works of G. K. Chesterton,* ed. Lawrence J. Clipper (San Francisco: Ignatius Press, 1987). Originally published in 1910 in *Illustrated London News.*

Edmund Burke Delabarre, 'A Student's Impressions of James in the Late '80s,' was originally published in the January 1943 issue of *Psychological Review.*

Elizabeth Glendower Evans, 'William James and His Wife,' was originally published in the September 1929 issue of *Atlantic Monthly*. Reprinted with permission.

Théodore Flournoy, 'The Artistic Temperament,' was originally published in *The Philosophy of William James* (New York: Holt, 1917).

Josephine Clara Goldmark, 'An Adirondack Friendship,' was originally published in the September–October 1934 issue of *The Atlantic Monthly*. Reprinted with permission.

George Angier Gordon, 'A Profoundly Religious Man,' excerpt from *My Education and Religion* by George A. Gordon. Copyright 1925; copyright © renewed 1953 by Ruth M. Gordon. Reprinted by permission of Houghton Mifflin Co. All rights reserved.

Henry James, 'A Brother's Notes,' is reprinted with the permission of Scribner, an imprint of Simon & Schuster, from *Notes of a Son and Brother* by Henry James. Copyright 1914 Charles Scribner's Sons; copyright © renewed 1942 by Henry James.

Henry James III, 'A Firm, Light Step,' excerpt from the introduction to *The Letters of William James*, vol.2 (Boston: Atlantic Monthly Press, 1920).

Horace Meyer Kallen, 'Remarks on R. B. Perry's Portrait of William James,' was originally published in the January 1937 issue of *Philosophical Review*.

Walter Lippmann, 'An Open Mind: William James,' was originally published in the December 1910 issue of *Everybody's Magazine*.

Arthur Oncken Lovejoy, 'William James as Philosopher,' was originally published in *The Thirteen Pragmatists and Other Essays* (Baltimore: Johns Hopkins University Press, 1963). Reprinted by permission of The Johns Hopkins University Press.

Dickinson Sargeant Miller, 'A Memory of William James,' published by permission of the Houghton Library, Harvard University; bMS Am 1092.10 (122).

Hugo Münsterberg, 'Professor James as a Psychologist,' was originally published in the 8 February 1907 issue of *Harvard Illustrated Magazine.*

George Herbert Palmer, 'William James,' was originally published in the September 1920 issue of *Harvard Graduates Magazine.*

Ralph Barton Perry, 'Professor James as Philosopher,' was originally published in the 8 February 1907 issue of *Harvard Illustrated Magazine.*

James Jackson Putnam, 'William James,' was originally published in the December 1910 issue of *Atlantic Monthly.*

Josiah Royce, 'A Word of Greeting to William James,' was originally published in the June 1910 issue of *Harvard Graduates Magazine.*

George Santayana, 'William James,' was originally published in *Character and Opinion in the United States* (New York: Doubleday Anchor, 1920).

F. C. S. Schiller, 'William James,' excerpt from *Must Philosophers Disagree* by F. C. S. Schiller. Copyright 1934. Reprinted by permission of Macmillan.

Edwin Diller Starbuck, 'A Student's Impressions of James in the Middle '90s,' was originally published in the January 1943 issue of *Psychological Review.*

'William James: A Belated Acknowledgment' was originally published in the April 1919 issue of *Atlantic Monthly.*

William James Remembered

HENRY JAMES

(1843–1916)

Fifteen months younger than William, Henry James Jr., as he was growing up, often felt that he lived in his brother's shadow. According to his memoirs, *A Small Boy and Others* and *Notes of a Son and Brother,* Henry saw William as the more aggressive, gregarious, talented, and precocious of the two boys. Although Henry was favored by his mother, who called him her angel and prized his gentle, contemplative nature, Henry aspired to be more like William. Reflecting on one of their childhood trips to England, Henry recalled William's 'deeper stirrings and braver needs' that contrasted with his own 'fatalism of patience, spiritless in a manner.' Henry did, however, belatedly acknowledge his own 'inwardly active, productive and ingenious side.'[1] This inner life sustained him throughout his youth; while William wanted to engage actively in the life around him, Henry was content with observing minute details and soaking up impressions.

Nevertheless, his penchant for introspection made him feel less interesting than his brother. Even when William was engrossed in a solitary activity such as drawing, he seemed to vibrate with more energy than his younger brother, 'his head critically balanced and his eyebrows working.'[2] William made no effort to dispel Henry's image of him: he often bullied his more docile brother, and refused to allow him to join his friends by declaring, '*I* play with boys who curse and swear!'[3]

In 1862, when Henry attended Harvard Law School at his father's insistence, William, a student at the Lawrence Scientific School, seemed much older and more sophisticated. 'I thought of William at the time as having, or rather as so much more than having already graduated,' Henry wrote; 'the effect of contact with his mind and talk, with the free play of his spirit and the irrepressible brush of his humour, couldn't have been greater had he carried off fifty honours. I felt in him such authority, so perpetually quickened a state of intellect and character.'[4]

Still, despite the difference in their temperaments that distanced them as children, the two brothers became close confidants as they grew into adulthood; their letters reveal a relationship that was both intimate and sustaining. 'Often in Paris I felt as if I had a hundred things to say to you,' Henry wrote to William in 1873 during one European trip.[5] William, responding from home (his parents' home, where, at thirty-one, he still lived), called Henry 'my in many respects twin brother.'[6]

Although much of their correspondence was devoted to family matters and details about their various emotional and physical ailments, they also discussed their work—with William commenting on Henry's fiction more than Henry commented on William's philosophy. Henry came to value his brother's responses, even when he disagreed with them. 'It is a great thing to have some one write to one of one's things as if one were a 3d person, & you are the only individual who will do this. I don't think however you are always right, by any means.'[7] William, for example, thought Henry's novel *The Europeans* 'thin' and empty. Henry conceded that the book was not his strongest, yet he cautioned William that he was taking 'these things too rigidly and unimaginatively—too much as if an artistic experiment were a piece of conduct, to which one's life were somehow committed.'[8] William, for his part, could not distinguish his brother's 'experiments' from the work to which he believed (correctly) that Henry had committed his life.

In the selection that follows we see the two brothers in Geneva, where they had been enrolled in school during the winter of 1859–60. William turned eighteen in January 1860, Henry seventeen in April. Despite his envy of William's place among his peers, Henry's delight in the color and texture of European life remained a strong motivation for him in his future travels. Eventually he decided to make his home in Europe: first he thought about settling in Paris, then Rome, and finally chose England.

Henry's success came far earlier than William's. While William did not become well known until after 1890, when his *Principles of Psychology* finally was completed, Henry, almost a decade before, already had published *The American, The Europeans, Confidence, Washington Square,* and *The Portrait of a Lady.* His essays, reviews, and stories appeared frequently in major journals, and in both Europe and America he was considered a literary lion.

Although Henry lived apart from the rest of his family, he took a strong interest in their affairs and played an important role during family crises.

With exemplary patience he often cared for his sister Alice when she suffered breakdowns or illness, taking her into his London apartment or finding near-by accommodations for her. It was Henry—along with Alice's companion Katharine Loring—who kept a vigil at Alice's bedside as she died of breast cancer in London in 1892. William always confided in Henry about recurring problems with their brothers Garth Wilkinson and Robertson. And when Henry James Sr. declined into his final illness, while both William and Henry were in London, the family sent for Henry to return to America, insisting that William stay away. Henry's gentle nature and his calm and nurturing manner endeared him to William, his wife, and their children.

NOTES

1. Henry James, *A Small Boy and Others, Autobiography,* ed. F. W. Dupee (Princeton: Princeton University Press, 1983), 170.
2. Henry James, *A Small Boy and Others,* 147.
3. Henry James, *A Small Boy and Others,* 147.
4. Henry James, *Notes of a Son and Brother, Autobiography,* 307.
5. *Correspondence,* 1:186 ([8 January 1873]).
6. *Correspondence* 1:193 (6 April 1873).
7. *Correspondence* 1:308 (14 November [1878]).
8. *Correspondence* 1:308 (14 November [1878]).

A Brother's Notes

What essentially most operated, I make out, however, was that force of a renewed sense of William's major activity which always made the presumption of any degree of importance or success fall, with a sort of ecstasy of resignation, from my own so minor. Whatever he might happen to be doing made him so interesting about it, and indeed, with the quickest concomitance, about everything else, that what I probably most did, all the while, was but to pick up, and to the effect not a bit of starving but quite of filling myself, the crumbs of his feast and the echoes of his life. His life, all this Geneva period, had been more of a feast than mine, and I recall the sense of this that I had got on the occasion of my accompanying him, by his invitation, toward the end of our stay, to a students' celebration or carouse, which was held at such a distance from the town, at a village or small bourg, up in the Vaud back-country, that we had, after a considerable journey by boat and in heterogeneous and primitive conveyances, tightly packed, to spend two nights there. The Genevese section of the Société de Zoffingue, the great Swiss students' organisation for brotherhood and beer, as it might summarily be defined, of which my brother had become a member, was to meet there certain other sections, now vague to me, but predominantly from the German-speaking Cantons, and, holding a Commerce, to toast their reunion in brimming bowls. It had been thought the impression might amuse, might even interest me—for it was not denied that there were directions, after all, in which I *could* perhaps take notice; and this was doubtless what after a fashion happened, though I felt out in the cold (and all the more that the cold at the moment happened to be cruel), as the only participant in view not crowned with the charming white cap of the society, becoming to most young heads, and still less girt with the parti-coloured ribbon or complementary scarf, which set off even the shabby—for shabbiness considerably figured. I participated vaguely but not too excludedly; I suffered from cold, from hunger and from scant sleeping-space; I found the Bernese and the Bâlois strange representatives of the joy of life, some of them the finest gothic grotesques—but the time none the less very long; all of which, however, was in the day's work if I might live, by the imagination, in William's so adaptive skin. To see that he was adaptive, was initiated, and to what a happy and fruitful effect, that, I recollect, was my measure of content; which was filled again to overflowing, as I have hinted, on my finding him so launched at the Academy after our stretch of virtual separation, and just fancying, with a freedom of fancy, even if with a great reserve of expression, how much he might be living and learning, enjoying and feeling, amid work that was the right work for him and comrades, consecrated comrades, that at the worst weren't the wrong. What was not indeed, I always asked myself, the right work for him, or the right thing of any kind, that he took up or looked at or played with?—failing, as I did more than ever at the time I speak of, of the least glimpse of his being below an occasion. Whatever he played with or worked at entered at once into his intelligence, his talk, his humour, as with the action of colouring-matter dropped into water or that of the turning-on of a light within a window. Occasions waited on him, had always done so, to my view; and there he was, that springtime, on a level with them all: the effect of which recognition had much, had more than aught else, to say to the charming silver haze just then wrapped about everything of which I was conscious. He had formed two or three young friendships that were to continue and to which even the correspondence of his later years testifies; with which it may have had something to do that the Swiss *jeunesse* of the day was, thanks to the political temperature then prevailing, in a highly inflamed and exalted state, and particularly sensitive to foreign sympathy, however platonic, with the national fever. It was the hour at which the French Emperor was to be paid by Victor Emmanuel the price of the liberation of Lombardy; the cession of Nice and Savoie were in the air—with the consequence, in the Genevese breast, of the new immediate neighbourhood thus constituted for its territory. Small Savoie was to be replaced, close against it, by enormous and triumphant France, whose power to absorb great mouthfuls was being so strikingly exhibited. Hence came much hurrying to and fro, much springing to arms, in the way of exercise, and much flocking to the standard—

'demonstrations,' in other words, of the liveliest; one of which I recall as a huge tented banquet, largely of the white caps, where I was present under my brother's wing, and, out of a sea of agitated and vociferous young heads, sprang passionate protests and toasts and vows and declaimed verses, a storm of local patriotism, though a flurry happily short-lived.

JAMES JACKSON PUTNAM

(1846–1918)

In the spring of 1873, during his busy first semester of teaching at Harvard, James complained to his brother Henry that he regretted being 'cut off . . . from the men with whom I used to gossip on *generalities* Holmes, Putnam, Peirce, Shaler & John Gray, and last not least yourself.'[1] James Jackson Putnam had been a close friend of James's since 1866, when they were students at Harvard Medical School, and both served as House Pupils at Massachusetts General Hospital in 1869.

Putnam shared James's interest in the workings of the mind and nervous system, and at the beginning of their respective careers both focused on anatomy and physical pathology in their attempts to understand personality and behavior. As a practitioner of the new field of neurology in late-nineteenth century Boston, Putnam exerted considerable influence on the medical scene there. In 1872, after returning from two years of study in Europe, he took a position as Electrician at MGH, where he was involved in the processes of galvanization and administration of electric current, customary treatment for nervous illnesses at the time. The following year, after he established the hospital's first out-patient clinic for mental illness, his title became 'Physician to Out-Patients with Diseases of the Nervous System.' For much of his career he also taught at Harvard Medical School.

Putnam soon became more than an intellectual colleague. Together with his brother Charles and Henry Bowditch, also physicians, he and James hiked often in Keene Valley in the Adirondacks of New York. They first took rooms at Beede's Boarding House but soon decided to purchase some land themselves and construct a small cottage—they called it the Shanty—for vacations. In 1876, when the Beedes put the Boarding House up for sale, the four men bought it for themselves. The camp still exists today, with a plaque commemorating the ledge, described in this essay, where James sequestered himself to read daily.

Putnam, like James, sought out new ideas in medicine and psychology. He was interested in James's experiments with hypnosis and automatic writing, and became a member of the American Society for Psychical Research because he believed that such investigations could help physicians understand the subconscious. He experimented with therapies in his work with patients at MGH. In 1898, when the government of Massachusetts threatened to impose registration and licensing restrictions on medical practitioners, James enlisted Putnam's support in opposing legislative bills that he thought would quash the work of 'mind-curers' and other practitioners who did not have medical degrees. Mind-curers, James wrote to Putnam, 'are proving by the most brilliant new results that the therapeutic relation may be what we can at present describe only as a relation of one person to another person; and they are consistent in resisting to the utmost any legislation that would make "examinable" information the root of medical virtue, and hamper the free play of personal force and affinity by mechanically imposed conditions.'[2]

Putnam cautioned James that many physicians, himself included, were suspicious of certain mind-healers, especially Christian Scientists. 'We are more in the way of seeing the fanatical spirit in which they proceed and the harm that they sometimes do than you are,' he wrote to James.[3] In a few years, however, Putnam was accused of this same type of fanatical spirit by colleagues who questioned his enthusiasm for the ideas of Sigmund Freud.

James differed with Putnam on his assessment of Freud, and Putnam eventually became impatient with James's enthusiasm over Leonora Piper, a medium championed by his friend. Despite intellectual differences, however, their friendship endured until James's death. Putnam served as an honorary pall bearer at James's funeral. This essay appeared in *The Atlantic* four months later.

NOTES

1. *Correspondence* 1:196 (6 April 1873). James here refers to Oliver Wendell Holmes Jr., James Jackson Putnam, and his Harvard colleagues Charles Peirce and Nathaniel Shaler. Both Holmes and Gray were lawyers.

2. *Letters* 2:69–70 (2 March 1898).

3. *Letters* 2:72–73 n.2 (9 March 1898).

William James

The news of Professor William James's death overwhelmed with deep sorrow the large circle of his friends and colleagues in every land, and the still larger circle of those who without knowing him had felt for him a sense of personal affection. But the grief at the loss of this warm-hearted friend and charming companion, this inspiring teacher and courageous advocate of justice, must soon have allowed room for the thought of what a noble and useful life he had led, and for gratitude that his frank, straightforward ways had made it possible to think of him as still animating the varied scenes with which he was identified so closely. He was so eager, so soldierly in spirit; his philosophy had so little of what he used to call 'the Dead-Sea-apple flavor,' that it will be a lasting pleasure to think how he would act if present; what humorous, generous, illuminating, or indignant utterance he would bring forth.

Those who knew him personally think of him most easily as he appeared in private life, and indeed it was easy to forget—so simple were his tastes and so unaffected his manner—that he was a great man and lived also in the eye of the world.

Surrounded at home by all that he really cared for,—family, friends, books, everything except robust health,—he did not seek the fame that found him. Yet he prized the honors that had come to him so abundantly, although mainly because of the assurance which they brought him that he had done and was doing the best work he was qualified to do.[1]

I well remember the earnestness with which he said to me, two years ago, that the results he had achieved were, in kind, just those he had aspired to

1. He was a member of the National Academies of America, France, Italy, Prussia, and Denmark; and was Doctor of Letters of Padua and Durham, a Doctor of Laws of Harvard, Princeton, and Edinburgh, and a Doctor of Science of Geneva and Oxford.

achieve; that he had asked no more than to succeed—by dint of personal weight and by striking a note appropriate to his day and time—in accentuating certain tendencies in the minds of thinking men which he believed to be wholesome and of vital significance.

James's ideals were generous. He cared less to see his private views prevail than to see philosophy counting as a real influence in men's lives. He longed to see the day when the advocates of a philosophic doctrine should recognize that the best warrant for its value lay, not in their ability to defend its claims against all comers, but in its power to inspire them with a desire for ever-increasing knowledge, greater liberality, a more courageous life. His attitude was at once an appeal against indifferentism, and for the recognition of a common meeting-ground of all philosophic tendencies of thought. In this sense pragmatism was a move toward mediation and conciliation, and this was one of the main interests of his own life.

James's foreign colleagues were quick to note this tendency and promise of the new-world thinker's work. The distinguished historian, Guglielmo Ferrero, has written eloquently, in a letter to the *Figaro* of September 22, of results already won among the philosophers of the Continent by this refreshing breath: 'Neither in Europe nor in America will men soon forget the simple, modest courage with which this student of philosophy proclaimed that men have need, not alone of philosophic and scientific truths, but also of peace, happiness, moral balance and serenity, and declared that no philosophic doctrine can be considered adequate, however solid its logical foundations, unless it satisfies the aspirations that lie deep within the mind.'

Many of his papers and addresses, though not strictly popular in tone and matter, were purposely kept free from needless technicalities, and so carried a wide appeal. People of all sorts found that through one or another of his writings, and equally through the impression of the writer, that went with them, they got something which made them do their own work better and led them to adopt a broader, a more considerate, and a kindlier view of life.

He, in his turn, was always eager to show sympathy and to notice signs of merit. Biography, and especially autobiography, was his favorite reading, but his search for noteworthy personal chronicle was by no means confined to the lives of famous men. His *Religious Experiences* will testify that he was fond of discovering and making known all outspoken lovers of the truth, especially if obscure. He went about like a herald or torch-bearer, among those who seemed to him deserving of recognition or in need of stimulation, as if calling to them, 'If you have anything to say on which you are willing to stake yourselves, follow me and I will help you to get heard.' This habit sometimes brought him into queer company and exposed him to many jests. He was not, however, greatly disturbed by this, thinking more of the chance that he might find some grains of intellectual or moral wheat which would otherwise have remained unfound. With all the warmth of a very warm nature, he tried to bring it about that every one whose needs he knew should be given the opportunity to set himself free, to choose for himself, to develop on his own lines.

This sense of the value of individuality in thought and act, which lay so deep in his heart and was woven into the texture of his thoughts, was chosen by him as the theme of his speech on the reception of his degree of LL.D. from Harvard University in 1903. He spoke as one who, in spite of his long contact with the university, had always looked on it somewhat from without. So he could clearly see, he said, 'two Harvards.' One of these had certain special educational functions, and served, also, in a very visible way, as a sort of social club. The other was 'the inner, spiritual Harvard. . . . The true Church was always the invisible Church. The true Harvard is the invisible Harvard in the souls of her more truth-seeking and independent and often very solitary sons. The university most worthy of imitation is that one in which your lonely thinker can feel himself least lonely, most positively furthered and most rightly fed.' In this respect he believed that Harvard 'still is in the van.'

James's love of personal liberty made him always ready to break a lance in its defense, even when in so doing he incurred the displeasure of many a respected friend and colleague. He came forward, unasked, as an advocate of those who wished to keep the privilege of consulting Christian Scientists and other irregular practitioners, when their standing was at issue before the legislature; he was an ardent defender of the rights of the Philippine Islanders, and a tireless supporter of all measures tending toward universal peace. Since his death several of those who stood with him on these and kindred issues have written warmly and gratefully of his aid. His belief that the Anti-Imperialist League had a real task to perform in national affairs never ceased, and he was one of its vice-presidents until his death.

This is no place to discuss the merits of the public questions here alluded to. I will say only that I have several letters written by him immediately after his speech at the State House, urging that no legislative action should be taken against the Christian Scientists and 'Mind Healers,' in which he declares that it was solely a love of right and the public welfare that had prompted him to come out against his medical colleagues. 'If you think I like this sort of thing you are mistaken. It cost me more effort than anything I have ever done in my life. But if Zola and Colonel Picquart can face the whole French army, cannot I face their disapproval? Far more easily than the reproach of my own conscience.'

To know William James thoroughly one should have seen him in company with a great variety of his friends in turn, so many notes did the gamut of his nature hold. These various notes were by no means out of harmony with each other; it was rather that he had many striking traits which no one person could bring out with equal emphasis. It was an especially rare treat to see him in friendly contest with one or several colleagues from whose views his own diverged. Such encounters brought out his own attitude and theirs as if with a rapid series of flash-light illuminations. He realized also that the fire of genius is distributed widely among men, as radium is found in minute quantities among baser minerals, and his generous instinct and intellectual zeal prompted him to seek its traces out.

Throughout his abundant social life he was so frank and so obviously friendly that it was impossible to take offense at anything he said, and this made it easier for him than for most men to strike the personal note in human intercourse. He could get at once upon a footing which made a basis for intimacy, if occasion called for this; a footing, which, in any case, left each new acquaintance feeling the gates of his own mind unlocked for him. He said jokingly, one day, that when he met a new person he asked him first his age and then his income, and this was almost literally true. Furthermore, these friendly relationships that he was so ready to establish did not always end with social courtesies. Generous in deed as he was in word and thought, he gave without stint, now, perhaps, a contribution of money to a friend in need, now a book from his library, now time and friendly counsel, offered to show appreciation and sympathy or to meet distress. This sense of kindliness was thorough-going. He had made it a principle, so he told me, to abstain from unfavorable personal criticism unless called for by some need. It was a rare event to hear him pass an unfriendly judgment, and he disliked to hear it done by others. He appreciated keenly the peculiarities of his acquaintances, and could characterize them with accuracy and wit. But such comments were always kindly or marked by a light and playful touch, devoid of sting.

My first meeting with William James was in 1866, at the Harvard Medical School, then on North Grove Street, and in thinking of him there

I am reminded of the old dissecting-room in the basement of that building, where the students gathered every afternoon to recite and listen to the demonstrator of anatomy. Perhaps I recall this with especial distinctness for the reason that James congratulated me on having made a good recitation; but I was greatly impressed at once with the frankness of his expression, the generosity of his manner, and the peculiarly attractive quality of his voice. There must be few of his friends who have not felt the same glow that I felt that day, at the sound of his ever-ready and welcome words of praise. He was five years my senior, but his education had been of an unusual sort and he had come late to medicine, so that we were fellow students. I learned afterwards that he had spent much time in Europe as a boy and youth, had then studied for one or two years at the Lawrence Scientific School, and had finally decided to follow a strong instinct and make himself an artist. In pursuance of this plan he had entered the studio of Mr. William M. Hunt, then living at Newport. In Hunt's studio he made the acquaintance of Mr. John Lafarge and they became close friends. But he soon gave up painting and allowed his talent to lapse, though he always remained capable of expressing himself freely in line-drawings.

The next move was again toward natural science. He studied comparative anatomy for a time with that delightful teacher, Professor Jeffries Wyman, and later he made one of the company of naturalists and students who accompanied Professor Louis Agassiz on his journey of exploration among the rivers of Brazil. Here his skill in drawing came into good service.

James's foreign training had given him a thorough mastery of French and a good familiarity with German, and, better still, habits of mind and thought which helped him to take a more cosmopolitan, and thus a more independent and personal, view of American affairs. To hold and to express such views, on matters political, social, and moral, was soon to become an opportunity for great usefulness.

During the medical-school period and also later, I saw James from time to time at the house of his father, Mr. Henry James, on Quincy Street in Cambridge. His father, his mother, and his sister were then living and at home, and one or another of his brothers was usually there. My memory of this house, and of each one of its occupants, is a memory warm and mellow with half-pictured scenes of gayety, kindliness, and charm. William, the oldest of the five children, was very like his father in feature, in manner, and in mind, and his father was an excellent person to be like. Both of them had the instinct generously to espouse unpopular causes, where the principle of personal liberty seemed at stake, and in both the advocacy sometimes went to the verge of what many persons called the fondness for a paradox. But this impression usually disappeared upon more familiar acquaintance.

In conversation both of these men had a delightful sense of humor, and a remarkable richness of vocabulary. A peculiarity of both was the habit of delaying speech for an instant, while the mind was working and the telling sentence was framing itself for utterance—a brief interval during which the lips would gather slightly, as for a sort of smile, and the eyes and face take on an indescribable expression of great charm. Then would burst forth one of those longer or shorter epigrammatic or aphoristic sayings which all their friends recall so well, full of meaning, full of kindliness and humor, never sarcastic, but always keen. Occasionally, too, they were full of fiery wrath. This James humor has often been referred to as of Irish origin. If so, it certainly throve well on American soil. It pointed also to the wide vision of real culture and to experience with men and books, thus showing itself to be cosmopolitan or universal, rather than racial. Certainly old and young, rich and poor, foreigner and native, appreciated its great charm and penetration. Sometimes a mere trifle would call out one of these rich, explosive extravaganzas of speech. I remember listening one day with trepidation when Mr. James, Senior, gathered his face into a half-humorous, half-thunderous expression and then rolled out a series of denunciations on the people who insisted on misusing the word 'quite.'

As I remember James at home, during the period of which I have been speaking, he was somewhat quieter and gentler in manner than he afterward appeared to be, though always full of playfulness and fun. His laughter was never boisterous, but no one could be quicker than he to see the chance for merriment, let the joke be with him or against him.

He had been much of an invalid, but he never lost for long his courage or his buoyancy. He believed that one should industriously cultivate the bearing, the expression, and the sentiments that go with health, and one of his former pupils has recently told me of his making an appeal to his college class on this subject. He succeeded, too, as a rule, in practicing what he preached, in spite of a real tendency to occasional depression, which might easily have been allowed to get control of him. I believe that through these frequent contests with his health James materially modified his character and, indirectly, his philosophic tendencies and views. This lack of vigor kept him at that time much at home, and he had a small laboratory there where he did a good deal of work.

James's mother, quiet in temperament and manner, was a very real power in the family, beloved by all, and holding all together; and this was also true of her sister, Mrs. Walsh, who for a long time made her home with them.

All the members of the James family were gifted with rich, melodious voices, and William's had a resonance and charm which those who had once heard it, especially in conversation, never could forget.

James took his medical degree in 1869, but never practiced. He had already become greatly interested in physiology and comparative anatomy, and was early invited to teach these subjects to the undergraduates at Harvard. From physiology he slipped into psychology, and so onward until finally he became the chief figure in the department of philosophy, one of the best departments of the college.

From the time of our first meeting until a few months before his death I had the privilege of seeing James fairly often, and of knowing something of his intellectual interests and work. From 1876 onward he made almost yearly visits to a charming spot in the Adirondacks, where there lies, in the midst of mountains, brooks, and forests, a little group of rough houses forming a sort of camp. James was formerly part owner of this very satisfactory establishment, and appreciated to the fullest extent its simple but copious resources.

These visits meant an opportunity of meeting a variety of acquaintances and friends under the most informal of conditions, and usually meant also a fresh deal of health. As a walker, he used to be among the foremost, in the earlier years, and it was a pleasure to watch his lithe and graceful figure as he moved rapidly up the steep trails or stretched himself on the slope of a rock, his arms under his head, for resting. He had the peculiarity, in climbing, of raising himself largely with the foot that was lowermost, instead of planting the other and drawing himself up by it, as is so common. This is a slight thing, but it was an element counting for elasticity and grace. There were periods when he took the longest walks and climbs, but after a time he felt that very vigorous exertion did not agree with him; and this belief, combined with his love of talk with some congenial person on some congenial subject, usually kept him back from the vanguard and rather at the rear of the long line, where he could walk slowly if he liked and find the chance to pause from time to time in order to enjoy and characterize in rich terms the splendid beauty of the steep forest-clad slopes, with the sun streaming through the thick foliage and into the islets between the tall trees.

There were certain spots which he particularly liked to visit, and even to visit alone or with a book—for he was always industrious and often did his fifty pages of solid reading daily. One such place, a ledge forming the verge of a superb precipice, with two fine pine trees overhead and the heavily wooded valley of the Ausable River rising steeply toward the north and descending into a broad plateau toward the south, was named for him many years ago by a warm friend and admirer. Another beautiful spot, well up on a steep side of Round Mountain, I remember reaching with him toward the end of a still and golden September day. We had been walking for a number of hours through the thick, dark woods, and this beautiful bit of cliff, nearly inclosed by the dense spruces of the forest, and carpeted with moss of a rich, yellowish-green tint, afforded the first chance for the afternoon sun to stream in and for the trampers to obtain a glimpse of the hazy valley winding off far beneath, and of the sun-deserted mountains closing in the deep ravine, along one side of which runs the narrow trail. I recalled this spot to his memory in a letter written several years later (in 1899), when he was in Europe, seeking health at Nauheim. He wrote back, saying, 'Your talk about Keene Valley makes me run over with homesickness. Alas, that those blessed heights should henceforward probably be beyond my reach altogether! It is a painful pang!'

Fortunately, this prediction was not fulfilled. He improved greatly on his return to America after this trip, came several times again to revisit old haunts, and even did a fair amount of walking.

He was very fond of stirring poetry, and one or another of our fellow campers has spoken of verses by Kipling or Walt Whitman or Goethe as associated with the thought at once of him and of some special mountain-top or forest walk. Occasionally, also, in the afternoon, he would read us portions of his own writings, at which he almost always was at work, and thus we had the first chance at bits of several of his best papers.

James was married in the spring of 1878 to Miss Alice H. Gibbens, and began at once to improve in health and to lead a fuller and more active life. He soon became widely known in Europe both through his writings and his fairly frequent visits, and it was felt by all his colleagues there that the Harvard faculty had rarely been represented by a brighter light than he.

In the autumn of 1892 he established himself in Florence with his wife and children for the winter, and thus amusingly describes their housekeeping:—

> If we can escape freezing this winter the retrospect of next spring will doubtless be a good one. Our apartment (just moved into) is snug, clean and sunny, and though devoid of every "domestic convenience" except one stop-

> cock and a hearth in a kitchen some ten feet by six, seems a place in which housekeeping can go on. Our cook, Raphaello, with whom we converse by means of raw Latin roots without terminations, seems nevertheless to grasp our meaning and evolves very savory dinners out of the nudity of his workshop. A one-sou fan is his principal instrument—by it he keeps the little fires from going out. I ought to say that we have a big Bernese governess, who looks like Luther in his more corpulent days, and, knowing more Italian than we do, has been quite useful as interpretess. But her appetites are ungovernable, she has no tact, and we shall have little use for her when the boys get to school, so we shall soon say farewell and give her a recommendation to some very full-blooded family.
>
> I'm telling you nothing of our summer, most all of which was passed in Switzerland. Germany is good, but Switzerland is better. *How good* Switzerland is, is something that can't be described in words. The healthiness of it passes all utterance. The air, the roads, the mountains, the customs, the institutions, the people. Not a breath of art, poetry, æsthetics, morbidness, or 'suggestiveness.' It's all there, solid meat and drink for the sick body and soul, ready to be turned to and do you good when the nervous and gas-lit side of life has had too much play. What a see-saw life is, between the elemental things and the others. We must have both; but, aspiration for aspiration, I think [that] of the over-cultured and exquisite person for the insipidity of health is the more pathetic. After the suggestiveness, decay, and over-refinement of Florence this winter, I shall be hungry enough for the eternal elements to be had in the Schweiz.

From the very beginning of their married life in Cambridge, Mr. and Mrs. James showed a hospitality which made them a marvel to their friends. In season and out, all were made welcome. This was especially true of visitors from Europe, whether those at whose hands James had received hospitality in his turn when abroad—for he was everywhere a welcome guest—or those who came to Cambridge attracted by his writings and reputation. All such visitors were made at home, for shorter or for longer periods, and only the friends of their hosts realized how much trouble was taken to make their stay successful.

What his home was to others, to him it was more, a thousand-fold. Every one who watched him saw clearly that he owed a distinct portion of his steady growth in tranquillity and power of accomplishment to the home influences—intellectual, physical, and moral—that formed the main background of his life. If the vital force was native and resident in him, its development was fostered by the untiring devotion which was constantly at his command. And this he himself well knew. Seconded by his wife, he made friends in every land, some of them through personal intercourse, which he always sought, and some through correspondence only. He was as sociable as Montaigne, both from principle and from true love of his fellow men.

One of the many foreign friendships which he greatly valued and frequently referred to was that with M. Renouvier, the able editor of the *Critique Philosophique.* There was a strong personal and intellectual sympathy between these two men. James was also an occasional contributor to the *Critique.* He wrote French with fluency and grace, and infused into it some of the elements that made his English style so engrossingly effective.

He had thought much, also, cosmopolitan as he was, about the relative advantages of the life in Europe and in America, and was always ready to talk about this subject. With his sensitiveness and his fine taste, he loved the cultivated, æsthetic atmosphere of France and England, and there were times when he longed for it and felt that he must gratify the longing. But he was at heart an American, and even a way-breaker, as well as an artist. One of his friends remembers his quoting from Gray's 'Eton,' the lines ending, 'And snatch a fearful joy,' with reference to the satisfaction and at the same time the sacrifices which American conditions offer and require. His attitude on this question illustrates his attitude on many questions. He could feel a warm glow in favor of two opposing sets of interests, each in turn, and yet one could predict which, in the end, would prove the stronger. I recall hearing him speak one day, in the dining-room of our Adirondack camp, of certain 'bitter-sweet' articles of food, of which it was 'hard to say whether one likes or dislikes them most.' But there are many bitter-sweets in life, and he was alive to the value of both elements that they contained. His readers will recall a charming essay[2] in which he describes a journey in the mountains of North Carolina and tells of passing by a large number of unkempt, squalid clearings, littered with the stumps and boughs of fresh-cut trees, and savoring of destruction, devastation, and discomfort. As he was in the act of drawing this lesson, he said to the mountaineer who was driving him,—

'What sort of people are they who have to make these new clearings?'

'All of us,' the man replied. 'Why, we ain't happy here unless we are getting one of these coves under cultivation.'

2. 'On a Certain Blindness in Human Beings.' *Talks to Teachers,* p.231.

James 'instantly felt' that he 'had been losing the whole significance of the situation.' 'The clearing which to me was a mere ugly picture on the retina, was to them a symbol redolent with moral memories and sang a very pæan of duty, struggle, and success.'

Few persons have written more charmingly or more lucidly than Professor James, or with greater evidence of personal conviction. This last feature of his books and papers was indeed so marked, what he said came so obviously from his heart, that to speak of his 'style' seems inappropriate. He was through and through an artist, in writing as in speech, and yet he used his art so obviously as a way of making his meaning clear that the reader thinks of his charming and telling manner mainly in terms of the conclusions that it enforced. When one reads his books it is a pleasure to assume one's self in full accord with him, even in the face of disagreement, so delightfully does he call learning, humor, fancy, abundant and apt citation, the homeliest of illustrations and the most daring of analogies, to the aid of his incisive argument. In all this he shows himself not only expert in knowledge and in literary skill, but a broad reader and an intimate knower of human thoughts and passions in wide range. He was of course a delightful correspondent, and he wrote copiously and to many persons. Even when very ill or very busy he managed to keep in touch in this way with a large number of his friends, though he was sometimes forced to call in the ready service of his wife as amanuensis.

He began to make scientific communications within a few years after his entrance on academic work. The earlier papers dealt with physiological questions. Even in these his psychological and philosophical interests were foreshadowed, while, on the other hand, his early training as a physiologist affected all his later work. One of the early papers, on 'The Law of Forward Action in the Nervous System,' in which he showed that the impulses in nerve fibres run always in one or the other direction, according to the function of the nerves concerned, is cited as important by the eminent English physiologist, Sherrington. His well-known papers on the absence of dizziness in deaf-mutes, on 'The Sense of Effort,' and on the 'Perception of Space,' are partly of physiological and partly of psychological interest.

It would be out of the question to review here his contributions in the psychologic field, but attention may be called in passing to his insistence on the very important part played by sensation in the feeling of emotion and even of consciousness itself. This doctrine, which was brought out at about the same time by the Swedish psychologist Lange, promptly became famous, the world over. It has a decided interest here as being closely related to some of his later philosophical generalizations. Sensations of various subtle kinds, as those coming from the circulatory and digestive apparatus, well known to be excited in the strong emotions, were recognized by him as deserving of more attention than they had received; and when he came to analyze the feeling of emotion closely it seemed to him that the honest observer could not assert that anything else was there. Strip off 'sensation' from emotion and what is left? he asked. At a later day the sense of consciousness was analyzed in the same fashion.

I cannot discuss the merits of these difficult subjects here, but I desire to point out that just as he felt that he must fully reckon with the influence of *sensation*, the most tangible element in *emotion*, before he would allow that anything else was there, so he felt that the influence of *experience* should be fully reckoned with before other means of judging of the *truth* were turned to.

This seems to me a distinct illustration of the way in which his mind worked. Although thoroughly alive to the existence of influences in the world which can only be reached through a free use of a trained imagination, his love of simplicity and directness led him to estimate at their full value the factors that had the merit of being relatively commonplace, and therefore more familiar to the ordinary mind, and to exert all his powers of observation to note more of these than others had discovered.

The earliest of his philosophical papers, so far as I am aware, was one written for the *Critique Philosophique;* and the next, on much the same subject, was that which was published later as the first part of *The Sentiment of Rationality.* This was first given as an address in 1879, and was finally brought out, in 1897, together with other valuable papers, in a volume called *The Will to Believe, and Other Essays in Popular Philosophy.*

His first enterprise in actual book-making was in 1885, when he edited *The Literary Remains of Henry James,* the preface to which was partly his own work, partly made up from extracts from his father's writings. All those who wish to gain insight into the evolution of Professor James's mind by noting the influences which were early at work on him, should read this admirable volume. The theology there defended is sufficiently simple and sufficiently well adapted for men's needs to have commanded James's respect, and both the character of the sentiments and the splendid language of the father strongly remind one of the son's thought and style.

His next book was the important two-volume *Psychology,* published in

1890 and written for the most part during a trip to Europe. This book proved an immense success. It has continued to win popularity and fame and has been translated into a number of languages, the latest being the Italian. Professor James told me only recently that this success had surprised him greatly. He had not taken especial pains, he said, to make a monumental work. But his mind and thoughts were so untrammeled, so keen and fresh, that he could not help writing a good book. He was one of the few scientific writers whose productions became a source of revenue. He made sundry trips to Europe, largely on the income derived from the *Psychology*, the *Talks to Teachers*, and the *Religious Experiences*, and the sale of his last two books also has been large.

In 1898 he delivered the Ingersoll lecture on *Personal Immortality*.

In 1899 he gave and published his now famous *Talks to Teachers on Psychology; and to Students on Some of Life's Ideals*, a book of great charm, great wisdom, and true scientific penetration.

In 1901 and 1902 he delivered at Edinburgh his first English lecture course, the Gifford Lectures, which at once appeared in book form as the *Varieties of Religious Experiences; a Study in Human Nature*. It was understood that he had long been collecting the materials for this book, for his object was not so much to give his own religious convictions as to show under how many and how varied aspects, convictions that could be called religious had impressed themselves on a variety of men and had helped to mould their lives. In the closing chapter he makes statements which indicate how he felt at that time on certain subjects which were being studied by his English colleagues of the Society for Psychical Research. He always took intense and appreciative interest in the investigations of both the English and the American branches of this society, though he did not bear so active a part in them as many people have supposed. The more prominent workers, both in England and America, were his personal friends, especially Richard Hodgson, the devoted secretary of the American branch. For a number of years James served as president of this branch.

Finally, in 1907 and 1909, respectively, came out the two books on *Pragmatism* and on *Pluralism*, and a third, *The Meaning of Truth* (1909), which formed an explanatory supplement to the course on pragmatism. He also wrote a large number of scientific papers and minor addresses, such as the fine tribute to Colonel Robert Gould Shaw, and several delightful biographical sketches, as those on Professor Louis Agassiz and on Thomas Davidson.

Professor James's attitude toward the general problems of philosophy is well known. He called himself a 'radical empiricist,' a 'pragmatist,' a 'pluralist,' and it is fair to say that these terms, indicative of his beliefs, indicate also important features of his own character. It is evident that he approached the deeper problems of life as a lover of men and a sympathizer with human needs, but also with the conscientiousness of a person trained to careful observation, and yet fully realizing that in the desire to make observation 'careful' it is very easy to make it narrow. He insisted on making 'experience' the touchstone for determining the value or the truth of a belief. But experience was construed by him in a far wider sense than by many others, and he was always ready to extend its scope. If a man could truly say that his life was made richer in any important respect by the acceptance of a given doctrine, vision, or intuition, then, in so far, the doctrine should count as true for him. He felt strongly that each person should strive to satisfy the demands, not only of his reason, but also of his aspirations and his sense of the power to accomplish something new and real, which every man possesses in some measure. Just because he felt the deep practical significance of the task which philosophy assumes, in trying to explain the rationality of a world filled with suffering and sorrow, he shrank from encouraging the acceptance of interpretations which might sound well but which a deeper searching of one's observation did not verify as helping to a truer and a sounder life. He objected strongly to the method of education which enabled the scholar glibly to 'throw the rule at the teacher' but left him unable to do the sum to which the rule applied.

It is safe to say, of course, that but few of the colleagues with whom he joined issues over philosophic problems would consent to be classed as opposing these propositions stated in this broad way. Every one acknowledges the claims of observation, thoroughness, and honesty, and so every one is a pragmatist and an empiricist. But James believed in drawing trenchant distinctions as an aid to clearer thought and more fruitful discussion, and conscientiously believed that the existence of a distinct difference of *emphasis* between his views and those of certain of his colleagues pointed to the practical need of a distinctive name. He longed to go to the furthest possible limit in his estimate of spiritual freedom and the possibility of a real unity and harmony underlying the distracting signs of multiplicity and discord in the world, but he felt that he should best help this cause, which he had so much at heart, by indicating distinctly the features by which each man might hope to recognize the sought-for angel of his truth, when met, and by making it perfectly clear what degree of success he himself had had. He came, eventually, to direct his search, not for *the* truth but for *truths*. For the attempt to assert *the* truth makes it necessary to depart from the pathway of experience—so he thought—and to trust one's self to forms of reasoning which, after years of study, he had found himself unable to accept as binding. His description, in *The Pluralistic Universe*, of this contest in his mind is full of the deepest interest.

In this crusade against an intellectualism which he considered *ultra*, James found a powerful ally in the admittedly great French philosopher and psychologist, Bergson, who with keen arguments asserts that the ultimate facts of life are only to be appreciated by immersing ourselves in life's stream and feeling it. Life implies motion, and motion we can create but cannot picture or describe. What we can do is to use the intellect for approaching nearer and nearer to the point from which, with the aid of intuition, we may get the sense of dipping into the fountain of reality.

Closely related to James's confidence in experience was his belief in the creative power of a voluntary act. He recognized that the practical issues with which philosophy indirectly concerns itself are so momentous for the everyday life of men, that it is unwise to wait too long before committing one's self to the view which seems the best. He therefore urged that every one, after looking at the facts as fairly as he could, should choose and act, even at the risk of choosing and acting from reasons that he might afterwards judge to have been mistaken. In thus acting, men might be, he thought, not only discovering the truth, but helping to create it.

It might be supposed, by one who did not know Professor James, that with his fixed confidence in experience as the proper touchstone of the truth, he would have been led straightway into the materialistic camp, or, at least, into the camp of those who though idealists are practically determinists. But not only was it untrue of Professor James that he took that road, but a fair reading of his arguments makes one agree with him that he was at liberty, logically, to refuse to take it. Every book, every essay, of his is redolent with the doctrine that if a man takes his whole self into account, realizing that he is not only a reasoning being but a feeling and aspiring being, and that his very reasoning is colored by emotion, then choices, preferences, leaps-in-the-dark, the 'presentiment of the eternal in the temporal,' become justifiable in so far as they are real. This was one of the pragmatic outcomes of his *radical* empiricism.

While his course of lectures upon pragmatism was in progress I wrote to him, saying that although the practical value of his recommendations to rigid honesty in applying the test of experience seemed undeniably of value, yet I thought the *tendency* of his doctrine might be to encourage, among some persons, a too narrow conservatism of a materialistic stamp. He wrote back, saying for himself at least,—'Surely you know there is an essence in me (whatever I may at any moment appear to say) which is incompatible with my really being a physico-chemico-positivist.'

This quality in Professor James's mind which enabled him to maintain his stout adherence to scientific accuracy and to assert the necessity for taking experience as the court of last resort, yet at the same time to recognize the existence of influences that transcend the evidence of the senses, kept him in touch at once with science and with religion, and made it possible for him to believe in a real spiritual freedom.

Instinctively devout and possessing religious sentiments, and sympathizing doubtless with his still more strongly religious father, he found difficulty, in spite of his critical attitude with regard to the doctrine of an all-absorbing 'Absolute,' in reconciling his conception of an imperfect, perhaps essentially disjointed and pluralistic universe, helped along by the combined efforts of the spiritual powers resident in men, with a belief in the possible and probable existence of a greater spiritual personality, between whom and ourselves and all the phenomena of the world a perfect intimacy must exist. We cannot prove this, he declares, but there is no argument or evidence which can prevent us from assuming it if we will, and if our assumption is sound our acts help to make the truth efficient for our needs.

It is idle to say, he would insist, that this procedure is unscientific; that the truly scientific man does not assume but always proves the truth. For not only does every progressive scientific man necessarily use his imagination in forecasting the results, but the attitude of holding back from a decision for the chance of a greater certainty is in itself an emotional, and not alone a rational, attitude. There are times when you must '*believe what is in the line of your needs,* for only by such belief is the need fulfilled. . . . You make one or the other of two universes true by your trust or mistrust,—both universes having been only *maybes,* in this particular, before you contributed your act.' Applying this principle to the question of religious belief, he says [This] 'command that we shall put a stopper on our heart, instincts and courage, and *wait*—acting of course meanwhile more or less as if religion were *not* true—till doomsday, or till such time as our intellect and sense working together may have raked in evidence enough—

this command, I say, seems to me the queerest idol ever manufactured in the philosophic cave.' Again, 'Better face the enemy than the eternal Void.'

In the same essay from which the last sentence is quoted, James points out that the chief and primary function of the intellect is to bring practical results to pass; to answer the question, 'What is to be done?' and says, 'It was a deep instinct in Schopenhauer which led him to reinforce his pessimistic argumentation by a running volley of invective against the practical man and his requirements. No hope for pessimism unless he is slain.' In the whole set of inspiring essays which *The Will to Believe* leads off as with a trumpet's note, this thesis, that the will, if strong enough to lead to action, is a real factor in the world's progress, is maintained with strong emphasis; and in the lectures on the *Pluralistic Universe* the same theme is taken up again and reinforced.

Even in his psychology he foreshadowed a certain portion of this philosophic attitude by asserting it as at least possible, and scientifically quite as admissible as the opposite assumption, that in the act of attention the will adds something new to the forces theretofore present in the world. This was a great step for an academic psychologist to take.

Though frankly iconoclastic and outspoken, and a hard-hitter in an intellectual combat, Professor James made no enemies, but usually drew closer and closer, as time went on, the ties of early friendships. Soon after his complete retirement, his colleagues of the department of philosophy at Harvard asked him to let them have his portrait painted, to be hung upon the walls of the Faculty Room in University Hall. When the portrait was finished, Professor James entertained the whole division of philosophy at his house. The occasion was a memorable one, and especially so for the reason that Professor Royce, who had always been one of James's most loyal friends and admirers, made an exceedingly warm-hearted and eloquent address. I quote here a few of his sentences, though the choice is difficult where everything was so good: —

> Nothing is more characteristic of Professor James's work as a teacher and as a thinker than is his chivalrous fondness for fair play in the warfare and in the coöperation of ideas and of ideals. We all of us profess to love truth. But one of James's especial offices in the service of truth has been the love and protection and encouragement of the truth-seekers. He has done much more than this for the cause of truth; but this at least he has always done.
>
> He has lately warned us much against thinking of truth as a mere abstrac-

> tion. And indeed it has always been his especial gift to see truth incarnate,—embodied in the truth-seekers,—and to show his own love of truth by listening with appreciation, and by helping the cause of fair play, whenever he found somebody earnestly toiling or suffering or hoping in the pursuit of any genuine ideal of truth. . . . Other men talk of liberty of thought; but few men have done more to secure liberty of thought for men who were in need of fair play and of a reasonable hearing than James has done.

James was one of the first among professional psychologists to recognize the full bearing of the contributions which medical observation—that is, the psychology of the unusual or the slightly twisted mind—has made to the more classical psychological attitudes and insights. In the early portion of his short but stirring address, *The Energies of Men,* he says, 'Meanwhile the clinical conceptions, though they may be vaguer than the analytic ones, are certainly more adequate, give the concreter picture of the way the whole mind works, and are of far more urgent practical importance. So the "physician's attitude," the "functional psychology," is assuredly the thing most worthy of general study to-day.'

The truth of these propositions has been amply verified, and the fact that he made them is but one more illustration of his power to see and seize upon the significant elements of a situation, as a skillful commander recognizes the points of strength and weakness of his adversary's lines.

William James was a manly and a radiant being. Loving and loved, he made all men think, and helped many a doubting soul to feel a man's glow of hope and courage, each for his own work. This was a noble task.

GEORGE HERBERT PALMER

(1842–1933)

When George Palmer entered Harvard as a student in 1860, thirty instructors taught nearly one thousand students and only one course was offered in philosophy. 'In most colleges,' Palmer remembered, 'the little Philosophy attempted was usually taught by the President, a minister. If an independent teacher was employed, he also was a minister. Under Puritanism Theology and Philosophy were pretty closely identified.'[1] Palmer himself entered Andover Seminary in 1865, imagining that he would preach for a few years and then, he hoped, be nominated for a professorship of philosophy.

Larger opportunities opened up for Palmer when Charles William Eliot took over the presidency of the college in 1869 and created a department of philosophy. In 1872, Palmer joined the faculty as an instructor in philosophy; by 1876 he chaired the department. During his tenure—he retired in 1913—its members included James, Josiah Royce, George Santayana, Hugo Münsterberg, and Francis Bowen (whose eulogy by Palmer evoked James's admiration).

Although Palmer and James felt affection for one another, they recognized irreconcilable differences in personality and outlook that prevented their becoming close friends. James thought Palmer too cautious, too bound by his background as a Congregational minister. Yet he remarked about Palmer, 'For a non-original man, he seems to me the ablest I know.' Palmer taught Philosophy 4 (a course in ethics), and in the 1880s joined some of his American colleagues in taking up the ideas of Hegel. 'It is a strange thing, this resurrection of Hegel in England and here, after his burial in Germany,' James wrote to Charles Renouvier. While James believed that this revival of Hegelianism would give 'a quasi-metaphysic backbone' to liberal Christianity and serve as a 'reaction against materialistic evolutionism,' he still preferred the 'fertile' ground sown by evolutionism to the philosophy of Hegel that he thought 'is absolutely sterile.'[2] From Palmer's memoir we can see that he believed James may not have been so certain of his anti-Hegelian feelings.

In 1887, Palmer, who had been a widower for many years, married Alice Freeman, the thirty-two-year-old president of Wellesley College. After their wedding, held at the home of former Massachusetts Governor William Claflin, Alice Freeman Palmer moved into her husband's house at 11 Quincy Street, giving up her position at Wellesley to take part in the social life of Cambridge. Palmer adored his wife, who died in 1903. He counted among his most important works his memorial to her, *The Life of Alice Freeman Palmer.*

A short, thin man with near-sighted blue eyes and a moustache, Palmer was modest, cautious, and a meticulous if not ground-breaking scholar. His books include *The Field of Ethics* (1901), *The Nature of Goodness* (1903), *The Life and Works of George Herbert* (1905)—the poet for whom he was named—and *The Problem of Freedom* (1911).

As a teacher Palmer earned his students' affection for his warm interest and sincerity. 'What a strange, kindly little man he had been!' wrote Rollo Walter Brown. 'He had shown them how great is the security to be found in self-development and self-direction. He had performed the impossible feat of making goodness seem exciting. And he had made religion the most reasonable and the most desirable thing in the world.'[3] Some, however, recalled Palmer's teaching with less enthusiasm. George Santayana, describing Palmer's course in ethics, remembered, 'His lectures were beautifully prepared, and exactly the same year after year. . . . The method was Hegelian adapted to a Sunday School; all roses without thorns.' Yet, like Brown, he remarked on Palmer's 'sweet reasonableness. That his methods were sophistical and his conclusions lame,' he added, 'didn't really matter.'[4] In fact, even Santayana admitted that he and his fellow students, who were 'crude, half-educated, conscientious, ambitious young men who wished to study ethics, gained subtler and more elastic notions of what was good than they had ever dreamt of: and their notions of what was bad became correspondingly discriminating and fair.'[5]

In a department noted for the ferocity of opinions among the faculty, Palmer often seemed an oasis of serenity. 'In our lectures,' he recalled, 'we were accustomed to attack each other by name, James forever exposing the follies of the idealists, particularly of Royce and me, Royce in turn showing how baseless all empiricism is, lacking a metaphysical ground.'[6] Students discovered, however, that in Palmer's class they would be subjected to none of this warfare: Philosophy 4 stood out as one of the most popular courses in the department.

NOTES

1. George Palmer, *The Autobiography of a Philosopher* (Boston: Houghton Mifflin, 1930), 20.
2. *Letters* 1:208 (27 December 1880).
3. Rollo Walter Brown, *Harvard Yard in the Golden Age* (New York: Current Books, 1948), 73.
4. George Santayana, *Persons and Places.* (London: Constable, 1944), 1:253–54.
5. Santayana, *Persons and Places,* 254.
6. Palmer, *Autobiography,* 52–53.

William James

In view of the publication of the letters of William James, I am asked to state how he appeared to his colleagues in the daily course of his work as a Harvard professor. In brief he showed among us the same surprising, rich, brilliant, and profitable variety of speech and act which appeared in his home, his books, and his championship of an unpopular cause. His nature was so abundant and original that it never became standardized or usual. We, who met him most intimately, found in him every day something fresh to wonder at and admire. I might then properly enough decline the work of description and say that James was indescribable. But I cannot content myself so. I loved the man, and far away I hear his prompting voice. When Professor Bowen died, I, as his successor, was called on to prepare a minute on him for the Faculty Record. As James and I came out together from the meeting where this had been read, he turned to me with one of his sudden bursts, 'Palmer, I mean to die before you, so that you can operate on me too.' Alas! he had his cruel wish, and I drew up his official minute. But such a man claims something more personal. I will set down a few random recollections of such sayings and incidents, slight in themselves, as bear his mark. The connected history of his life, discussion of his philosophy, and criticism of his many books, I leave to others. Mine is the pleasanter, if harder, task of setting forth an exceptionally engaging personality.

Whenever that alert figure comes to my mind—he of the handsome face, upright bearing, energetic movement, swift step, and tempered voice—there always comes with it the adjective 'manly.' In every tense fibre of his being James was a man, one of his own plural centres of creative causation, a being unconstrained by the surrounding world, master of himself and it, happy in subjecting its complicated and interesting enginery to the control of his own large powers. How large those powers were he knew well, but did not exaggerate. He treated them respectfully, cultivated them carefully, and joyously sent them forth on errands for the public good. His own stamp was on all he thought, did, or said. I doubt if he ever knew fear, vanity, or social constraint, or if a sense of incompetence ever held him back from what he wished to do. Yet courage did not blind him. When he was in Florence, writing his Gifford Lectures, he was well aware that his heart might stop its beating any day. Yet he wrote on. Each fortnight he and I exchanged letters. His were full of his usual charm, playfulness, and eager interest in all the world was doing, though in a few closing sentences he usually acknowledged his peril. A similar coolness was shown in small things. Once, when lecturing to a large class on formal logic, he was caught in the intricacies of Mood and Figure and for the moment puzzled. Merely remarking, 'You will have to wait a few minutes,' he turned his back to the class, his face to the wall, and after a brief meditation, turning back, went on with his lecture as if nothing had happened.

Commonly one so indifferent and masterful is apt to neglect social amenities. But James had a delicate consideration of others, an observant tactfulness in putting all at ease. Few persons are habitually so kind. In consequence a troop of cranks attended him through life, in each of whom he found some merit and—more costly—some need. His last paper was an attempt to sift grains of gold out of a muddy stream. What outlays of time and money he spent on half-baked philosophers! And how keen was the advice he gave, if only they had had the wit to take it! When an aspiring Sophomore brought him his program of study for the following year with only philosophical electives on it, James turned from him with disgust. 'Jones, don't you philosophize on an empty stomach!'—a rebuke too harsh for older dreamers. To them he would patiently listen, gently suggest corrective reading, and try to arrange for them opportunities for lectures or publication. His judgment of men was not good; it was corrupted by kindness. In our Committee, when voting on candidates for the higher degrees, he generally favored the merciful side. 'Of course Smith is n't a genius. But, poor devil, how he has worked!' His over-estimate of Charles Peirce, and too ample acknowledgment of his own debt to Peirce's thought, I believe to have sprung quite as much from pity as from admiration.

This inclination toward the under-dog, and his insistence on keeping the door open for every species of human experiment, brought James into alliance with causes which his social set looked on with some disfavor. But friendship never dulled his sense of justice nor his zeal in vindicating it.

When the doctors, like trade-unionists, were making one of their periodical assaults on Christian Science, James appeared at the State House arguing against his natural friends. Or, again, he never concealed from himself how large a part fraud and self-deception play in Spiritualism. He and I, as members of a Committee of the Psychical Society, attended 'cabinet séances' every Saturday for an entire winter, and at the close reported that in our opinion all these materializing phenomena were fraudulent. Still, discrimination was necessary. The following year he invited Mrs. Piper to give a series of trance interviews at his house; and he believed—as did I—that there was significant matter in her visions. While never, I think, fully convinced that beings of another world communicate with us, he was unwilling to treat the subject as a closed question. Closed questions and the many varieties of scientific obscurantism were abhorrent to him and never failed to call forth his energetic, if sometimes comical, protest. Once, long before the days of spelling reform, he came to me with, 'Is n't it abominable that everybody is expected to spell in the same way? Let us get a dozen influential persons to agree each to spell after his own fashion and so break up this tyranny of the dictionary.' I had to say that my philistine soul preferred order to oddity.

Yet no one ever called James odd or bumptious. Self-assertion and loose radicalism were alien to his beauty-loving and serious temperament. His bearing and utterance were always quiet and distinguished. Only he insisted on using his own eyes and mind, and thought the best contribution he could make to the sleepy world was a pungent statement of just how things looked to him. Yet in this he was not insistent. His work in the classroom was uneven, his lectures—somewhat dependent on mood—often lacking continuity. If a student did not immediately 'catch on' he might go from one of them no richer than he came. But the same student next week was sure to be stirred by some passage so striking and searching that its truth became henceforth a veritable part of his mind and a way was opened to a whole new tract of formulative thought. Few teachers have had more grateful pupils than James.

On the rare occasions when he spoke in Faculty or Committee meetings it was usually with a hesitation compounded in about equal measure of modesty, punctilious truthfulness, and literary exactitude. What he said was important and some shining phrase would ultimately carry the meaning home. So, too, in his writing. His search for the just word was as relentless as that of Flaubert. It filled with corrections the manuscript of his books. But who among our writers has lodged in the public mind so many subtle thoughts on difficult subjects? Whether we agree or dissent, with what delight we read his pages! The famous saying is just: Of the pair of extraordinary brothers, the psychologist wrote like a novelist, the novelist like a psychologist. William James's style may not be classical. Smoothness and easy flow he did not value. But their glorious opposites march superb—force, unexpectedness, epigram, coruscating abundance. His, too, is perfect frankness and a command of all the resources of the language. A friend who makes many public addresses tells me his test of a good one is whether he 'wallowed,' that is, moved unobstructedly, through his matter as the whale does through the sea, twisting and turning at his pleasure, tossing up foam for mere sport, and plunging or rising as the fancy strikes. James always wallowed.

In our Department of Philosophy it was a tradition that differences of opinion were to be honored and their open announcement in our lecture-rooms encouraged. When a new instructor was to be chosen, we looked for one who would bring to our ranks a philosophic attitude not previously represented. We thought our students were best stimulated to form convictions of their own if they were invited to consider opposing views presented by those who heartily believed them. Among ourselves, therefore, we could not easily quarrel, for our divergences were expected and approved. We were a group singularly diverse in judgment and temperament, and at the same time the warmest of friends. Each saw in his colleagues men of such worth and eminence that to honor them was a matter of course. There was literary enjoyment and intellectual discipline in committee meetings attended by James, Royce, Everett, Münsterberg, and Santayana. Few college departments have been so united, for ours was an organic unity and not one of sameness. At some time each of us except James served as Chairman. He disliked administration and thought himself unfit for it.

And if there was such hearty tolerance of difference among his colleagues, James accepted the principle no less for the workings of his own mind. Consistency was counted negligible, fidelity to facts the sole obligation. We used laughingly to say that you could not tell what beliefs James would hold to-day, but only that they would be different from those of last week. And while his mind was certainly hospitable to an astonishing variety of ideas which are usually thought to conflict, it was a sane and usually evolutional variety, where the later did not quite forget the earlier. So soon as he had seen anything through, his interest flagged. To hold attraction for him a subject must offer opportunity for adventure and exploration. In the Medical School he began his teaching with Comparative Anatomy, soon found bones and muscles things of no consequence apart from functions, and so crossed to Physiology. He had been engaged with this but a short time when he announced to me that bodily functions were subsidiary to mental and could only be understood from the point of view of Psychology. Accordingly he came over into College teaching, organized the first laboratory of experimental psychology in America—raising the money himself—gave delightful instruction for several years to large courses of beginners, led a little band of graduates in psychological research, and amused his leisure with building up his monumental book. But when this was published he refused all further teaching of psychology. 'Nasty little subject! Nothing in it! All one cares to know lies outside!' He had the title of his professorship changed and declared he would leave Harvard if obliged to continue as director of its laboratory. He now turned to Epistemology, Metaphysics, Religion, carrying into all his later fields the acquisitions and training of the old. With all its brilliancy, his was no flippant, loose, or disorderly mind, but one of untiring advance. He would not rest at any spot attained, nor even notice conventional restraints; but after studying the discoveries of others, would sail uncharted seas, his own originality his compass.

The general direction of his intellectual movement I am inclined to think was shaped by reaction from two strong opposing influences of his youth. Everybody knows how philosophers divide over mind and matter and the importance to be attached to their seeming contrast. The extreme empiricist holds that to the constitution of the physical world, as manifested in its steadfast laws, all our knowledge is to be referred; while the idealist finds in laws of mind the ultimate reality and regards material phenomena as but exhibits of their working. Naturally between these extreme views fall many varieties. Now the father of William James, a student of Swedenborg, was loved and honored by him profoundly. He has written an exquisite sketch of his life and character. But James grew up believing that the powers of that admirable man had been hindered in efficiency, if not in growth, by a mystical idealism. He came, therefore, to dread such blinding beliefs for himself. In early manhood, too, he formed a close acquaintance with Chauncey Wright, a powerful personality and intrepid thinker, who, following J. S. Mill, carried agnosticism to an extreme beyond that master. For a time James found in Wright's hard empiricism a welcome escape from the idealism which had oppressed him. It gave close contact with the actual world. But by degrees its avoidance of ultimate issues and restriction to mere fact exasperated him. Expressing to me his aversion from a philosophy which so emptied life of significance, he exclaimed: 'Chauncey is the damnedest rationalist that ever I saw.'

Henceforth he seemed to oscillate between these two gulfs, making it his daily prayer that he might fall into neither. Twice he ventured up to the idealist edge and looked on the devouring flood below. One winter Dr. W. T. Harris presided over an informal philosophical club in Boston for the reading of Hegel. Among its irregular members were C. C. Everett, Eliot Cabot, E. B. Andrews, Thomas Davison [*sic*], William James, and myself. I do not think James obtained anything from the strange jargon. Again a few years later he attended a seminary of mine on Hegel's Logic, and once more found it intolerable and incomprehensible. He washed his hands of the pernicious stuff in his amusing paper on 'Some Hegelisms.' But I thought it always held a terrifying fascination for him. Though he called his philosophy 'Radical Empiricism' and liked to try how complete a world might be constructed by ingenious manipulation of material elements, yet to the last he kept ample room in his empiric universe for spiritual forces. Man is free. An approachable God exists, reverence for whom is the beginning of wisdom, and religion the most urgent of human concerns. He himself was a peculiarly devout man, and though living at a distance, liked to begin his day with the service at Appleton Chapel.

Perhaps the grounds of endearment, and its long reach beyond admiration, must always remain unstateable. They certainly appear but slenderly in this meagre sketch. I can only say that we, who for more than thirty years were blest with James's presence, loved him with increasing fervor. We found in him a masterful type of human being, developed almost to perfection. We found an ever fresh and genial companion, of whom we could say with Chaucer that 'dulnesse was of him y-drad.' We found the tenderest of friends, who was at our side in every affliction, great or small. We found a noble soul, high-bred and democratically minded, incapable of doing anything to be seen of men, but who, perceiving that our age stands in extreme need of patient thought and lucid speech, earned the gratitude of two continents by what he gave. Who that came close to such a being could fail to love? In him there was nothing to excuse.

JOSIAH ROYCE

(1855–1916)

Born in the small mining town of Grass Valley, California, Josiah Royce had early ambitions to be a hunter or a trapper. When he entered school, however, he discovered other interests: mathematics, for one, and engineering. A precocious student, he entered the preparatory program at the University of California after his first year of high school. He was not yet fifteen.

By the time he graduated from the University of California in 1875, Royce had decided to study philosophy and, at the suggestion of Daniel Coit Gilman, the school's president, set off to study in Germany—stopping first in Boston. In the summer of 1875, at a dinner party hosted by George Dorr and his wife, Royce first met James.

James saw something special in Royce, despite Royce's social awkwardness. A non-stop talker with a harsh, unpleasant voice, Royce looked decidedly odd: short and stocky, with an unusually large head, bright red tousled hair, eyelashes so light they seemed nonexistent, and intense blue eyes. His full lips gave the appearance of a permanent pout. But Royce was obviously bright, displaying a sense of irreverence that attracted James immediately.

After a year in Germany, Royce enrolled at Johns Hopkins University, where his mentor Gilman had assumed the presidency. At the end of his first year he again came to Cambridge, visited James, and poured out his soul (as he put it in this memoir), asking for advice. James encouraged him to continue his studies, assuring him that it was possible to follow a career in philosophy—especially for someone as talented as Josiah Royce.

Royce graduated from Johns Hopkins in 1878, receiving one of the first four doctorates awarded there. He found to his dismay, however, that the only position offered was from the English Department at the University of California at Berkeley. Stimulated by the intellectual communities of Baltimore and Cambridge and longing to teach philosophy, he was reluctant to return to what he saw as the wasteland of California.

James sympathized with Royce's plight. In the spring of 1881 James advised Royce of a possible vacancy at Harvard and promised his support in helping Royce obtain it. But not until 1882, when James took a sabbatical leave, did the vacancy occur. Royce was exultant. He then managed to extend this temporary position and in 1885 was offered permanent status.

Royce was a polished lecturer whose talks fit so neatly into the class sessions that it seemed to one student 'that the lecture had been prepared first and then a period of time carved out of eternity that would just include it.'[1] And he was also an industrious writer, 'working like 3 men and thinking like 100,' as James put it to his friend George Howison.[2] James admired Royce's 'unscholastic' form, and envied his ability to write for a wide audience. In addition to his many philosophical studies, Royce wrote a history of California, and a novel, *The Feud of Oakfield Creek* (1887), which he dedicated to James.

Anyone who knew James and Royce acknowledged that they seemed to be complete opposites in every way: James, charming and gregarious, Royce socially inhibited and lonely; James, trim and smartly attired, Royce short, stocky, and frumpy; James celebrating religious plurality, Royce, as Alice James put it, carrying 'his Infinite under his arm.'[3] They frequently attacked one another in class, and students observed them in heated discussions as they walked to their homes on Irving Street. In light of James's objections to Royce's absolutism, and Royce's disappointment in James's pragmatism, it is all the more surprising that the two men were such close friends. Certainly Royce's admiration for James was underscored by his gratitude for James's encouragement and professional help. But his regard went beyond gratitude. While James was spending his 1892–93 sabbatical year in Europe, Royce wrote plaintively, 'Cambridge without you is like toast unbuttered, like the heart without blood.'[4]

James himself best described the quality of their relationship in a letter he wrote to Royce in 1900, when James was in Nauheim seeking a health cure.

> Different as our minds are, yours has nourished mine, as no other social influence ever has, and in converse with you I have always felt that my life was being lived importantly. Our minds, too, are not different in the *object* which they envisage. It is the whole paradoxical physics-moral-spiritual fatness, of which most people single out some skinny fragment, which we both cover

with our eye. We 'aim at him generally'—and most others don't. I don't believe that we shall dwell apart forever, though our formulas may.[5]

NOTES

1. Rollo Walter Brown, *Harvard Yard in the Golden Age* (New York: Current Books, 1948), 56.

2. WJ to George Howison. Scott, 60 (21 October 1889).

3. Comment of Alice James to Henry James, on Royce's taking Gifford lectures when William James refused them in 1899 and 1900. Quoted in Clendenning, *The Life and Thought of Josiah Royce* (Madison: University of Wisconsin Press, 1985), 239.

4. Josiah Royce to WJ. Clendenning, *Letters of Josiah Royce,* 299 (17 October 1892).

5. WJ to Josiah Royce. *Letters* 2:136 (26 September 1900).

A Word of Greeting to William James

My word of greeting to our host ought to be delivered *ex tempore*. If I cannot meet the requirement of the occasion in this respect, one sufficient reason for my failure is the difficulty of separating out, in my mind, and in my speech, the things that it is possible to say from amidst the great mass of the things which flock to my mind at such a time. My relations to our host have lasted so long,—have been so manifold,—that I can select only with difficulty. What he has meant to me has been of such intimate importance in my own personal life that it is especially hard to judge what part of my own account of him will appeal to others with any of the deeper meaning that this account inevitably has for me.

Yet there is one matter to which I may at once refer,—a matter that has been indeed momentous for my own private fortunes, but that is also known and interesting to all of us alike. Nothing is more characteristic of Professor James's work as a teacher and as a thinker than is his chivalrous

A dinner was held at the house of Prof. James on Jan. 18, to celebrate the completion of his portrait, and the presentation of it to the University. The portrait was subscribed, on the occasion of Prof. James's retirement, by the members of the Division and the Visiting Committee on Philosophy as a symbol of the affection and esteem of his colleagues. The following were present at the dinner:

Specially invited guests: Pres. Lowell, Pres. Eliot, Mr. H. L. Higginson. Members of the Visiting Committee: Messrs. R. C. Robbins, G. B. Dorr, R. C. Cabot, R. H. Dana, W. R. Warren, J. Lee, and the Rev. G. A. Gordon. Members of the Division of Philosophy: Professors James, Palmer, Münsterberg, Royce, Peabody, Santayana, Holt, Yerkes, Woods, Perry, and Dr. Fuller. Informal remarks were made by Prof. Palmer, who represented the subscribers, by Pres. Eliot and Prof. Royce, who spoke as Prof. James's associates throughout his career, by Pres. Lowell, who represented the University and received the portrait in its behalf, and by Prof. James. The portrait was painted by Miss Ellen Emmett, of New York, and is to hang in the Faculty Room, University Hall.

fondness for fair play in the warfare and in the coöperation of ideas and of ideals. We all of us profess to love truth. But one of James's especial offices in the service of truth has been the love and protection and encouragement of the truth-seekers. He has done much more than this for the cause of truth; but this at least he has always done. He has lately warned us much against thinking of truth as a mere abstraction. And indeed it has always been his especial gift to see truth incarnate,—embodied in the truth-seekers, and to show his own love of truth by listening with appreciation, and by helping the cause of fair play, whenever he found somebody earnestly toiling or suffering or hoping in the pursuit of any genuine ideal of truth. How many eager seekers, neglected by the world,—men who fought on the side of unpopular causes, have come to him for sympathy, and have found it,—not in the form of any easy acceptance of their own opinions,—but in the form of a sympathy that has sustained them in the freedom of their faith and in the sincerity of their life, because he told them that if the spirit of earnest endeavor was in them, and if some real light had come to their souls, it was better to offer what they had, and to fight for their own best, than to accept tamely the restraints of this or of that transient form of present-day orthodoxy. Other men talk of liberty of thought; but few men have done more to secure liberty of thought for men who were in need of fair play and of a reasonable hearing than James has done.

Now I suppose that it is altogether, or almost altogether because of James's chivalry of soul that I myself first obtained that opportunity in life which results in my being here with you at all. In speaking of my personal relation to him, I therefore have to dwell upon a matter that in this respect does indeed tend to characterize him. My real acquaintance with our host began one summer day in 1877 when I first visited him in the house on Quincy St., and was permitted to pour out my soul to somebody who really seemed to believe that a young man might rightfully devote his life to philosophy if he chose. I was then a student at the Johns Hopkins University. The opportunities for a lifework in philosophy in this country were few. Most of my friends and advisers had long been telling me to let the subject alone. Perhaps, so far as I was concerned, their advice was sound; but in any case I was so far incapable of accepting that advice. Yet if somebody had not been ready to tell me that I had a right to work for truth in my own way, I should ere long have been quite discouraged. I do not know what I then could have done. James found me at once—made out what my essential interests were at our first interview, accepted me, with all my imperfections, as one of those many souls who ought to be able to find themselves in their own way, gave a patient and willing ear to just my variety of philosophical experience, and used his influence from that time on, not to win me as a follower, but to give me my chance. It was upon his responsibility that I was later led to get my first opportunities here at Harvard. Whatever I am is in that sense due to him.

There are a great many people living who could give almost this very account of their own careers. My own case is but one of a multitude. No other philosopher in our country compares with James, I think, in his effectiveness as a man who has helped active and restless minds not only to win their own spiritual freedom, but to express their ideals in their own way.

Sometimes critical people have expressed this by saying that James has always been too fond of cranks, and that the cranks have loved him. Well, I am one of James's cranks. He was good to me, and I love him. The result of my own early contact with James was to make me for years very much his disciple. I am still in large part under his spell. If I contend with him sometimes, I suppose that it is he also who through his own free spirit has in great measure taught me this liberty. I know that for years I used to tremble at the thought that James might perhaps some day find reason to put me in my place by some one of those wonderful, lightning-like epigrams wherewith he was and is always able to characterize those opponents whose worldly position is such as to make them no longer in danger of not getting a fair hearing, and whose self-assurance has relieved him of the duty to secure for them a sympathetic attention. What, I used to say, would be *my* feeling if James were to wither me with such a word as he can use about Thomas Hill Green, or perhaps about some other so-called Hegelian?—The time has passed, the lightning in question has often descended,—never indeed on me as his friend, but often on my opinions, and has long since blasted, I hope, some at least of what is most combustible about my poor teachings. Yet I am so glad of the friendly words that still sustain me, that these occasional *segnende Blitze,* when incidentally they are sown over the earth where my opinions chance to be growing, only make me love better the cause that James loves, and that he has so nobly served, the cause of fertilizing the human soil where our truth has to grow,—this cause, and the friend who through all these years has borne with me so kindly, and has in so many ways been my creator and my support. He is my teacher. I am his pupil, and I bring him a pupil's homage tonight.

Next to fearing James's lightning, I have long used for years to live in a love which I think he never fully understood,—the love of just watching and listening for whatever James has had to say by way of comment upon current events and upon new problems. For years, I say, I have never known precisely what to think of any new matter until I have carried it to James, and have waited to hear his first absolutely spontaneous comment upon it. I find that he usually forgets these first comments. They escape him without reflection. They leave no trace in his mind of being remarkable or worthy of being remembered. Yet they often possess a quality that he will much object to hearing me mention,—the quality of being absolutely true,—not true in the merely 'pragmatic' sense. They are like his lightning,—only they do not by any means always consume. They reveal. It is hard to say how many of these comments have sunk into my soul, or how often I find myself reporting them to my classes, with a greater or less temptation to repeat them as if they were my own.

For a pronounced opponent of philosophical absolutism, such as our host is, it is indeed remarkable how many absolute truths he has been heard to utter, and how many he has also written down in his books. The wind bloweth where it listeth; and so is every one that is born of the Spirit.

GEORGE ANGIER GORDON

(1853–1929)

When George Gordon emigrated to America from his native Scotland in the summer of 1871, he had no hopes other than making money and extricating himself from a society that he thought was oppressive and feudal. His first job was in a safe factory, followed by work as a stonemason, a painter, and an assistant editor of a small newspaper. In December 1871, however, he called on the Reverend Luther H. Angier of the Fourth Presbyterian Church in South Boston to discuss joining the parish. Angier was much impressed by the young man, and came to serve not only as his minister but also as his adviser and confidant. As testimony to the sense of communion he felt for Angier, Gordon incorporated Angier's surname into his own.

Although Gordon never had thought of himself as an intellectual, Angier encouraged him to pursue studies in theology and philosophy. In 1874 Gordon enrolled at the Bangor Theological Seminary; in 1878 Angier spoke to his friend Charles William Eliot about Gordon's admission to Harvard as a special student. Gordon remembers his first meeting with Eliot as a kind of Judgment Day. 'When, on June 15, 1878, at nine o'clock in the morning, I first met him, by appointment, this was the impression he made upon me. No one could have been kinder or more considerate; at the same time, something in his look and bearing said plainly, "I am observing you; you must prove your worth."'[1]

Gordon was much more comfortable with some of his professors, most notably George Herbert Palmer, whom he remembers with great affection as 'luminous, simple, learned, rich, subtle in intellect, a great teacher, a great character, a great friend.' He praised Palmer's ability to make vivid the personalities of such philosophers as Socrates, Plato, Berkeley, and Kant, and to show the connections among apparently disparate schools of thought.[2]

Evidently Gordon did prove his worth at Harvard. After two years as a special student, he was admitted to the class of 1881 and graduated *magna cum laude* with honors in Philosophy. Upon graduation he was offered a position teaching ethics at Johns Hopkins University. Eliot, however, wanted Gordon to continue studying in England and Germany, after which he might return to Harvard to teach Ecclesiastical History.

But Gordon could not afford to be a student any longer. His father had just died, and he found himself the sole support of his mother and two younger siblings. He decided to accept a ministry instead, and in August 1881 became minister at the Second Congregational Church in Greenwich, Connecticut.

Gordon remembers his time in Greenwich as rich and satisfying. The affluent, liberal, and open-minded community welcomed his freshness and youth. But in January 1883, Gordon received another invitation—this time from the prestigious Old South Church in Boston, which was seeking a successor to its departing minister. Charles Eliot had put Gordon's name up for consideration.

Although his parish in Greenwich tried to keep him, Gordon could not refuse the repeated requests to move to Boston. On 2 April 1884 he was installed at the Old South Church. Gordon offended some members of his conservative parish by his denial of a personal Devil and his interest in questioning the tenets of Christianity. 'The intellect of our churches,' he wrote, 'was facing the task of finding a new and more adequate philosophy of the Christian religion, the experience of Christian men, and the meaning of God's great world in time.'[3] Gordon was, for his time, an unconventional minister who believed individuals should and must challenge accepted doctrine and think for themselves. He believed 'Men under authority are men without training in the powers of the mind, and in character as it bears upon the things of the mind. . . . Intellectual anarchy is the inevitable issue of cancelled authority; it is a beginning in independent intellectual life, it is a start toward the far-away goal of competent judgment.'[4]

Gordon himself was not at all sure that he had a genuine call to preach. 'The fact is,' he remembered, 'I was induced to try by very dear friends who thought they knew me better than I knew myself. I accepted their judgment tentatively, and I am free to confess that the call was so feeble that if I had met with any serious reverse, with anything other than the unqualified kindness and unbounded encouragement which I did meet, I should have turned back.'[5]

Part of the unbounded encouragement he received came from William James, with whom he remained friends even after he left Harvard. Gordon and his wife socialized with the Jameses, and the two men shared their writings with one another. Gordon, a prolific writer, published dozens of books on questions of theology, including *Christ of to day* (1895), *Immortality and the new theodicy* (1897), *New Epoch for Faith* (1901), *Through Man to God* (1906), and *Ministry as a Profession* (1907).

NOTES

1. George Angier Gordon, *My Education and Religion* (Cambridge: Riverside Press, 1925), 293.
2. Gordon, *My Education and Religion,* 194.
3. Gordon, *My Education and Religion,* 241.
4. Gordon, *My Education and Religion,* 240.
5. Gordon, *My Education and Religion,* 176.

A Profoundly Religious Man

There was William James, no longer among the living; he, too, was thirty-six when I was his pupil, a young man, working slowly upon his great book 'Principles of Psychology,' a book which upon its publication placed him at once among the famous men in his subject all over the world. He was brilliant, erratic, for weeks at a time languid and nearly useless, and then all at once for two or three weeks following he would be incomparably original and suggestive. He was not great as a metaphysician, but he was in psychology a man of genius, and his gift of expression has made his books literature.

When he retired from active teaching and became Professor Emeritus, I, as one of his oldest pupils, ventured to write him a letter in which, among other things, I said that I was happy that I knew him before he became famous; that I never knew a fairer mind, one more sensitive to evidence for or against himself, one more candid or more willing to give even the Devil his due. He was a noble and most lovable man, and at the same time occasionally provoking owing to his eccentricity. Professor Palmer was a wise but frank religionist; Professor James was equally religious, but he was fond of hiding it; the truth, however, could not be concealed. He was too high in tone, too fine in fiber, too deep in his sympathy with the best in the life of his kind, to be other than a profoundly religious man.

Professor James's father was a remarkable character, a kind of glorified Greek Fury. When I came to know him he was old, white-haired, lame, and wore a skull-cap. On one occasion his son sent me for a book to his father's house on Quincy Street, where William James lived before he was married. I thought it was strange to send me, an unknown student, to an unknown home, to unknown inhabitants, to find a book, but I went. The old man met me at the door with the question, 'What do you want?' 'I want a book,' I replied. 'What's your name, and who are you?' I told him my name and who I was. 'Are you one of William's students?' 'I am.' He looked me all over with a good deal of suspicion, still glaring at me with eyes like flames of fire. 'Come in,' he finally said. I went in and I looked him over, and I was perfectly sure that I could take care of him physically, if it should come to that. I sat down. 'Are you a believer?' he asked. I said that I counted myself on that side. Then every sentence was kinder than the one that went before, and mellower, and before the conversation ended he had taken me into his heart, a great heart it was, and he told me some things about his two sons, of whom he was very proud, William and Henry. They were always debating when they were boys, he said, and I learnt afterward from another friend that this was true. The old man further reported that Henry was quicker both in speech and in argument than William; William was deeper, and usually, before the debate ended, got the better of his brother. Henry announced one day, 'I believe in God; but I have no use for the church.' William said, 'If you believe in God, you have got to believe in the church because God is the church.' This remarkable statement staggered the younger brother, being a sort of solar plexus blow, and it ended the debate for that day.

William James was the simplest and most confiding person with his students. His eyes were weak, and he invited some of the more mature of us to come and read our examination-books to him. Then he would ask us what we thought we ought to get on the book. There was, however, in reserve a judgment, absolutely upright, that could not be twisted by kindness or by comradeship; in that true mind there was a standard that was fixed as fate. We debated with him, but without avail. This sort of thing will show the comradeship that existed between James and his students, and his absolute integrity as a teacher. He loved and trusted us, but we could not fool him, if indeed we had ever wanted to do so.

I recall an incident in his section that contributed to my admiration for him, an incident which in most cases would have destroyed the influence of another type of man. He was explaining some subtle point in psychology, and he wished to use a mathematical illustration. He went to the blackboard and was in the midst of his process when one of the men in the section who was an expert mathematician inquired respectfully, 'Professor James, are you sure that you are right there?' He continued with his figuring, and the further he proceeded in the illustration the profounder became the confusion into which he went. At last he turned and said, 'Well, I knew that once, but I must have forgotten all about it; let it go.' This confession of absolute candor in his confusion called forth a round of applause, and greatly increased our admiration for our teacher and our loyalty to him.

When Professor James died, his wife wrote me a note asking me to officiate at his funeral, in which she said, 'I want you to officiate at the funeral as one of William's friends and also as a man of faith. That is what he was; I want no hesitation or diluted utterance at William's funeral.'

The letters that follow have long been precious to me, yet am I glad to share them with his friends and mine.

95 Irving Street, Cambridge, Jan. 24, 1907

Dear Gordon:

I am deeply touched by your letter—on the whole the finest compliment I ever received. To be held in such remembrance by men like you spells indeed success for a teacher. Within a year or two I seem to be getting 'recognized' as I never was before, and feel in consequence as if my place in the world was warmer. No one can tell how he really appears to 'outsiders,' least of all, perhaps, after they have tried to tell him; so I am well content to take the conclusion without chopping logic over the premises. You and I seem to be working (along with most other decent people) towards the same end (the Kingdom of Heaven, namely), you more openly and immediately. I more subterraneanly and remotely, but I believe we are converging upon the same thing ultimately, and the best thing I can hope for is that our successes may not be too uneven.

With thanks—and thanks—believe me ever

Affectionately yours

Wm. James

95 Irving Street, Cambridge, 30. IV. '09

Dear Gordon:

Your letter has given me acute pleasure, both substantively that *you* should show such sympathy with what I am trying to do, and representatively as the first swallow of what I hope may be a summer flock. You seem to be the first person to have read the book through, and from its effect on you I am encouraged to hope for a similar effect on others. My intent is indeed deeply conciliatory, as you may see by the advertisement which I wrote and which I enclose.

Have you read Elwood Worcester's Fechnerian book of devotion, which seems to me a very living word indeed?

What a reader you must be! It is very good of you to write to me at such length, and so warmly. I much regretted not being able to get to your anniversary dinner. I have perforce to cut all such things out of my life nowadays—you had enough without me!

Believe me, again, dear Gordon, with heartfelt thanks, in which the good wife joins

Yours always truly

Wm. James

95 Irving Street, Cambridge, Oct. 31, 1909

Dear Gordon:

I have just finished reading your 'Religion and Miracle,' and have found it even more full of the 'Spirit' than your previous books—extraordinarily rich and superabounding in moral and rhetorical momentum as well, of course, as true in the thesis it urges with such convincing power. I should think it would have a strong effect in the Church, I mean on the Clergy, for I found myself wondering often, as I read, how much your very respectable Old South Congregation really relished the wild-horse freedom of some of your rushes of feeling and thought—they must feel a little breathless, like poor Mazeppa.

How times have changed in theology! How could people ever have taken these paltry miracles as the cornerstone of the whole system? God's 'credentials,' forsooth! Bah!

Always truly yours

Wm. James

95 Irving Street, Cambridge, March 24, '09

Dear Gordon:

I have just had to refuse a gracious invitation to the dinner to be given to you. I regret exceedingly to have done this, for I should like above all things to swell any crowd assembled to do you honour, but dinners and crowds do me nothing but harm nowadays and my 'doctor's orders' are to abstain peremptorily. You are having so splendid a career that I grow prouder than ever of having had anything to do with you in your infancy, and I hope that fifteen years hence I may still be alive to witness your 85th jubilee.

With warmest regards from both of us, to Mrs. Gordon as well as to yourself, believe me

Ever truly yours

Wm. James

JOHN JAY CHAPMAN

(1862–1933)

Perhaps the most notorious event in John Chapman's life was his self-mutilation. After assaulting a man who he believed—mistakenly, as it turned out—was trying to steal his sweetheart, Chapman fled home, stuck his left hand in a fire, and burned himself so severely that the hand had to be amputated.

Such impulsive behavior was characteristic of Chapman. As a young student, he became so emotionally upset over the rigorous requirements and religious attitude of St. Paul's School that he suffered a breakdown and had to be tutored at home. 'I regarded the place,' he reflected later, 'as a religious forcing-house, a very dangerous sort of place for any boy to go, especially if he were inclined by nature toward religion.'[1] At Harvard, which he attended from 1880 to 1884, he delved passionately into both academic and social activities, withdrawing only to take up his violin and practice feverishly. In 1900, after a bout of influenza, he plummeted into a physical and emotional breakdown that lasted for nearly ten years.

Chapman found the profession of law, his field of training at Harvard, too dull for his taste. Instead, as an editor and writer he became a vociferous advocate of political reform. His monthly journal, *The Political Nursery,* appeared from March 1897 to January 1901 and was available to subscribers—William James included—for one dollar a year. '[D]o you see Jack Chapman's "Political Nursery?"' James wrote to his friend Fanny Morse. 'If not, *do* subscribe to it; it is awful fun. He just looks at things, and tells the truth about them—a strange thing even to *try* to do, and he does n't always succeed.'[2] Among the issues Chapman commented upon were New York City politics, the Dreyfus case, racial prejudice, and the works of such Harvard philosophers as Josiah Royce and William James.

Although James was amused by Chapman's audacity, and deemed his views a possible 'gospel for our rising generation,'[3] he sometimes scolded Chapman for being elitist. Chapman's criticism of Charles William Eliot's reforms at Harvard, for example, struck James as 'nothing but *priggishness.*' 'What keeps me from going the whole distance with you,' James wrote to Chapman,

> is the implication . . . of there being a thing called 'higher' learning, or ideal education, or something the University is supposed to be faithful to *against* the vulgar demands of the world. . . . I don't believe in any 'higher' learning, except as one item amid the very broad and miscellaneous demands of human beings for the instruction they want. To be acquainted with the works of human genius is a permanent demand, the interests of which may be depended upon to take care of themselves without artificial protection by institutions fitted to that effect by being relieved from inferior work.[4]

James apparently read Chapman's articles and books more regularly than Chapman read the works of his esteemed professor. As Chapman admits in this selection, he read attentively only 'The Will to Believe,' an essay that 'exasperated [him] greatly.' '"But why all this pother,"' Chapman thought, '"—what *difference* does it make whether a man believes or not? Why is this question important enough to be discussed?". . . My own studies have led me to believe that there may be men who in some matters are sometimes influenced by the form of their religious tenets, and act and feel as they would n't have acted and felt but for some dogma; but this is so rare and so complex, and is of course rapidly disappearing.'[5] James disagreed. 'I am sorry for your paragraph about your supposed connection between belief and conduct,' he replied. 'It is by no means busted; on the contrary, it is one of the most tremendous forces in the world.'[6]

Their correspondence suggests a mutual respect tempered with acknowledgment of each other's shortcomings. Chapman tells us here that James lacked 'the gift of expression,' although he had 'the gift of suggestion. He said things which meant one thing to him and something else to the reader or listener.' James, recommending Chapman's *Practical Agitation* to George Palmer, commented that the style was 'all splinters.' Nevertheless, he responded to Chapman's energy and buoyancy, exclaiming in one of his last letters to Chapman, 'You, dear Jack, are the only reincarnation of Isaiah and Job, and I praise God that he has let me live in your day. *Real* values are known only to *you!*'[7]

NOTES

1. M. A. DeWolfe Howe, *John Jay Chapman and His Letters* (Boston: Houghton Mifflin, 1937), 158.
2. *Letters* 2:128 (13 April 1900).
3. *Letters* 2:124 (2 April 1900).
4. WJ to John Jay Chapman, 7 October 1909. Houghton.
5. John Jay Chapman to WJ, Perry 2:236 (30 March 1897).
6. WJ to John Jay Chapman, Perry 2:237 (5 April 1897).
7. *Letters* 2:329 (30 January 1910).

William James

None of us will ever see a man like William James again: there is no doubt about that. And yet it is hard to state what it was in him that gave him either his charm or his power, what it was that penetrated and influenced us, what it is that we lack and feel the need of, now that he has so unexpectedly and incredibly died. I always thought that William James would continue forever; and I relied upon his sanctity as if it were sunlight.

I should not have been abashed at being discovered in some mean action by William James; because I should have felt that he would understand and make allowances. The abstract and sublime quality of his nature was always enough for two; and I confess to having always trespassed upon him and treated him with impertinence, without gloves, without reserve, without ordinary, decent concern for the sentiments and weaknesses of human character. Knowing nothing about philosophy, and having the dimmest notions as to what James's books might contain, I used occasionally to write and speak to him about his specialties in a tone of fierce contempt; and never failed to elicit from him in reply the most spontaneous and celestial gayety. Certainly he was a wonderful man.

He was so devoid of selfish aim or small personal feeling that your shafts might pierce, but could never wound him. You could not 'diminish one dowle that's in his plume.' Where he walked, nothing could touch him; and he enjoyed the Emersonian immunity of remaining triumphant even after he had been vanquished. The reason was, as it seems to me, that what the man really meant was always something indestructible and persistent; and that he knew this inwardly. He had not the gift of expression, but rather the gift of suggestion. He said things which meant one thing to him and something else to the reader or listener. His mind was never quite in focus, and there was always something left over after each discharge of the battery, something which now became the beginning of a new thought. When he found out his mistake or defect of expression, when he came to see that he had not said quite what he meant, he was the first to proclaim it, and to move on to a new position, a new misstatement of the same truth,—a new, debonair apperception, clothed in non-conclusive and suggestive figures of speech.

How many men have put their shoulders out of joint in striking at the phantasms which James projected upon the air! James was always in the right, because what he meant was true. The only article of his which I ever read with proper attention was 'The Will to Believe,' a thing that exasperated me greatly until I began to see, or to think I saw, what James meant, and at the same time to acknowledge to myself that he had said something quite different. I hazard this idea about James as one might hazard an idea about astronomy, fully aware that it may be very foolish.

In private life and conversation there was the same radiation of thought about him. The center and focus of his thought fell within his nature, but not within his intellect. You were thus played upon by a logic which was not the logic of intellect, but a far deeper thing, limpid and clear in itself, confused and refractory only when you tried to deal with it intellectually. You must take any fragment of such a man by itself, for his whole meaning is in the fragment. If you try to piece the bits together, you will endanger their meaning. In general talk on life, literature, and politics James was always throwing off sparks that were cognate only in this, that they came from the same central fire in him. It was easy to differ from him; it was easy to go home thinking that James had talked the most arrant rubbish, and that no educated man had a right to be so ignorant of the first principles of thought and of the foundations of human society. Yet it was impossible not to be morally elevated by the smallest contact with William James. A refining, purgatorial influence came out of him.

I believe that in his youth, James dedicated himself to the glory of God and the advancement of Truth, in the same spirit that a young knight goes to seek the Grail, or a young military hero dreams of laying down his life for his country. What his early leanings towards philosophy or his natural talent for it may have been, I do not know; but I feel as if he had first taken up philosophy out of a sense of duty,—the old Puritanical impulse,—in his case illumined, however, with a humor and genius not at all of the Puritan type. He adopted philosophy as his lance and buckler,—psychology, it was called in his day,—and it proved to be as good as the next thing,—as pliable as poetry or fiction or politics or law would have been,—or anything else that he might have adopted as a vehicle through which his nature could work upon society.

He, himself, was all perfected from the beginning, a selfless angel. It is this quality of angelic unselfishness which gives the power to his work. There may be some branches of human study—mechanics perhaps—where the personal spirit of the investigator does not affect the result; but philosophy is not one of them. Philosophy is a personal vehicle; and every man makes his own, and through it he says what he has to say. It is all personal: it is all human: it is all non-reducible to science, and incapable of being either repeated or continued by another man.

Now James was an illuminating ray, a dissolvent force. He looked freshly at life, and read books freshly. What he had to say about them was not entirely articulated, but was always spontaneous. He seemed to me to have too high an opinion of everything. The last book he had read was always 'a great book'; the last person he had talked with, a wonderful being. If I may judge from my own standpoint, I should say that James saw too much good in everything, and felt towards everything a too indiscriminating approval. He was always classing things up into places they didn't belong and couldn't remain in.

Of course, we know that Criticism is proverbially an odious thing; it seems to deal only in shadows,—it acknowledges only varying shades of badness in everything. And we know, too, that Truth is light; Truth cannot be expressed in shadow, except by some subtle art which proclaims the shadow-part to be the lie, and the non-expressed part to be the truth. And it is easy to look upon the whole realm of Criticism and see in it nothing but a science which concerns itself with the accurate statement of lies. Such, in effect, it is in the hands of most of its adepts. Now James's weakness as a critic was somehow connected with the peculiar nature of his mind, which lived in a consciousness of light. The fact is that James was non-critical, and therefore divine. He was forever hovering, and never could alight; and this is a quality of truth and a quality of genius.

The great religious impulse at the back of all his work, and which pierces through at every point, never became expressed in conclusive literary form, or in dogmatic utterance. It never became formulated in his own mind into a statable belief. And yet it controlled his whole life and mind, and accomplished a great work in the world. The spirit of a priest was in him,—in his books and in his private conversation. He was a sage, and a holy man;

and everybody put off his shoes before him. And yet in spite of this,—in conjunction with this, he was a sportive, wayward, Gothic sort of spirit, who was apt, on meeting a friend, to burst into foolery, and whose wit was always three parts poetry. Indeed his humor was as penetrating as his seriousness. Both of these two sides of James's nature—the side that made a direct religious appeal, and the side that made a veiled religious appeal—became rapidly intensified during his latter years; so that, had the process continued much longer, the mere sight of him must have moved beholders to amend their lives.

I happened to be at Oxford at one of his lectures in 1908; and it was remarkable to see the reverence which that very un-revering class of men—the University dons—evinced towards James, largely on account of his appearance and personality. The fame of him went abroad, and the Sanhedrim attended. A quite distinguished, and very fussy scholar, a member of the old guard of Nil-admirari Cultivation,—who would have sniffed nervously if he had met Moses—told me that he had gone to a lecture of James's 'though the place was so crowded, and stank so that he had to come away immediately.'—'But,' he added, 'he certainly has the face of a sage.'

There was, in spite of his playfulness, a deep sadness about James. You felt that he had just stepped out of this sadness in order to meet you, and was to go back into it the moment you left him. It may be that sadness inheres in some kinds of profoundly religious characters,—in dedicated persons who have renounced all, and are constantly hoping, thinking, acting, and (in the typical case) praying for humanity. Lincoln was sad, and Tolstoi was sad, and many sensitive people, who view the world as it is, and desire nothing for themselves except to become of use to others, and to become agents in the spread of truth and happiness,—such people are often sad. It has sometimes crossed my mind that James wanted to be a poet and an artist, and that there lay in him, beneath the ocean of metaphysics, a lost Atlantis of the fine arts; that he really hated philosophy and all its works, and pursued them only as Hecules might spin, or as a prince in a fairy tale might sort seeds for an evil dragon, or as anyone might patiently do some careful work for which he had no aptitude. It would seem most natural, if this were the case between James and the metaphysical sciences; for what is there in these studies that can drench and satisfy a tingling mercurial being who loves to live on the surface, as well as in the depths of life? Thus we reason, forgetting that the mysteries of temperament are deeper than the mysteries of occupation. If James had had the career of Molière, he would still have been sad. He was a victim of divine visitation: the Searching Spirit would have winnowed him in the same manner, no matter what avocation he might have followed.

The world watched James as he pursued through life his search for religious truth; the world watched him, and often gently laughed at him, asking, 'When will James arise and fly? When will "he take the wings of the morning, and dwell in the uttermost parts of the sea"?' And in the meantime, James was there already. Those were the very places that he was living in. Through all the difficulties of polyglot metaphysics and of modern psychology he waded for years, lecturing and writing and existing,—and creating for himself a public which came to see in him only the saint and the sage, which felt only the religious truth which James was in search of, yet could never quite grasp in his hand. This very truth constantly shone out through him,—shone, as it were, straight through his waistcoat,—and distributed itself to everyone in the drawing-room, or in the lecture-hall where he sat. Here was the familiar paradox, the old parable, the psychological puzzle of the world. 'But what went ye out for to see?' In the very moment that the world is deciding that a man was no prophet and had nothing to say, in that very moment perhaps is his work perfected, and he himself is gathered to his fathers, after having been a lamp to his own generation, and an inspiration to those who come after.

ELIZABETH GLENDOWER EVANS

(1856–1937)

Elizabeth (Gardiner) Evans was born in New York to Edward and Sophia Gardiner. When her father, an architect, died after a fall from his horse in 1859, Elizabeth, her mother, and four siblings were taken into the Boston and Brookline, Massachusetts, homes of her wealthy paternal grandfather, William Howard Gardiner. Evans described herself as a serious and thoughtful girl, who devoted herself to religion when she was about twelve. 'Going to church became my one interest. Oh, how I gloried in it!' she recalled.[1]

At twenty-one years old, her aspirations for the future centered on work as a missionary. But those plans changed after she met Glendower Evans in Bar Harbor, Maine, where the two were vacationing with their families. They fell in love immediately and became engaged, but did not marry until 1882 on the day after Evans took his examination for the Massachusetts Bar. He joined the prestigious Boston law firm of Shattuck, Holmes & Monroe, where he was a colleague of Oliver Wendell Holmes Jr.

Glendower Evans had a profound influence on his wife. Although Glendower was the same age as she, Elizabeth thought of him as more worldly and sophisticated, especially concerning philosophical matters. She came to realize that, for Glendower, 'the religion in which he had been reared dropped from him as an outgrown overcoat, while with me it was the very life of my life.'[2] Suddenly she began to question her beliefs, then came to develop a personal definition of spirituality that precluded membership in any church but served to guide her in ethical and moral decisions for the rest of her life.

When Glendower Evans died suddenly in 1886, Elizabeth hardly could conceive of a future without him. She depended on the emotional support of their friends, including William James, who had singled out Glendower for attention when he had been James's student. William and Alice had enjoyed visiting with the young couple and continued to include Elizabeth in their social plans.

To distract her from her grief, Lizzie Putnam, the sister of Charles Putnam, who had been Glendower's physician, suggested that Elizabeth Glendower Evans (as she became known upon her husband's death, when she appended his full name to her own) become a trustee of the Lyman and Industrial Schools, a reform institution. Although Evans had no experience in such work, her developing ideas on social issues interested her in the job, and she accepted the position. With Putnam's encouragement and especially with the guidance of her close friend and neighbor Louis Brandeis, Evans began a distinguished career in social reform.

She also began her formal philosophical education, taking classes with Josiah Royce and George Herbert Palmer, and joining the Philosophical Conference, an informal club that met at Royce's home in 1903–4. Other club members included Richard Cabot, a physician active in the development of social work; his wife, Ella Lyman Cabot, who taught philosophy at Radcliffe; Frances Hall Rousmaniere, a graduate student at Radcliffe; William Ernest Hocking, soon to receive a doctorate in philosophy from Harvard; and Mary Calkins, a Wellesley philosophy instructor studying as a special student at Harvard. 'As to the spirit of the occasion,' Royce wrote to Cabot, explaining the group, 'I intend neither a purely scholastic exercise, nor yet, in any sense, a social entertainment other than such as talking together of good things involves. We shall all be busy folk, with some things to say, and many things to think over.'[3]

Evans became increasingly busy in the next few years. In 1908 she toured England to learn about English socialism, and returned to America with a renewed commitment to both socialism and feminism. She worked alongside Florence Kelley, Jane Addams, Robert La Follette, and Felix Frankfurter as a speaker, a lobbyist, and a writer on social and political issues, including women's suffrage. As a director of the American Civil Liberties Union in the 1920s, she took a strong public stand in support of Sacco and Vanzetti.

Despite James's admiration for Evans, sometimes he found her fervent involvement in social causes personally tiring. 'She is an absolutely amiable woman,' he wrote to Henry, after Evans had spent a few weeks with him and Alice in Europe, 'but fitted for a heroic life exclusively and scuffs away every common remark and consideration in a way so curt that it dries one up. Were some great work on hand, revolution, siege, or shipwreck, she'd take the lead as a duck takes to water, without an effort or an interfering thought.'[4] Nevertheless, Evans remained a close friend of the family, continuing to visit and correspond with them even after James's death.

NOTES

1. Elizabeth Glendower Evans, *Memoir*. Manuscript on microfilm at the Schlesinger Library, Harvard.

2. Evans, *Memoir*.

3. Josiah Royce to Richard Cabot. *The Letters of Josiah Royce*, ed. John Clendenning 464 (9 October 1903).

4. WJ to Henry James, *Correspondence* 2:265 (31 March 1893).

William James and His Wife

I

William James and his wife have been a part of my life ever since my husband—we were then engaged—was a Harvard student in 1879. Mr. James was at that time an instructor in physiology, and well do I remember my husband's talk of his extraordinary personality, of the discursive quality of his mind, and more especially how it would dart off from the subject matter of his lectures and discuss for the full hour some philosophical question far afield. Instructor and pupil met outside the classroom and laid the basis of a friendship which grew with the years.

My husband's mind, like that of William James, had a 'What are you?' quality toward each fact which it encountered, and likewise was quick to note what was happening far and wide. In his college days he had talked to me about the formation in England of a Psychical Society for the study of ghosts, crystal reading, trances, and other phenomena, eternally believed in by simple souls, and eternally damned as bosh by scientists and average sensible persons; and I remember his playful comments upon truth seekers who knew there was nothing to be investigated in these so little understood phenomena in this so little understood world.

Thus it was on the cards that when we were married and my husband was beginning to practise law in Boston he should get in touch with Mr. James and together they should interview Mrs. Piper, whose psychical powers to this day are still explored. It was my husband's part to observe and keep the record while James spoke or wrote to the medium. And when, presently, a branch of the English Psychical Society was to be established in Boston, my husband agreed readily to act as its secretary. His activities were cut short by his death. But Mr. James never relinquished his studies of this elusive subject.

While I was knowing of Mr. James only as an intriguing personality, one day a woman of most unusual appearance came to call at my mother's house in Marlborough Street. She was neatly dressed in grey; in figure she was short and thickset. She had great dark luminous eyes, an abundance of soft brown hair, and a girlish wild-rose complexion, which together gave extraordinary beauty to somewhat heavy features. She spoke in a resonant organlike voice, which made the most ordinary words sound significant. And she had a smile which lit up her face, and seemed to light up the world. I, who was always short of small talk, had no notion of what to say, and my mother and sister for the most part sat silent. But my husband, who was always a host in himself, was fortunately present, and he saved the occasion from awkwardness. Our visitor was Mrs. William James.

It was years later that Mrs. James told me how she had happened to make this call. She said that her husband had spoken one evening of a student he had been seeing at his rooms. 'Such a brilliant fellow,' he said, 'and with a rarely cultivated mind. He told me that he was engaged to be married to a Boston girl, and he showed me her picture'; and then he added, 'Oh, Alice, I hope we may see something of these young people.'

After Mrs. James's first visit to me, I used from time to time to seek her out in Cambridge, where I would find her perhaps with a little one in her arms, or an older child clinging to her skirts, and I used to unburden the problems which at that time seemed to me to be unanswerable. And she would answer out of her own experience, speaking in her sonorous voice, which seemed to carry a message from Heaven.

And to this day do I remember, when my husband died after his brief, brief years, how Alice James came and sat beside me, and said, 'Oh, what can we know? But what can we not know? I think of my little Herman [her third boy, who died when he was eighteen months old, and in her thought lived with her always among her other children]—where is he now? He does not tell me. But as well might I have asked him, before he was born, what his life in this world would be. How could he have conceived of sight and hearing and of moving about freely in this wonderful world? Had I tried to tell him, he would have shrunk back in terror and begged to stay safely in his mother's womb.'

Fourteen years later she wrote:—

> No one who knew your husband could forget him. Often and often I think of him when I see you, and of how he must rejoice in your full and generous life. You see, dear Bessie, I believe [in], I almost feel immortality, or peradven-

ture something infinitely better; but life and immortality are surely calling to us all—and more than ever I want to listen.

It is very strange that I have no recollection when I first saw William James. My first remembrance of him is when he came to our house in Otis Place about five weeks before my husband died, and he came then as one well acquainted. He had with him his eldest son, Harry, then a boy of perhaps eight years old. He did not sit down, but he spoke for a few minutes to my husband of the psychical work which the two of them had in hand; and no one of us guessed that the indisposition from which my husband was then suffering was so soon to have a fatal climax.

When my husband died on March 28, 1886, the very first letter I received was from William James:—

> I can hardly express the sorrow I feel at your husband's being thus cut off almost before he had begun to show what was in him. . . . The whole thing is one of those incomprehensible, seemingly wasteful acts of Providence, which, without seeing, we can only hope may some day be proved to spring from a rational ground. I shall remember him as one of the most manly high-spirited men I have ever known. . . . Somewhere in the universe that gallant spirit remains and now is.

A few weeks later he wrote:—

> There is no *full* consolation. Evil is evil and pain is pain, and it is our part to bear them valiantly; I think the only thing we can do is to believe that the Good power of the world does not appoint them of its own free will, but works under some dark and inscrutable limitations, and that we by our patience and good will can somehow strengthen his hands.

In these two letters one gets a glimpse into the philosophy which strengthened and deepened in Mr. James as his thought matured. Radical Empiricism, he came to call it. He argued that our world in its fundamental make-up is something unfinished, is problematic in its outcome, and is eternally at war with itself.

'God himself,' he says, 'may draw vital strength and increase from our fidelity. For my own part, I do not know what the sweat and blood and tragedy of life mean, if they mean anything short of this. If this life be not a real fight, in which something is gained for the Universe by success, it is no better than a game of private theatricals from which one may withdraw at will. But it feels like a real fight. . . .'

And equally at war was William James with the absolute view of the world which was eloquently expounded by his friend and colleague, Josiah Royce, whose parlor lectures in Boston and elsewhere secured him a following among those with the leisure to attend such gatherings.

I myself in those early days became an ardent follower of Royce, whose philosophy I took as an intellectual statement of truths which Emerson uttered as 'affirmations of the soul.' And nothing is more characteristic of William James than the eight-page letter which he wrote to little me, all in his own beautiful handwriting, as easily read as if it were print, in answer to my perhaps flippant claim that he was caricaturing Royce.

He writes, playfully at first: —

Cambridge, Mass., Dec. 11, 1906

Dear Bessie,

I shall continue to love every word *you* say, however wicked—thus should pragmatists and absolutists take each other!

Your wickedest word is to accuse me of caricaturing the absolute. As pragmatism is little more than an attempt to think clearly, that charge would kill me dead, if true, so, in spite of you, I *must* reply to it on paper.

Vaguely, everyone is both monist and pragmatist. One lives in the detail of one's experiences; and one supplements those in sight by a *more,* which most of us imagine consolingly.

'T is when you try to be not vague but definite about the more that the trouble arises. You can take it as quantitative addition, indefinite in amount, and merely prolonging the finite, or you can take it as totalizing and surrounding the finite, altering the form of experience therefore (or rather presenting it in another form than that in which we get it): Eternal or absolute form.

If you take it as *prolongation,* your consolations are probable at best, and your world a meliorism. If you take it as totalizing, your consolations are certain or necessary and your world a dogmatic optimism. (It flows from the very form of totality that it should lack nothing, for it does n't refer beyond itself. You surely don't mean *this* when you accuse me of caricaturing!) *As realized 'eternally,'* then, everything is good. Evil is seen along with what overrules it, monistically.

Is it a caricature to say that we ourselves are advised to seek peace by ascending as far as possible to the eternal point of view? What can such peace come from in that case but from the abstract reflexion that *in* the whole every part is needed and symphonic? No perception of the particular atonements is needed for this, by us; the Absolute Experient has the perception, but for us the monistic form *per se* is a guarantee of the total excellence.

How is it a caricature to say that this permits of quietism? You yourself write of issues being 'guaranteed' by the larger order. Guaranteed *anyhow*, without specification of remedy. It permits equally of strenuosity, of course. It *dictates* nothing, but *justifies* all *fact* qua element of absolute experience. It thus helps sick souls more than pragmatism does; and as their needs are the sorest, it has always seemed to me that this is a towering merit, to be weighed against Absolutism's demerits.

But after all, *how* does an Absolute make so for Optimism, blindfold on our part, clear-sighted on that of Eternal?

Surely by the 'overruling' content which it postulates as complementing the bad parts of experience. The 'more,' whether you take it empirically or absolutely, is more content of experience, which in neither case *you* (the finite experient) see, but only suppose or believe, but the atoning and redeeming character of which you suppose guaranteed when you *totalize* experience, and only possible or probable when you simply *prolong* it. The pragmatic value of the absolute consists in nothing but these *atoning facts.* The pragmatist postulates them by faith, *sans phrase,* the absolutist by his extra machinery, which is supposed to certify them.

In any case *our* only way of realizing them is as a prolongation. The only thing *we* gain by assuming the eternal point of view is the *permission of blindfold optimism.* To those who don't care for it, the invariable reply is: 'Go back to the finite point of view.' Hate and deplore things to your heart's content; for the 'now,' the evil part *as such,* exists in the Absolute to be deplored exactly as we deplore it. Only as overruled is it justified, only as He sees it.

And that is what I meant by the 'shuffle.' The Absolute has become only an abstract name, like 'Nature,' for the indefinitely prolonged content of experience, and we are all pragmatists again together. There may *be* an Absolute, of course: and its pragmatic use to us is to make us more optimistic. But it is n't forced on us by logic, as Royce and Bradley think, and its cash equivalent is the *atoning experience believed in.* Pardon so long a rigmarole,

Yours affectionately, W.J.

In this letter James makes clear how he was saved from inevitable dilemmas by his free appeal to 'faith,' elsewhere defined by him as meaning 'the kind of belief a person may have in a doubtful case, and may carry a sense of heart in your throat, ready-to-back-outness; or a sort of passionate refusal to give up, or anything in between, and it is the same state, when applied to some practical affair of your own, or to a theologic creed.'

The book in which he first specifically set forth and justified this use of faith was called *The Will to Believe, and Other Essays,* and it utters a great call to the capacity for heroism in man, to his will to take big risks and fling himself, to sink or to swim, into the effort to achieve some noble purpose.

II

As a popular lecturer, Mr. James came to be in great demand all across the country. His voice was so splendid, his use of words and the way he spoke them were so unique, and the problems which he discussed were at once so close to the common experience of man and so filled with his own peculiar wisdom, that his lectures were hailed as an intellectual treat of the first order. Yet he himself always treated them as matters of slight importance and deprecated every word of praise.

Of his *Talks to Teachers,* still treasured as priceless wisdom by all engaged in the teaching craft, he wrote me on a post card:—

> Thanks for your note of thanks. But pray don't wade through the Teacher part, which is incarnate boredom. I sent it to you merely that you might read the essay on a certain Blindness, which is really the perception on which my whole individualist philosophy is based. W. J.

Regarding his *Varieties of Religious Experience,* a most wise and most beautiful book, he wrote me:—

> You are sweet to take my book so seriously. I thought, when writing it, that it could have no originality, but the reception it gets makes me feel that it is original in temper at least. No previous book of mine has got anything like the prompt and *thankful* recognition that has come to me in letters about this—many of them from strangers. But I can't myself say on reflection that I do anything [except] leave the subject just where I find it, and everybody knows that the real life of religion springs from what may be called the mystical stratum of human nature. . . . Still the volume is selling well and will no doubt help to sell my other books. I want now if possible to write something serious, systematic, and syllogistic; I've had enough of the squashy popular-lecture style.

Of another book entitled *Pragmatism—A New Name for Some Old Ways of Thinking*, he wrote:—

> Your two delightful letters, one to me full of forgiveness and the other to Alice full of communicativeness, have duly come to hand. Let me thank you for all the pleasant things you say of my book—only don't, *don't* take it too damned serious. It will doubtless please you to hear that I have news from Longmans, Green & Co. yesterday that they are going to press with a third thousand.

His essay on 'The Moral Equivalent of War' has a message which the world is slowly coming to understand. People of my generation first thought seriously of war, not as a romantic tradition of the past, but as belonging to America in our own day and generation, when President Cleveland made his sudden threat of war upon England over the borderland of Venezuela, and Mr. James wrote an anti-war pronouncement that still speaks to-day.

> Three days of mob hysteria can at any time undo peace habits of a hundred years; and the only permanent safeguard against irrational explosions of the fighting instinct is absence of armament and of opportunity. Since this country has absolutely nothing to fear, nor any other country anything to gain from its invasion, it seems to me that the party of civilization ought immediately, at any cost of discredit, to begin to agitate against any increase of either army, navy or coast defense. That is the one form of protection against the internal enemy on which we can most rely. . . . I have not slept right for a week.

William James's outspoken protest against our adventure in the Philippines was deep and passionate. I myself was tremendously aroused over our war against the Filipinos, and I was thinking of going out there, so impossible did it seem to me to stay safe in a conquering land. Mr. James was full of sympathy with my feeling, and he wrote me (on a post card, and not forgetting to make his playful thrust at the Absolute): 'Your activity is splendid. Keep *mad!* but don't forget the higher unity! Much love. W. J.' And a few weeks later: 'Damn great empires! including that of the Absolute! You see how much crime it necessarily involves. Give me individuals and their "spheres of activity." Yours, Fanny Morse's, Jim Putnam's, and the like. . . . Love from us both. W. J.'

Then came the news of Aguinaldo's capture, betrayed in his fortress by our bribery of his native troops. This time William wrote in deadly seriousness:—

> I now write just as the news comes of Aguinaldo's capture. This may put alteration into your notion of going out there, but I hope you may go all the same, since mutual acquaintance is in any case the thing most needed, and you are framed for heroic efforts, bless your noble generous heart. I'm glad we got Aggie by a bunco-steering trick: it would have been a pity to mar the moral harmony of our operations by making a legitimate capture. As far as physical access to him goes, we have now made the great step forward of being just where we were three years ago. . . . When one thinks, however, that we could have had these conditions for the asking, and been thanked for them and kept the native good will, our own honor and world-prestige and everything, three years ago, and that we have lost all these things and Heaven knows how many more things besides in consequence of our masterly stroke of 'avoiding all entanglement' with the natives except to 'use them against Spain,' it makes one fairly sick. I doubt whether such would-be craftiness was ever before, except in the history of the Bourbons, identical with such actual stupidity. . . .

A post card containing two hundred and forty-five perfectly legible words, in his old playful strain, may well conclude these extracts from his letters:—

> Better a post card than *gar nichts, nicht wahr,* and I have been aiming at a letter to you for so long without writing it that I feel the smallest reality to be worth more than the largest prospect. Your two long typewritten letters were most interesting and gratitude-arousing. You must be glad that the Cuban teacher scrape proved on the whole so well worth doing—I feel less joy over your repentance at not passing your examination and your coming to do it again [I had skipped an examination in a special philosophy course for the sake of making the trip as an advanced guard to escort back a deputation of teachers to take a summer course at Harvard]. Soon you will be unhappy at not having a Ph.D., that Moloch of our time which threatens to destroy so many of our innocent children. But perhaps this grumpiness is all due to my jealousy at your being Royce's disciple instead of mine. Whosoever you are, be it with all your strength! . . . W. J.

III

It was the year after my husband's death that I first visited the James family in their summer home at Chocorua, New Hampshire. It was my impulse to refuse their invitation, so impossible did it seem to me to make visits. But then I decided that it was too stupid to close such an open door in my own face, so on an August morning I started on a six hours' journey to West Ossipee, some seven miles from their home. Alice met me at the station, and a desolate little figure I felt myself as I mounted into her open wagon. She gave my hand a warm clasp, exclaiming, 'You poor child, how you must wish you had not come!' And I confessed that she had read my mood aright.

Besides themselves, the James household consisted of Mrs. James's mother, Mrs. Gibbens, a gracious and beautiful woman; her married sister Mary and her husband, William MacIntire Salter, an ethical lecturer and quite one of the elect; her then unmarried sister Margaret, and the children. All of them, grown-ups and children, spoke in resonant organlike voices like Alice's and William's, and the talk about the table seemed always to be on some high theme. I used to pinch myself in an effort to discover whether I was still in the flesh or in some heavenly state. Alice was busy ripping the boys' suits, to turn them, and very thankful was I to be allowed a part in that humble service. William that summer was making a flying trip to Europe, and his letters, which Alice read aloud, were a noble substitute for his conversation.

One day, driving in the open wagon, Alice told me how she and William had come to find each other. She said that one morning at breakfast her husband's father, a prophetlike person,—Henry James, Sr., as he came to be called when his second son had made a name for himself in the literary world,—had announced: 'William, I have seen the woman you are to marry!' And he went on to describe a young schoolteacher named Alice Gibbens whom he had met the previous evening at the Radical Club, where Boston's free spirits were wont to congregate. William, evidently believing in his father's prescience, had counted the days until the Radical Club met again, and there he had found the woman surely born to be his own.

I am one who dearly loves a lover, so I listened eagerly to this tale. 'So it was love at first sight!' I exclaimed. But Alice's sister Margie, who was in the wagon with us, remarked, 'Well, Alice, it was n't what I call first sight with you. You kept William waiting a good two years.' Whereupon Alice turned to me with a deprecating look, exclaiming, 'But, Bessie, don't you think a woman has a right to take her time?'

With the happiest and the most harmonious family life to be imagined, William James was nevertheless a perpetually restless and unsatisfied soul. 'I am going away for a fortnight to be alone with God, after so much family immersion and unfulfilled household responsibilities,' he wrote. His wife always had the wisdom to speed his going; and he would write back letters commenting on 'the soap your dear hands packed' and using similar phrases rich with domestic tenderness. '*Zerrissenheit* or torn-to-pieces-hood,' he said was what the Germans called the constitutional disease from which he suffered. 'The days are broken into pure zigzag and interruption. . . . Give me twelve hours of work on *one* occupation for happiness. . . . Your account of 12 Otis Place is seductive enough. I think I might find there coolness, seclusion, and even a sense of continuity.'

When William went to Europe for his sabbatical year, taking with him his wife and four children, he wrote back letters eloquent of his torn-to-pieces state of mind. Apologizing for a long-delayed letter, he wrote from Gryon:—

> We have been distracted by the children living all the time, as it were, in one and the same bedroom with us, with inward perplexities about the educational problem and the future abode, and with my wildly zigzagging to and fro to find a proper place for ourselves and the boys. We have come to a temporary rest in this precipitous Alpine village, but although I start tomorrow again to look for a better abode, many of our perplexities are already solved by the experience of five weeks, and we begin to breathe more equably.

Here his letter was interrupted and was taken up two days later.

> I have been dashing round to find families to put the boys into. No easy task; one becomes so fastidious here that the crumpled rose leaf makes one say 'no'—the fact being, I suppose, that one dreads to alienate the little critters after all. But Switzerland is *good,* in spite of lake steamers blowing up and St. Gervais disasters—good through and through, and calculated to make the most pessimistic respect the Universe. I hope that your summer thus far has gone well in spite of labour troubles and presidential uproar.

It was always the habit of the James family to be amply hospitable. One day in Florence, when they were to have some formal company, William stipulated for champagne, which Alice conceded reluctantly as an unwarranted expense. At luncheon William came in bringing a friend, and he called for wine; a 'pop' was heard from the pantry, and in came the maid bearing the bottle of dinner champagne. 'Oh, not that, not that!' Alice exclaimed, stretching out her hands, so her husband averred, whereat he cried out, 'Oh, this is good! Champagne for luncheon, champagne for dinner!'

Another domestic climax was when William came home one day bearing an oil painting which he said was an original, and prodigiously cheap. Alice was wont to receive with a patient smile the photos and other knick-knacks with which he would come home laden, always measuring them against the cost of the children's education. But when the oil painting was produced she cried out, 'Oh, William, how *could* you!' Whereupon he seized the scissors and cut the picture to pieces. 'And will you believe me,' he said in telling me the story, 'that when I destroyed the picture Alice wept!'

It was my pleasant fortune to pass several months at a pension in Florence near the Piazza del Indipendenza where the James family had an apartment, and to accompany them, when the spring came, up to Hinter Meggin, near Lucerne, and then to Ver-chez-les Blanc, near Lake Geneva, and all this time I was practically a part of their household. Their children were charming little people. The baby, whom they called Tweedy, was about two years old, and very darling he looked, dressed in a bright red flannel frock. His name, given him in honor of a beloved family friend, I assumed was a nursery corruption of some more usual name, and William allowed that it simply would n't do. 'I shall write to Mr. Tweedy and tell him that we meant well, but that names are a thing we cannot control, so we have decided to call him Francis—Francis Robertson.' But the name Francis was apparently beyond control, for by the time Francis was twelve he had become Alexander, and now is generally known as Aleck.

Talking of the older boys once, William remarked, 'Harry has a steady disposition and can always be relied on to take what falls to him with equanimity. But when Bill does not get what he wants, he fills the welkin with his lamentations!'

Their one daughter Peggy, whose full name was Margaret Mary,—so called for her mother's two sisters,—was a strange little creature with dark blazing eyes, and with a most vivid inner life. Once asked her age, she answered, 'I am as old as the pangs of death.' When she was a little tot her grandmother one day read to the older boys Tennyson's *Ulysses,* with no thought that Peggy would take heed. She was then staying nights with Mrs. Gibbens, and in the early morning when she was thought to be asleep she was heard to say, '"Far on the ringing plains of windy Troy"—oh, Grandma, those are beautiful words!' The summer I was with the family in Switzerland I made her a pink gingham frock which she used to call her 'R-rose R-robe.' She was passionately devoted to *mon oncle,* as she called her Uncle Henry, who passed some days or weeks at a hotel in Lucerne, from which he would descend, or ascend, to see his brother at Hinter Meggin, when William would pour out his stream of talk while Peggy would cling to Uncle Henry's hand and attend him as closely as if she were his shadow.

It was a part of the plan, for that second summer in Switzerland, that William and Alice should pass a couple of weeks with Henry in London, leaving Peggy and Tweedy in some reliable Swiss family, and there was often discussion at table as to when the parents should go and where the children should be left. And Alice used to tell me how, when Peggy would go to bed, she would scream and scream with terror that she was to be left, she did not know when or where. I said to Alice, 'Is n't a mistake to discuss the matter before her? She will surely be happy when you are gone, but anticipation of it is getting on her nerves.' And Alice answered, 'Yes, that is what I say to William, and he agrees. But then he says, "Well, Alice, that's the sort of people we are; so let's be hearty about it!"'

As the oldest boy, it fell to the lot of Harry to get the first wear at clothes, which when outgrown were handed on to Billy. Harry's thoughtfulness for his little brother was exemplified when he remarked to his mother, 'It's all right for you to give Bill my coat, but I advise you not to ask him to wear my hat. The boys always laugh at it. I don't mind, but he would.' From his youngest childhood Harry was always a responsible eldest son, and he grew to be relied on by his mother as her right hand.

The winter of 1892–1893, as before mentioned, I passed with the Jameses in Florence, going, however, from there for some six weeks to join friends in Egypt and returning in April by way of Athens. In Greece I received the following letter from Alice:—

> . . . Your dear beautiful letters (which make me love you afresh) tell me of a most intense life fed by inner springs and outward beauty. I think you would be surprised to know how much you have given me of Egypt, and I am looking forward to more when you come and talk of it. What you wrote of Pæstum made a strong impression on me. A beautiful sight is worth going far to behold, for I find that it not only gives itself but in some mysterious way adds a new beauty to common sights, and Italy does help to circumnavigate the sea of thought and things at home.

You see I am in a fair way to leave the children with you for a couple of weeks if time and place and health all favour. I am delighted that you are coming for another draught of Florence—it is so fair in the warm sunshine and people seem so at home. This is the Italy they are conscious of, and its charm wipes out the memory of winter cold and fog. With the Spring comes a host of strangers.

The richest part of this rich year to me will be the feeling of goodness in the world, goodness of such different forms, but flowering and making life fragrant in strange places. And Florence has so many dear people to be remembered along with her beauty and olive trees. I should like to look as much like an olive tree as I can for the rest of my natural life. Billy says my hair is *green!* That is one step towards it. I shall write again before the fourteenth unless I hear from you in the interval.

From England the following summer she wrote:—

The heat here has been very oppressive and now I have had enough of London. The best thing I have had was a chance to hear the debate last Thursday in the House. Gladstone is the most impressive 'human' I have ever beheld or listened to. It seemed to me that one *must* believe what he believes. But the whole [Irish] question seems to me far less simple than we are wont to consider, and I begin to sympathize with dear old Dyer who said he was 'on both sides.' Balfour has a noble presence and beautiful voice. He made the only able speech on the side of the opposition. . . .

IV

When William was a young man he and some friends made a camp up in the Adirondacks, where many of his vacations were passed, which came to be called the Shanty. One day in the spring of 1899, when he was alone in the woods, he lost his trail and did not get back to the camp until the next day. From this mishap he suffered a heart strain which resulted in a serious illness and from which he probably never recovered. From Southern France his wife wrote:—

Hôtel d'Albion, Costebelle, Jan. 17, 1900

Your blessed letter of October 12th reached us in London just after William's break-down, when I was plunged into the deepest anxiety, and resolved not to let the family at home know of our deplorable situation. The very excellence of your letter, and the impossibility of writing you a free letter just then, kept me silent, for I thought each week that William *must* be better. But for many weeks the change seemed all in one direction till a month ago, when we took him to Lamb House [Henry James's home] really at the end of our resources. I will not dwell on the anxiety of those weeks. He did show faint signs of returning strength at Rye, where he spent hours sitting in the sunny garden covered with wraps.

Last Friday Henry came with us to Dover, where we spent the night, and the next day in a comfortable sleeping car we journeyed hither. And he has borne the journey well, and is improving daily in this wonderful air. He is in the garden all the morning and then in an easy-chair on our balcony. I am wonderfully encouraged, and as I shrank from telling you the measure of my grief, so I am doubly eager to let you know that better days are come. It seems to me that in addition to the functional disturbance of his heart my husband has had a complete nervous break-down, which naturally has aggravated all the cardiac symptoms. As yet he can only walk five minutes at a time and people tire him,—in other words he is still very weak,—but he is gaining.

Before we left [Henry's home in] Rye we had a little visit from Royce, which we all enjoyed. You have no idea how *good* he looked as he got out of the carriage. William has been reading his book, little by little, with the keenest delight in its excellence. He exults in its existence as a credit to American philosophy, and an honour to our University—in his own words, 'an honour to Irving Street.'

At Nauheim, where William had taken a cure, the Jameses met a Pole who told them 'monstrous things of his unhappy land.' 'Poland,' Alice comments, 'seems to be a country all by itself, of amazing sorrows and wrongs. . . .' If William were well, she and he would like to go there together. She would like to understand 'why Poland has no middle class, only nobles and peasants. . . .' Here William comes from his perch on the balcony where he has been watching the wild sunset. 'We have lighted our lamp and our bit of olive-wood fire, and he says he wants to write to you himself, so I gladly hold the pen for him.' He dictated the following:—

Don't think that this is the first time that my spirit has turned towards you since our departure. Away back in Nauheim I began meaning to write to you, and although that meaning was 'fulfilled' long before you were born, in Royce's Absolute, yet there was a hitch about it—in the finite, which gave me perplexity. I think that the real reason why I kept finding myself able to dictate letters to other persons—not many, 't is true—and yet postponing ever until next time my letter unto you was that my sense of your value was so much greater than almost anyone else's—though I would n't have anything in this construed prejudicial to Fanny Morse! Bound as I am by the heaviest of matrimonial chains, even dependent for expression on an alien pen, how can my spirit move with perfect spontaneity or 'voice itself' with the careless freedom it would wish for in the channels of its choice? I am sure you understand, and under present conditions of communication anything more explicit might be imprudent. . . .

Our present situation is enviable enough. A large bedroom with a balcony high up on the vast hotel façade, a terrace below it gravelled with snow-white pebbles containing beds of palms and oranges and roses, below that a downward sloping garden full of plants and winding walks and seats, then a wide hillside continuing southward to the plain below, with its grey-green olive groves bordered by great salt marshes with salt works on them, shut in from the sea by two causeways which lead to a long rocky island, perhaps three miles away, that limits the middle of our view due south, and beyond which to the east and west appears the boundless Mediterranean. But delightful as this is there is no place like home; Otis Place is better than Languedoc and Irving Street than Provence. And I am sure, dear Bessie, that there is no maid, wife or widow in either of these countries that is half as good as you. But here I must absolutely stop, so with a good-night and a happy new year to you, I am as ever,

Affectionately your friend,

William James

On April 13 he again dictated:—

Your delightful letter of the 28th surprised us yesterday and I must individually send you one word of thanks before the day goes by. It is awfully damaging to me to write letters, although I have just got off a tremendously long one *eigenhändig* to Fanny Morse. I have been on the point of writing to you over and over again since your last. . . .

You write delightfully about Royce; and happy is he to have so eager and appreciative a pupil! When shall I have one? After this, I can't have you, I fear. . . .

Good-bye, dear Bessie. I am getting much better as to nervous strength, and Alice is *very* well, and more of an angel than ever. In a month I shall know something authentic about the heart's condition and about our future program. Keep well! and busy!

Another letter of that year of exile was written from Rome on November 16 by Alice: —

You have been a saint and an angel to write us such splendid letters and I have not been ungrateful, if silent. Such a disturbed, bewildered, anxious summer trailing its uncertainties even to this place, where at last, thank Heaven, they are in full retreat. *For William is decidedly better and gaining all along the line, nerves, heart, ability to walk and to work.* So mysterious tawny Rome already seems like a friend, and we can look forward to being quiet for three months. . . .

I am glad that William has been away during election, for he takes the country's errors so to heart. Next year he will be stronger. You little know how we long to get home. It is a pity that I should be in Rome when there are so many students to whom it would be the chance of a life.

I love to think of you flitting about Cambridge and taking so triumphantly all those difficult courses in Philosophy. I heard Mr. Palmer give one lecture to his Annex class nearly twenty years ago and I have never forgotten it. How I longed to join that very class, and how I wish now that I had had the course! We generally rue the day when courage gives out. It seemed to me then that I had no right to take the time for anything so delightful. But Peggy shall do all the good things—and better than I. . . .

After a year in Europe, William's condition was sufficiently mended to allow his return to Cambridge. There follows another breach in our correspondence until February 27, 1905, when, referring to some scheme which had seemed great to me, but which had fallen flat, William wrote: —

Darling Bessie,

What a golden heart and headlong generosity you are possessed by! . . . If you won't let me repay you in truth (i.e. in radical empiricism) you will let me pluck you from Long Island [the Boston Almshouse], where your generosities will have landed you.

After explaining all the letters he had thought of writing and had not written during a long illness I had suffered, he said, 'You were there in the absolute—and would keep!'

In an undated letter he wrote from Chocorua:—

> It is pleasant to be able to be all together under our own rooftree again, and I am glad to say that my health seems to be improving satisfactorily.
>
> It seems strange to be out of communication with you, even by hearsay, for so long. Pray write, a p.c. if nothing else, and let us know how it goes with you. Will it be possible to have you here sometime? Our place and life seem more primitive than ever after the things we have been seeing abroad, *but our hearts are still affectionate,* so please say you will come. Date can be arranged later.
>
> Alice sends her warmest love, and so do I.

And again in an undated letter from Cambridge, as William and his wife were preparing to get off on one of their many trips to Europe, he wrote:—

> Good-bye at last! May we each be better, nobler, loftier, more worthy of the other's friendship than ever before, when next we meet. Each is meant to include Alice, who has been living on a higher level than I ever knew her for the past month. Working fifteen hours a day *straight,* eating almost nothing, yet amiable to the last degree always. . . .
>
> *Lebewohl!*
>
> Yours— W. J.

V

William James in his appearance was the embodiment of youth to the end of his days. His figure, about five feet eight inches in height, was light and buoyant, so that he seemed to spring as he walked. He usually dressed in rough brown tweeds, often wore a Norfolk jacket, and looked like a sportsman rather than a professor. At Chocorua he wore knickerbockers.

His hospitality was unbounded, as was that of his wife. But in him it was joined to a nervous tension that made it sometimes uncertain in its expression. The story runs that on one occasion when they were having something of a party he dashed into the hall and, seizing a student found there, cried: 'This place is hell! Here is the way to escape'—and he thrust his guest out through the back door. Later the student was found searching for his hat. He had wanted to stay, he had explained, 'but Professor James seemed to want me to go.' Felix Frankfurter, a professor at the Harvard Law School, tells a somewhat similar story. When he was about to graduate from the Law School he went to call on Professor James, to be asked, 'What are you now going to do?' He said he was going to New York to practise law. 'Yes, you are like all the rest; you are going to New York to make money!' Mr. James answered, and the young man felt himself to be almost put out of the door. Did Mr. James's indignant words weigh with Felix when, after a few months in a big law office, he threw up private practice to act as an assistant prosecutor to Henry I. Stimson (now Secretary of State in President Hoover's cabinet) and presently to follow him into public service in Washington?

Alice James often told of evenings when her husband would exclaim, 'Are we *never* to have an evening alone? Must we always talk to people, every night?' And she would answer, 'I will see that whoever calls to-night is told that you are strictly engaged.' So they would settle down for their quiet evening. Presently the doorbell would ring and Alice would go to the entry, to make sure that her instructions were carried out; but close behind her would be William, exclaiming, 'Come in! Come right in!'

Their house at 95 Irving Street, Cambridge, was of New England architecture, with a gambrel roof and wood-colored shingles. It had a sizable entrance hall, and the biggest library I have ever seen, with books on all the walls up to the ceiling, an open fire almost always burning, a long writing desk, a window seat running across four windows, two sofas, one on either side of the fire, and easy-chairs in sufficient number to accommodate several groups of people. Beside the fireplace was an entrance into the parlor, and well can one see William frequently darting from his desk into the adjoining room to take part in his young people's fun, proving how entirely he was a man of two worlds.

Jessie Hodder tells that once when she was visiting the Jameses at Chocorua she was asked to read some French book aloud. As she was about to start, William silently slipped out of the room, and she, who is always sensitive to the moods of others, inferred that he was sparing himself the torture of presumably hearing the language mispronounced. But, walking to and fro outside the windows, he apparently 'listened in,' and presently returned and took his place with the others. Later he asked whether she had learned

French as a child, and expressed his surprise that one who had learned the language as an adult should have acquired the accent of a native.

In formal conversation William could never be counted on to take the lead. But on summer mornings such as those in Switzerland, with only my sister, myself, and Peggy at the table,—Alice would be busy upstairs with Tweedy,—he would pour out a stream of talk, German words and English run together, of a quality so human, so imaginative, and so unique that one could not seem to bear it that all the world was not present to hear.

On one occasion, returning from the Shanty, he stopped for a night at Major Henry L. Higginson's outlying summer home on Lake Champlain, where he encountered the friend with whom I had gone to Cuba, Miss Grace Minnes. They talked together, she addressing him as 'Professor' James. 'Oh, don't call me Professor!' he exclaimed. 'Why, what shall I call you?' she asked. 'Call me Percival!' was his characteristic answer, perhaps indicating in that romantic word the many people to whom his heart was open.

The following letter was obviously written by Percival, full as it is of a romantic desire simply to stretch out his hand to a friend across a continent, and equally full of pure fun.

Berkeley, Cal., Sept. 2, '98

Dear Elizabeth,

You will be surprised at hearing from me at this distance; but at intervals all through this summer I have had stirrings of romantic appreciation of your character (which character grows upon me more and more, and which I won't pretend to diagnosticate for your own self-elation) that have brought me to the verge of a letter to tell you of the same—for why, when we feel most friendly towards a person, should we stay as dumb as a Boston Back Bay Fish?—but the letter has each time been postponed till now. Yes! Elizabeth, there is that about you, a touch of—what shall I call it?—magnanimity, that makes the thought of your existence in the world and of your friendship and toleration very, very consoling and helpful when one is in certain sorts of spirits about one's self and life. I wish to say to you this, for it is literally true; but I will say no more, for you probably find this enough. Let the word give you one momentary gleam of egotistic pleasure—for you deserve one. . . .

I have been away for five weeks, which seem much more—seen much grand scenery, some good people, and a very interesting city and civilization.

I have a fortnight more of it, but shall get off to Monterey by myself for a week, for the social giggle, innocent and good as it is, seems to be a sort of poison to me. I shall be tremendously glad to get back to Alice and the Brats, and all that 'home' means, and hope soon after to have the pleasure of seeing you. Meanwhile, dear Bessie, I am your faithful friend,

Wm. James

The next letter, written in a quite different style, shows that William could be tart as well as sweet. One of his many protégés was a person who wrote admirable syllogistic articles but who was apparently incapable of earning even a crust of bread, and who once at least called William back from a trip in Nova Scotia to give him the money saved by thus cutting short his stay. William spoke to me of this man's needs and I spoke of them to a friend, and together we chipped in. But something was evidently wrong with our giving, for William wrote:—

Dear Bessie,

I have received enough from *your* friends for P—— the unfortunate, so give yourself no more concern about him. I return with thanks Mrs. H——'s check, which can now go to some other 'object.' Christ died for us *all*—*nicht wahr?* . . .

Thine truly,

William James

It may be added that William's wife finally intervened between 'P—— the unfortunate' and William's out-of-bounds generosity by recommending P—— to pick cranberries on the Cape as a means of relieving his wants—advice which gave him high displeasure. In a final letter to me on the subject, William quoted the views of certain philosophers who claimed that pity was a vice, to be exterminated along with its object. 'I believe that to be a lie,' he had commented. But he went on to say that the 'canalization of pity was an engineering feat' demanding great skill—and that this especial 'object' put a sore tax upon his patience.

Oh, his patience! Who ever had so vast a supply? Numberless struggling authors and students sought his counsel and his financial aid. And always they met with an appreciative hearing, and money paid out almost recklessly.

William James died on August 26, 1910. He had been in Europe for some months, suffering cruelly from deranged nervous functions. When finally it was decided that he had best return home, he and his wife and his brother Henry made the journey with an unexpected degree of comfort. 'Oh, how good it is to be at home!' he exclaimed when they reached Chocorua. Nevertheless, two days later he collapsed, and the end came quickly.

Jessie Hodder was staying at a nearby hotel. She heard that her friend since her early married days, the friend who used to speak of her husband as the most brilliant philosophic student he had ever known, lay dying, and she describes the great cloud that hung over the mountain as if it were a portentous sign of the passing of a Great Soul.

I read the news of William's death in the paper as I was traveling from Milwaukee to the LaFollettes' home in Madison. I felt as if it eclipsed the light of the sky. It seemed impossible—impossible that such a vital creature should be lying still and cold, to be covered in the silence of the grave from the eyes that delighted in him. His wife wrote me in her own characteristic vocabulary, bidding me 'think of William as I love to, free from pain, and full of the joy of life, his feet beautiful upon the mountains whence he bringeth good tidings.'

THÉODORE FLOURNOY

(1854–1920)

Although William James and Théodore Flournoy saw one another only a few times during their twenty-year friendship, their correspondence reflects unusual warmth.[1] When they met in 1889 at the First International Congress of Physiological Psychology in Paris, they found common bonds both personally and professionally. Both men were interested far more in psychological theory than in experimental data, both took seriously the field of psychical research, and both were married with growing families and the burdens of household concerns.

Flournoy, who taught psychology at the University of Geneva, never managed to relinquish his responsibilities as director of the university's laboratory (as James had done at Harvard), and he complained continually about the task. 'I do not speak to you of my laboratory, which bores me more and more and in which I accomplish nothing worth while,' he wrote to James in 1892.[2] Six years later he compared his laboratory to 'a heavy cannon ball which I pull along like a convict.'[3] And five years after that he lamented having to go to his laboratory 'to face a dozen Russians, not knowing either what to tell them or what to have them do.'[4]

Flournoy preferred to consider questions about the influence of subconscious forces on personality, and on 'supernormal or metaphysical phenomena.'[5] He regretted that many scientists refused to focus on such phenomena, instead allowing 'theosophists, mystics, and occultists' to study them.[6] 'I try to penetrate into the spiritualistic world of our city,' he wrote to James. 'I have been asked to give two talks in a series of public lectures, after the New Year, and I shall do them on Verifiable Hallucinations, Visions in the Crystal Ball, etc.'[7]

James and Flournoy wrote each other often about their respective work in psychical research. Flournoy made a clear distinction between *spiritism,* which he defined as 'a pretended scientific explanation of certain *facts* by the intervention of spirits of the dead,' and *spiritualism*, 'which is a religio-philosophical belief, opposed to materialism and based on the principle of value and the reality of individual consciousness.'[8] For Flournoy, understanding the work of the medium could lead to a deeper understanding of the subconscious. He based his own 'psychological theory of mediumship' on the belief that each medium was predisposed 'to mental dissociation and a sort of infantile regression, a relapse into an inferior phase of psychic evolution, where his imagination naturally begins to imitate the discarnate, utilizing the resources of the subconscious, the emotional complexes, latent memories, instinctive tendencies ordinarily suppressed, etc., for the various roles it plays.'[9]

Flournoy's publications include *From India to the Planet Mars* (1900), the result of his six years of study with the Swiss medium 'Hélène Smith,' and *Spiritism and Psychology*, (1911), which he dedicated to William James and Marc Thury, a colleague at the University of Geneva.

NOTES

1. Robert Le Clair, *The Letters of William James and Théodore Flournoy* (Madison: University of Wisconsin Press, 1966).
2. Le Clair, *Letters*, 17 (30 December 1892).
3. Le Clair, *Letters*, 77 (11 December 1898).
4. Le Clair, *Letters*, 148 (22 December 1903).
5. T. Flournoy, *Spiritism and Psychology*, trans. Hereward Carrington (New York: Harper, 1911), vii.
6. Flournoy, *Spiritism and Psychology*, vii.
7. Le Clair, *Letters*, 29 (18 December 1893).
8. Le Clair, *Letters*, ix–x (18 December 1893).
9. Le Clair, *Letters*, viii (18 December 1893).

Artistic Temperament

William James was an artist by virtue of an originality and perfection of literary style which made him one of the most brilliant writers of his own country. But above all he was an artist in his extraordinarily vivid and delicate feeling for concrete realities, his penetrating vision in the realm of the particular, and his aptitude for seizing on that which was characteristic and unique in everything that he met. I do not here refer to external and material realities (although it is true that James appreciated as few do the beauties of nature, and having a remarkable facility for drawing, he entertained for a time the idea of becoming a painter), for in the life of the soul he saw a still more mysterious and fascinating spectacle, and it is to the observation of this that he resolved to devote himself. He was a born psychologist and a psychologist of genius precisely because of this artistic insight, which in him, by a rare exception, was combined with the exact scientific spirit.

Between these two turns of mind there is, as you know, a profound contrast; for the artistic mind looks at everything in its concrete particularity and presents it as individual, while the scientific intellect analyzes, abstracts, and generalizes. All science is general, as Aristotle said, and when it deals with particular objects it at once dissolves their particularity, analyzing them into elemental factors, classifying them and referring them to general laws, until all their individuality is lost. But it is just this unique individuality, intact, immediate, and real, which is the exclusive interest of art. Now James's temperament led him to see that both these points of view are indispensable to a complete knowledge of mental life, and that psychic facts must be observed in their integrity, as indivisible pulsations of the continuous 'stream of consciousness' (to borrow his favorite expression); while at the same time they must be analyzed introspectively, and related to their extrinsic causes and conditions. One might reverse the familiar saying that 'every landscape is a state of the soul,' and say that for James every state of the soul was a landscape, in which he perceived with the eye of an artist the color, the atmosphere, and the indefinable charm of the whole; while at the same time his scientific eye distinguished the minutest detail and divined even the geologic structure of the earth beneath. This rare combination of two so diverse perceptive faculties gave to James's psychology a quality that was both spiritual, in that the most subtle manifestations of consciousness were never violated, and at the same time searchingly physiological and even seemingly materialistic, in that the mechanical side of our psychic life, the organic and cerebral conditions, were attentively observed. But it is not of his psychology that I wish especially to speak to you to-day.

This same artistic capacity, this fineness of perception, by means of which James, in analyzing his own subjective states was able to recognize the uniqueness and irreducible individuality of each, also enabled him to penetrate the recesses of other persons' consciousnesses far better than other psychologists have ever succeeded in doing. By a kind of admirable divination he fathomed without disturbing them, minds that were very different from his own. Thus he was in touch with the moods and phases of the inner life of others, which to most of us are inaccessible, imprisoned as we are by the fixed barriers of our own egoism. Every work of James testifies to this aptitude, which besides being innate had been consciously exercised and developed, for seizing the living reality wheresoever it was to be found, and in persons howsoever different. So happy a faculty necessarily broadened both his personality and his philosophy far beyond the narrow individual horizon within which the devisers of philosophic systems are too often confined.

Little touches that testify to this breadth and penetration abound in James's life and in his writings. It is not only other philosophers whom he endeavors intimately to understand, but also men of a mentality quite different from his own; behind whose abstract statements he sympathetically sees, and so realizes what the immediate experience was which has inspired them. Even the most humble derelicts of our race are still of interest to him when he suspects something in them which has been sincerely lived. If in a museum, for instance, he runs across a couple of simple souls engaged in the blissful contemplation of a mediocre canvas, instead of passing on with a smile at their naïveté, he reflects rather that at least these untutored souls are experiencing the authentic aesthetic emotion which is very often quite missed by the learned critics in whom intellectualism has dried up the springs of feeling. If he meets one of those original characters whom good society treats disdainfully as a crank, because he does not comply with accepted conventions, James instinctively feels himself attracted toward that person, not only with the curiosity of a naturalist for a rare specimen, a species which he must not miss, but with the sincere affection of a human being for his fellow-man, and with the interest of one experimenter in life for another participator in the same experiment. And we must note that in order to excite James's interest, it is not necessary for this other person's experience to present anything exceptional or sublime. However modest a human existence may be, however meagre or insipid it appears from the outside, it possesses nevertheless when seen from within its own intimate and peculiar quality, its unique importance, and a personal significance which most of us scarcely suspect where our fellow-men are concerned, but which James always felt and endeavored to penetrate.

For instance, once when traveling in North Carolina, he passed through a desolated region where the natural forest had been ruthlessly sacrificed to make room for some miserable settlers' habitations. James reproached himself for his first feeling of revulsion at the melancholy spectacle, and blamed himself for not at once having had the sympathetic imagination to divine how much these objects, destitute as they were of beauty from the point of view of the tourist, represented for the dwellers themselves by way of toil and vicissitudes endured, and security finally won. In short here a victory had been gained over nature. However much an ugly locality may strike us with its sorry aspect when we see it merely as passers-by, it may yet be that it has a very different message for those who live there and who have toiled, suffered, and perhaps triumphed; and it is this accumulated inner significance which we ought to discern, because it is that, rather than the cheerless outward aspect of the place, which constitutes its essential reality. James has left us in this connection two admirable lay sermons on that intellectual and spiritual blindness which prevents our seeing into the soul of our neighbor whenever the conditions of his life differ at all from our own, and which makes us stupidly insensible to all that determines his valuation of things and his deepest interests in life.[1]

James's artistic sensitiveness to all the concrete forms of psychical existence was not confined to the case of other men; it extended on occasion

1. *Cf.* James's two essays entitled 'On a Certain Blindness in Human Beings' and 'What Makes a Life Significant?' in the latter part of his volume *Talks to Teachers on Psychology: and to Students on Some of Life's Ideals*. New York, 1899, pp.229 and 265.

even to the dim consciousness of the lower animals, in whom he sought to fathom the dull pulse of psychic life, and to divine what aspect the universe wore for their confused experience. From the inquiring look of his dog, from the vague apprehensiveness of cattle being driven to the slaughter-house, from the manifestations of pain in animals on the operating table, James sought to divine the way in which the mystery of things comes home to them. The quiet and more elusive states of consciousness as well as the brute joys and atrocious sufferings, which make up the existence of our humbler fellow-creatures, were all in his eyes fragments or pulsations of reality which no philosopher has any right to neglect. Even the lowly crab is summoned to the court of metaphysics by his inquiring genius, there to give its testimony in favor of the uniqueness of each individual consciousness; which in our passion for scientific generalization has been left so flagrantly out of account. 'It is only a crab,' says the naturalist, as he tosses it down among its fellows. 'Excuse me, it is I,' the animal would protest, and thus remind the philosopher that if the scientist supposes he has finally disposed of a living organism when he has pasted a label on it, or given it a place in his classification, he has quite missed the true inwardness of the situation. In reality every individual counts as itself and constitutes a unique and given fact whose existence one must recognize with a certain deference; nor may one flatter oneself that one can ever reduce it to a mere constellation of general laws or of abstract categories.

I could multiply indefinitely these little indications which show how supreme James was in discerning that which is original and unique in every creature, and in attaining a sympathetic insight into that which constitutes for each its own peculiar being. But the most typical and masterly example which he has left us of this fine comprehension of other minds that differed from his own is undoubtedly his celebrated book, *The Varieties of Religious Experience*.[2] This work has been a profound revelation to innumerable readers, initiating some into mysteries of the inner life which they had never even suspected, and freeing others from the heavy yoke of dogma, while it has given to all a broader outlook and a salutary lesson in toleration. There is indeed no realm in which different souls are ordinarily more completely shut off from one another than in that of religion, and no field in which the mutual lack of comprehension among human beings displays itself as more complete or more deplorable. James was the first per-

2. New York, 1902.

son to succeed in pulling down these barriers, to understand and to make others understand the infinite gradations of this peculiarly intimate order of experience. He has been in this field more influential than any one else. In the midst of our modern society, so profoundly torn by religious and anti-religious hatreds, he has set in motion a current of coöperation and mutual respect, a movement for human sympathy and fraternity by which all sincere persons may feel themselves encouraged, and may, in spite of the diversity of their temperaments and personal convictions, lend friendly assistance to one another.

We are not to conclude, however, from this openness of mind and gift of sympathetic intuition which made James take an interest in every aspect of mental life, that he was one of those over-refined æsthetes for whom humanity in its infinite variety is merely an absorbing spectacle. Without doubt to know all is to pardon all. But if James pardoned all, that is to say if he was infinitely indulgent to others (so long as they on their side were not intolerant or overbearing), he none the less appreciated differences of moral quality with rare subtlety, because he was himself a positive and preëminently moral individual. He had his own ideals that were the product of his own inner experience, of his rare moral intuition, his personal view of life, in a word of his own philosophy.

GEORGE SANTAYANA

(1863–1952)

George Santayana was born in Madrid, retained his Spanish citizenship throughout his life, and proclaimed himself 'Latin' in spirit and by blood. He arrived in Boston in 1872, an eight-year-old with no knowledge of English; he attended the Brimmer School, the Boston Latin School, and finally, in 1882, entered Harvard where, as student and teacher, he would spend the next two decades.

He was not immediately attracted to philosophy as a discipline. '[M]y whole experience since I left college and even before has been a series of disenchantments,' he confessed to James when he was in Europe on a fellowship. 'First I lost my faith in the kind of philosophy that Professors Palmer and Royce are interested in; and then, when I came to Germany, I also lost my faith in psycho-physics, and all the other attempts to discover something very momentous.'[1] He could not really understand why philosophers were so obsessed about 'absolute truth, which,' he remarked, 'is not to be made or altered by our discovery of it.'[2] Yet he came to decide that philosophy was, in a way, like art, and if it would not yield truth, still it might help to 'expose a half-discovered reality.'[3]

Santayana graduated with a doctorate in 1889—James called him 'the best *intellect* we have turned out here in many a year'[4]—and immediately was asked to teach a course on Locke, Berkeley, and Hume, for the small remuneration of $500. An allowance from his family made it possible for him to accept, and in the fall of 1889 he began his teaching career at Harvard.

Although he enjoyed the company of students and met with them in his rooms in Stoughton Hall, Santayana often seemed reserved, a darkly romantic figure sweeping through Harvard Yard in an exotic black cape, detached, somehow, from the life of the college. 'And why should he not have been detached,' asked Dickinson Miller. 'A bachelor, withdrawn from the entanglement of practical affairs, a Spaniard and Spanish subject established in America, a Roman Catholic by birth and nurture living amongst Protestants, nay Unitarians, an American professor finding his most congenial atmosphere in England, a poet teaching philosophy, a thinker of essentially modern philosophic training finding his most congenial sages amongst the ancient Greeks, a scholar with a taste for fashionable society.'[5] Santayana cultivated detachment, causing some people—Bertrand Russell, for one—to find him rather prim, and others—like John Chapman—to find him ultimately unknowable. 'He makes the impression on me,' Chapman commented, 'of not knowing more about life than a kid glove exposed for sale in a shop-window.'[6] But Santayana felt a sense of freedom in his position as an outsider. Writing from Paris, he told James that he found that speaking a foreign language among foreigners was 'exhilarating. You can say what is *really true.* You needn't remember that you are in Cambridge, or are addressing the youth entrusted to your paternal charge.'[7]

After Santayana had continued as an instructor for many years, James recommended to President Eliot that he be promoted to assistant professor. 'S. is a very honest and unworldly character,' James wrote, 'a spectator rather than an actor by temperament, but apart from that element of weakness, a man (as I see him) of thoroughly wholesome mental atmosphere. He is both a "gentleman" and a "scholar" in the real sense of the words, an exquisite writer and a finished speaker.'[8] In 1898, Santayana was appointed assistant professor for $2000 a year, with a renewal contract of five years. He left Harvard in 1912 as a full professor.

James admired Santayana's talent as a writer, but his praise revealed an underlying distrust of Santayana's way of thinking. Writing to Dickinson Miller about *The Life of Reason,* for example, James called the book 'great,' and predicted that it would 'be reckoned great by posterity.' But he was disturbed by its lack of '*rational* foundation.' Instead, James wrote, the book was 'merely one man's way of viewing things: so much of experience admitted and no more, so much criticism and questioning admitted and no more. Here is a paragon of Emersonianism—declare your intuitions, though no other man shared them; and the integrity with which he does it is as fine as it is rare.' But, according to James, while Emerson was 'receptive, expansive,' Santayana saw the world 'as if through a pin-point orifice that emits his cooling spray outward over the universe like a nose-disinfectant from an "atomizer."'[9]

Santayana was frustrated by James's inability—or unwillingness—to understand him. James offered him 'goodwill and kindness,' he said, but 'when he talked to me there was manikin in his head, called G.S. and entirely fantastic, which he was addressing. No doubt I profited materially by this illusion,' Santayana added, 'because he would have liked me less if he had understood me better; but the sense of that illusion made spontaneous friendship impossible.'[10] He wrote repeatedly to James that he believed they shared many ideas, but James insisted that they did not. 'I am very glad you find some of my ideas so congruent with yours,' he told Santayana. 'Yours are still one of the secrets of the universe which it is one of my chief motives to live for the unveiling of.'[11]

In his memoir Santayana characterizes James as a wistful romantic, one whose democratic impulses made him generous, tolerant, and lovable. Certainly Santayana had none of these characteristics: he was an elitist who believed that man's reason—that is, the intellectual capacity of cosmopolitan, well-educated, aesthetically sensitive men—mediated experience to produce art, poetry, literature, and philosophical works such as his own. Where James lived comfortably in a world buzzing with confusion and stimulation, Santayana did not: as he admitted to Sidney Hook, 'I love order in the sense of organized, harmonious, consecrated living.'[12] 'William James and George Santayana,' Dickinson Miller concluded, 'were a contrast almost too absolute and perfect to be real.'[13]

NOTES

1. George Santayana to WJ, Perry 1:405 (3 July 1888).
2. George Santayana to WJ, Perry 1:401 (18 December 1887).
3. George Santayana to WJ, Perry 1:401 (18 December 1887).
4. WJ to Martha Carey Thomas, Scott, 57 (22 March 1889).
5. Dickinson Miller, 'Mr. Santayana and William James,' *Harvard Graduates' Magazine* March 1921, 348.
6. John Chapman, *Selected Writings.* (New York: Farrar, Straus, 1957) 250.
7. George Santayana to WJ, Perry 2:400 (5 December 1905).
8. WJ to Charles Eliot, Scott, 140 (24 January 1896).
9. WJ to Dickinson Miller, *Letters* 2:234–35 (10 November 1905).
10. George Santayana, *Persons and Places,* vol.2 (New York: Scribner's, 1945), 166.
11. WJ to George Santayana, Perry 2:398 (8 February 1905).
12. George Santayana to Sidney Hook, 8 June 1934. 'Letters from George Santayana,' *The American Scholar,* Winter 1976, 79.
13. Miller, 'Mr. Santayana and William James,' 356.

William James

William James enjoyed in his youth what are called advantages: he lived among cultivated people, travelled, had teachers of various nationalities. His father was one of those somewhat obscure sages whom early America produced: mystics of independent mind, hermits in the desert of business, and heretics in the churches. They were intense individualists, full of veneration for the free souls of their children, and convinced that every one should paddle his own canoe, especially on the high seas. William James accordingly enjoyed a stimulating if slightly irregular education: he never acquired that reposeful mastery of particular authors and those safe ways of feeling and judging which are fostered in great schools and universities. In consequence he showed an almost physical horror of club sentiment and of the stifling atmosphere of all officialdom. He had a knack for drawing, and rather the temperament of the artist; but the unlovely secrets of nature and the troubles of man preoccupied him, and he chose medicine for his profession. Instead of practising, however, he turned to teaching physiology, and from that passed gradually to psychology and philosophy.

In his earlier years he retained some traces of polyglot student days at Paris, Bonn, Vienna, or Geneva; he slipped sometimes into foreign phrases, uttered in their full vernacular; and there was an occasional afterglow of Bohemia about him, in the bright stripe of a shirt or the exuberance of a tie. On points of art or medicine he retained a professional touch and an unconscious ease which he hardly acquired in metaphysics. I suspect he had heartily admired some of his masters in those other subjects, but had never seen a philosopher whom he would have cared to resemble. Of course there was nothing of the artist in William James, as the artist is sometimes conceived in England, nothing of the æsthete, nothing affected or limp. In person he was short rather than tall, erect, brisk, bearded, intensely masculine. While he shone in expression and would have wished his style to be noble if it could also be strong, he preferred in the end to be spontaneous, and to leave it at that; he tolerated slang in himself rather than primness. The rough, homely, picturesque phrase, whatever was graphic and racy, recommended itself to him; and his conversation outdid his writing in this respect. He believed in improvisation, even in thought; his lectures were not minutely prepared. Know your subject thoroughly, he used to say, and trust to luck for the rest. There was a deep sense of insecurity in him, a mixture of humility with romanticism: we were likely to be more or less wrong anyhow, but we might be wholly sincere. One moment should respect the insight of another, without trying to establish too regimental a uniformity. If you corrected yourself tartly, how could you know that the correction was not the worse mistake? All our opinions were born free and equal, all children of the Lord, and if they were not consistent that was the Lord's business, not theirs. In reality, James was consistent enough, as even Emerson (more extreme in this sort of irresponsibility) was too. Inspiration has its limits, sometimes very narrow ones. But James was not consecutive, not insistent; he turned to a subject afresh, without egotism or pedantry; he dropped his old points, sometimes very good ones; and he modestly looked for light from others, who had less light than himself.

His excursions into philosophy were accordingly in the nature of raids, and it is easy for those who are attracted by one part of his work to ignore other parts, in themselves perhaps more valuable. I think that in fact his popularity does not rest on his best achievements. His popularity rests on three somewhat incidental books, *The Will to Believe, Pragmatism,* and *The Varieties of Religious Experience,* whereas, as it seems to me, his best achievement is his *Principles of Psychology.* In this book he surveys, in a way which for him is very systematic, a subject made to his hand. In its ostensible outlook it is a treatise like any other, but what distinguishes it is the author's gift for evoking vividly the very life of the mind. This is a work of imagination; and the subject as he conceived it, which is the flux of immediate experience in men in general, requires imagination to read it at all. It is a literary subject, like autobiography or psychological fiction, and can be treated only poetically; and in this sense Shakespeare is a better psychologist than Locke or Kant. Yet this gift of imagination is not merely literary; it is not useless in divining the truths of science, and it is invaluable in throwing off prejudice and scientific shams. The fresh imagination and vitality of William James led him to break through many a false convention. He saw that experience, as we endure it, is not a mosaic of distinct sensations, nor the expression of separate hostile faculties, such as reason and the passions, or sense and the categories; it is rather a flow of mental discourse, like a dream, in which all divisions and units are vague and shifting, and the whole is continually merging together and drifting apart. It fades gradually in the rear, like the wake of a ship, and bites into the future, like the bow cutting the water. For the candid psychologist, carried bodily on this voyage of discovery, the past is but a questionable report, and the future wholly indeterminate; everything is simply what it is experienced as being.

At the same time, psychology is supposed to be a science, a claim which would tend to confine it to the natural history of man, or the study of behaviour, as is actually proposed by Auguste Comte and by some of James's own disciples, more jejune if more clear-headed than he. As matters now stand, however, psychology as a whole is not a science, but a branch of philosophy; it brings together the literary description of mental discourse and the scientific description of material life, in order to consider the relation between them, which is the nexus of human nature.

What was James's position on this crucial question? It is impossible to reply unequivocally. He approached philosophy as mankind originally approached it, without having a philosophy, and he lent himself to various hypotheses in various directions. He professed to begin his study on the assumptions of common sense, that there is a material world which the animals that live in it are able to perceive and to think about. He gave a congruous extension to this view in his theory that emotion is purely bodily sensation, and also in his habit of conceiving the mind as a total shifting sensibility. To pursue this path, however, would have led him to admit that nature was automatic and mind simply cognitive, conclusions from which every instinct in him recoiled. He preferred to believe that mind and matter had independent energies and could lend one another a hand, matter operating by motion and mind by intention. This dramatic, amphibious way of picturing causation is natural to common sense, and might be defended if it were clearly defined; but James was insensibly carried away from it by a subtle implication of his method. This implication was that experience or mental discourse not only constituted a set of substantive facts, but the *only* substantive facts; all else, even that material world which his psychology had postulated, could be nothing but a verbal or fantastic symbol for sensations in their experienced order. So that while nominally the door was kept open to any hypothesis regarding the conditions of the psychological flux, in truth the question was pre-judged. The hypotheses, which were parts of this psychological flux, could have no object save other parts of it. That flux itself, therefore, which he could picture so vividly, was the fundamental existence. The *sense* of bounding over the waves, the *sense* of being on an adventurous voyage, was the living fact; the rest was dead reckoning. Where one's gift is, there will one's faith be also; and to this poet appearance was the only reality.

This sentiment, which always lay at the back of his mind, reached something like formal expression in his latest writings, where he sketched what he called radical empiricism. The word experience is like a shrapnel shell, and bursts into a thousand meanings. Here we must no longer think of its setting, its discoveries, or its march; to treat it radically we must abstract its immediate objects and reduce it to pure data. It is obvious (and the sequel has already proved) that experience so understood would lose its romantic signification, as a personal adventure or a response to the shocks of fortune. 'Experience' would turn into a cosmic dance of absolute entities created and destroyed *in vacuo* according to universal laws, or perhaps by chance. No minds would gather this experience, and no material agencies would impose it; but the immediate objects present to any one would simply be parts of the universal fireworks, continuous with the rest, and all the parts, even if not present to anybody, would have the same status. Experience would then not at all resemble what Shakespeare reports or what James himself had described in his psychology. If it could be experienced as it flows in its entirety (which is fortunately impracticable), it would be a perpetual mathematical nightmare. Every whirling atom, every changing relation, and every incidental perspective would be a part of it. I am far from wishing to deny for a moment the scientific value of such a cosmic system, if it can be worked out; physics and mathematics seem to me to plunge far deeper than literary psychology into the groundwork of this world; but human experience is the stuff of literary psychology; we cannot reach the stuff of physics and mathematics except by arresting or even hypostatising some elements of appearance, and expanding them on an abstracted and hypothetical plane of their own. Experience, as memory and literature rehearse it, remains nearer to us than that: it is something dreamful, passionate, dramatic, and significative.

Certainly this personal human experience, expressible in literature and in talk, and no cosmic system however profound, was what James knew best and trusted most. Had he seen the developments of his radical empiricism, I cannot help thinking he would have marvelled that such logical mechanisms should have been hatched out of that egg. The principal problems and aspirations that haunted him all his life long would lose their meaning in that cosmic atmosphere. The pragmatic nature of truth, for instance, would never suggest itself in the presence of pure data; but a romantic mind soaked in agnosticism, conscious of its own habits and assuming an environment the exact structure of which can never be observed, may well convince itself that, for experience, truth is nothing but a happy use of signs—which is indeed the truth of literature. But if we once accept *any* system of the universe as literally true, the value of convenient signs to prepare us for such experience as is yet absent cannot be called truth: it is plainly nothing but a necessary inaccuracy. So, too, with the question of the survival of the human individual after death. For radical empiricism a human individual is simply a certain cycle or complex of terms, like any other natural fact; that some echoes of his mind should recur after the regular chimes have ceased, would have nothing paradoxical about it. A mathematical world is a good deal like music, with its repetitions and transpositions, and a little trill, which you might call a person, might well peep up here and there all over a vast composition. Something of that sort may be the truth of spiritualism; but it is not what the spiritualists imagine. Their whole interest lies not in the experiences they have, but in the interpretation they give to them, assigning them to troubled spirits in another world; but both another world and a spirit are notions repugnant to a radical empiricism.

I think it is important to remember, if we are not to misunderstand William James, that his radical empiricism and pragmatism were in his own mind only methods; his doctrine, if he may be said to have had one, was agnosticism. And just because he was an agnostic (feeling instinctively that beliefs and opinions, if they had any objective beyond themselves, could never be sure they had attained it), he seemed in one sense so favourable to credulity. He was not credulous himself, far from it; he was well aware that the trust he put in people or ideas might betray him. For that very reason he was respectful and pitiful to the trustfulness of others. Doubtless they were wrong, but who were we to say so? In his own person he was ready enough to face the mystery of things, and whatever the womb of time might bring forth; but until the curtain was rung down on the last act of the drama (and it might have no last act!) he wished the intellectual cripples and the moral hunchbacks not to be jeered at; perhaps they might turn out to be the heroes of the play. Who could tell what heavenly influences might not pierce to these sensitive half-flayed creatures, which are lost on the thick-skinned, the sane, and the duly goggled? We must not suppose, however, that James meant these contrite and romantic suggestions dogmatically. The agnostic, as well as the physician and neurologist in him, was never quite eclipsed. The hope that some new revelation might come from the lowly and weak could never mean to him what it meant to the early Christians. For him it was only a right conceded to them to experiment with their special faiths; he did not expect such faiths to be discoveries of absolute fact, which everybody else might be constrained to recognise. If any one had made such a claim, and had seemed to have some chance of imposing it universally, James would have been the first to turn against him; not, of course, on the ground that it was *impossible* that such an orthodoxy should be true, but with a profound conviction that it was to be feared and distrusted. No: the degree of authority and honour to be accorded to various human faiths was a moral question, not a theoretical one. All faiths were what they were experienced as being, in their capacity of faiths; these faiths, not their objects, were the hard facts we must respect. We cannot pass, except under the illusion of the moment, to anything firmer or on a deeper level. There was accordingly no sense of security, no joy, in James's apology for personal religion. He did not really believe; he merely believed in the right of believing that you might be right if you believed.

It is this underlying agnosticism that explains an incoherence which we might find in his popular works, where the story and the moral do not seem to hang together. Professedly they are works of psychological observation; but the tendency and suasion in them seems to run to disintegrating the idea of truth, recommending belief without reason, and encouraging superstition. A psychologist who was not an agnostic would have indicated, as far as possible, whether the beliefs and experiences he was describing were instances of delusion or of rare and fine perception, or in what measure they were a mixture of both. But James—and this is what gives such romantic warmth to these writings of his—disclaims all antecedent or superior knowledge, listens to the testimony of each witness in turn, and only by accident allows us to feel that he is swayed by the eloquence and vehemence of some of them rather than of others. This method is modest, generous, and impartial; but if James intended, as I think he did, to picture the *drama* of human belief, with its risks and triumphs, the method was inadequate. Dramatists never hesitate to assume, and to let the audience perceive, who is good and who bad, who wise and who foolish, in their pieces; otherwise their work would be as impotent dramatically as scientifically. The tragedy and comedy of life lie precisely in the contrast between the illusions or passions of the characters and their true condition and fate, hidden from them at first, but evident to the author and the public. If in our diffidence and scrupulous fairness we refuse to take this judicial attitude, we shall be led to strange conclusions. The navigator, for instance, trusting his 'experience' (which here, as in the case of religious people, means his imagination and his art), insists on believing that the earth is spherical; he has sailed round it. That is to say, he has seemed to himself to steer westward and westward, and has seemed to get home again. But how should he know that home is now where it was before, or that his past and present impressions of it come from the same, or from any, material object? How should he know that space is as trim and tridimensional as the discredited Euclidians used to say it was? If, on the contrary, my worthy aunt, trusting to her longer and less ambiguous experience of her garden, insists that the earth is flat, and observes that the theory that it is round, which is only a theory, is much less often tested and found useful than her own perception of its flatness, and that moreover that theory is pedantic, intellectualistic, and a product of academies, and a rash dogma to impose on mankind for ever and ever, it might seem that on James's principle we ought to agree with her. But no; on James's real principles we need not agree with her, nor with the navigator either. Radical empiricism, which is radical agnosticism, delivers us from so benighted a choice. For the quarrel becomes unmeaning when we remember that the earth is *both* flat and round, if it is experienced as being both. The substantive fact is not a single object on which both the perception and the theory are expected to converge; the substantive facts are the theory and the perception themselves. And we may note in passing that empiricism, when it ceases to value experience as a means of discovering external things, can give up its ancient prejudice in favour of sense as against imagination, for imagination and thought are immediate experiences as much as sensation is: they are therefore, for absolute empiricism, no less actual ingredients of reality.

In *The Varieties of Religious Experience* we find the same apologetic intention running through a vivid account of what seems for the most part (as James acknowledged) religious disease. Normal religious experience is hardly described in it. Religious experience, for the great mass of mankind, consists in simple faith in the truth and benefit of their religious traditions. But to James something so conventional and rationalistic seemed hardly experience and hardly religious; he was thinking only of irruptive visions and feelings as interpreted by the mystics who had them. These interpretations he ostensibly presents, with more or less wistful sympathy for what they were worth; but emotionally he wished to champion them. The religions that had sprung up in America spontaneously—communistic, hysterical, spiritistic, or medicinal—were despised by select and superior people. You might inquire into them, as you might go slumming, but they remained suspect and distasteful. This picking up of genteel skirts on the part of his acquaintance prompted William James to roll up his sleeves—not for a knock-out blow, but for a thorough clinical demonstration. He would tenderly vivisect the experiences in question, to show how living they were, though of course he could not guarantee, more than other surgeons do, that the patient would survive the operation. An operation that eventually kills may be technically successful, and the man may die cured; and so a description of religion that showed it to be madness might first show how real and how warm it was, so that if it perished, at least it would perish understood.

I never observed in William James any personal anxiety or enthusiasm for any of these dubious tenets. His conception even of such a thing as free-will, which he always ardently defended, remained vague; he avoided defining even what he conceived to be desirable in such matters. But he wished to protect the weak against the strong, and what he hated beyond everything was the *non possumus* of any constituted authority. Philosophy for him had a Polish constitution; so long as a single vote was cast against the majority, nothing could pass. The suspense of judgment which he had imposed on himself as a duty, became almost a necessity. I think it would have depressed him if he had had to confess that any important question was finally settled. He would still have hoped that something might turn up on the other side, and that just as the scientific hangman was about to despatch the poor convicted prisoner, an unexpected witness would ride up in hot haste, and prove him innocent. Experience seems to most of us to lead to conclusions, but empiricism has sworn never to draw them.

In the discourse on 'The Energies of Men,' certain physiological marvels are recorded, as if to suggest that the resources of our minds and bodies are infinite, or can be infinitely enlarged by divine grace. Yet James would not, I am sure, have accepted that inference. He would, under pressure, have drawn in his mystical horns under his scientific shell; but he was not naturalist enough to feel instinctively that the wonderful and the natural are all of a piece, and that only our degree of habituation distinguishes them. A nucleus, which we may poetically call the soul, certainly lies within us, by which our bodies and minds are generated and controlled, like an army by a government. In this nucleus, since nature in a small compass has room for anything, vast quantities of energy may well be stored up, which may be tapped on occasion, or which may serve like an electric spark to let loose energy previously existing in the grosser parts. But the absolute autocracy of this central power, or its success in imposing extraordinary trials on its subjects, is not an obvious good. Perhaps, like a democratic government, the soul is at its best when it merely collects and co-ordinates the impulses coming from the senses. The inner man is at times a tyrant, parasitical, wasteful, and voluptuous. At other times he is fanatical and mad. When he asks for and obtains violent exertions from the body, the question often is, as with the exploits of conquerors and conjurers, whether the impulse to do such prodigious things was not gratuitous, and the things nugatory. Who would wish to be a mystic? James himself, who by nature was a spirited rather than a spiritual man, had no liking for sanctimonious transcendentalists, visionaries, or ascetics; he hated minds that run thin. But he hastened to correct this manly impulse, lest it should be unjust, and forced himself to overcome his repugnance. This was made easier when the unearthly phenomenon had a healing or saving function in the everyday material world; miracle then re-established its ancient identity with medicine, and both of them were humanised. Even when this union was not attained, James was reconciled to the miracle-workers partly by his great charity, and partly by his hunter's instinct to follow a scent, for he believed discoveries to be imminent. Besides, a philosopher who is a teacher of youth is more concerned to give people a right start than a right conclusion. James fell in with the hortatory tradition of college sages; he turned his psychology, whenever he could do so honestly, to purposes of edification; and his little sermons on habit, on will, on faith, and this on the latent capacities of men, were fine and stirring, and just the sermons to preach to the young Christian soldier. He was much less sceptical in morals than in science. He seems to have felt sure that certain thoughts and hopes—those familiar to a liberal Protestantism—were every man's true friends in life. This assumption would have been hard to defend if he or those he habitually addressed had ever questioned it; yet his whole argument for voluntarily cultivating these beliefs rests on this assumption, that they are beneficent. Since, whether we will or no, we cannot escape the risk of error, and must succumb to some human or pathological bias, at least we might do so gracefully and in the form that would profit us most, by clinging to those prejudices which help us to lead what we all feel is a good life. But what is a good life? Had William James, had the people about him, had modern philosophers anywhere, any notion of that? I cannot think so. They had much experience of personal goodness, and love of it; they had standards of character and right conduct; but as to what might render human existence good, excellent, beautiful, happy, and worth having as a whole, their notions were utterly thin and barbarous. They had forgotten the Greeks, or never known them.

This argument accordingly suffers from the same weakness as the similar argument of Pascal in favour of Catholic orthodoxy. You should force yourself to believe in it, he said, because if you do so and are right you win heaven, while if you are wrong you lose nothing. What would Protestants, Mohammedans, and Hindus say to that? Those alternatives of Pascal's are not the sole nor the true alternatives; such a wager—betting on the improbable because you are offered big odds—is an unworthy parody of the real choice between wisdom and folly. There is no heaven to be won in such a spirit, and if there was, a philosopher would despise it. So William James would have us bet on immortality, or bet on our power to succeed, because if we win the wager we can live to congratulate ourselves on our true instinct, while we lose nothing if we have made a mistake; for unless you have the satisfaction of finding that you have been right, the dignity of having been right is apparently nothing. Or if the argument is rather that these beliefs, whether true or false, make life better in this world, the thing is simply false. To be boosted by an illusion is not to live better than to live in harmony with the truth; it is not nearly so safe, not nearly so sweet, and not nearly so fruitful. These refusals to part with a decayed illusion are really an infection to the mind. Believe, certainly; we cannot help believing; but believe rationally, holding what seems certain for certain, what seems probable for probable, what seems desirable for desirable, and what seems false for false.

In this matter, as usual, James had a true psychological fact and a generous instinct behind his confused moral suggestions. It is a psychological fact that men are influenced in their beliefs by their will and desires; indeed, I think we can go further and say that in its essence belief is an expression of impulse, of readiness to act. It is only peripherally, as our action is gradually adjusted to things, and our impulses to our possible or necessary action, that our ideas begin to hug the facts, and to acquire a true, if still a symbolic, significance. We do not need a will to believe; we only need a will to study the object in which we are inevitably believing. But James was thinking less of belief in what we find than of belief in what we hope for: a belief which is not at all clear and not at all necessary in the life of mortals.

Like most Americans, however, only more lyrically, James felt the call of the future and the assurance that it could be made far better, totally other, than the past. The pictures that religion had painted of heaven or the millennium were not what he prized, although his Swedenborgian connection might have made him tender to them, as perhaps it did to familiar spirits. It was the moral succour offered by religion, its open spaces, the possibility of miracles *in extremis,* that must be retained. If we recoiled at the thought of being dupes (which is perhaps what nature intended us to be), were we less likely to be dupes in disbelieving these sustaining truths than in believing them? Faith was needed to bring about the reform of faith itself, as well as all other reforms.

In some cases faith in success could nerve us to bring success about, and so justify itself by its own operation. This is a thought typical of James at his worst—a worst in which there is always a good side. Here again psychological observation is used with the best intentions to hearten oneself and other people; but the fact observed is not at all understood, and a moral twist is given to it which (besides being morally questionable) almost amounts to falsifying the fact itself. Why does belief that you can jump a ditch help you to jump it? Because it is a symptom of the fact that you *could* jump it, that your legs were fit and that the ditch was two yards wide and not twenty. A rapid and just appreciation of these facts has given you your confidence, or at least has made it reasonable, manly, and prophetic; otherwise you would have been a fool and got a ducking for it. Assurance is contemptible and fatal unless it is self-knowledge. If you had been rattled you might have failed, because that would have been a symptom of the fact that you were out of gear; you would have been afraid because you trembled, as James at his best proclaimed. You would never have quailed if your system had been reacting smoothly to its opportunities, any more than you would totter and see double if you were not intoxicated. Fear is a sensation of actual nervousness and disarray, and confidence a sensation of actual readiness; they are not disembodied feelings, existing for no reason, the devil Funk and the angel Courage, one or the other of whom may come down arbitrarily into your body, and revolutionise it. That is childish mythology, which survives innocently enough as a figure of speech, until a philosopher is found to take that figure of speech seriously. Nor is the moral suggestion here less unsound. What is good is not the presumption of power, but the possession of it: a clear head, aware of its resources, not a fuddled optimism, calling up spirits from the vasty deep. Courage is not a virtue, said Socrates, unless it is also wisdom. Could anything be truer both of courage in doing and of courage in believing? But it takes tenacity, it takes *reasonable* courage, to stick to scientific insights such as this of Socrates or that of James about the emotions; it is easier to lapse into the traditional manner, to search natural philosophy for miracles and moral lessons, and in morals proper, in the reasoned expression of preference, to splash about without a philosophy.

William James shared the passions of liberalism. He belonged to the left, which, as they say in Spain, is the side of the heart, as the right is that of the liver; at any rate there was much blood and no gall in his philosophy. He was one of those elder Americans still disquieted by the ghost of tyranny, social and ecclesiastical. Even the beauties of the past troubled him; he had a puritan feeling that they were tainted. They had been cruel and frivolous, and must have suppressed far better things. But what, we may ask, might these better things be? It may do for a revolutionary politician to say: 'I may not know what I want—except office—but I know what I don't want'; it will never do for a philosopher. Aversions and fears imply principles of preference, goods acknowledged; and it is the philosopher's business to make these goods explicit. Liberty is not an art, liberty must be used to bring some natural art to fruition. Shall it be simply eating and drinking and wondering what will happen next? If there is some deep and settled need in the heart of man, to give direction to his efforts, what else should a philosopher do but discover and announce what that need is?

There is a sense in which James was not a philosopher at all. He once said to me: 'What a curse philosophy would be if we couldn't forget all about it!' In other words, philosophy was not to him what it has been to so many, a consolation and sanctuary in a life which would have been unsatisfying without it. It would be incongruous, therefore, to expect of him that he should build a philosophy like an edifice to go and live in for good. Philosophy to him was rather like a maze in which he happened to find himself wandering, and what he was looking for was the way out. In the presence of theories of any sort he was attentive, puzzled, suspicious, with a certain inner prompting to disregard them. He lived all his life among them, as a child lives among grown-up people; what a relief to turn from those stolid giants, with their prohibitions and exactions and tiresome talk, to another real child or a nice animal! Of course grown-up people are useful, and so James considered that theories might be; but in themselves, to live with, they were rather in the way, and at bottom our natural enemies. It was well to challenge one or another of them when you got a chance; perhaps that challenge might break some spell, transform the strange landscape, and simplify life. A theory while you were creating or using it was like a story you were telling yourself or a game you were playing; it was a warm, self-justifying thing then; but when the glow of creation or expectation was over, a theory was a phantom, like a ghost, or like the minds of other people. To all other people, even to ghosts, William James was the soul of courtesy; and he was civil to most theories as well, as to more or less interesting strangers that invaded him. Nobody ever recognised more heartily the chance that others had of being right, and the right they had to be different. Yet when it came to understanding what they meant, whether they were theories or persons, his intuition outran his patience; he made some brilliant impressionistic sketch in his fancy and called it by their name. This sketch was as often flattered as distorted, and he was at times the dupe of his desire to be appreciative and give the devil his due; he was too impulsive for exact sympathy; too subjective, too romantic, to be just. Love is very penetrating, but it penetrates to possibilities rather than to facts. The logic of opinions, as well as the exact opinions themselves, were not things James saw easily, or traced with pleasure. He liked to take things one by one, rather than to put two and two together. He was a mystic, a mystic in love with life. He was comparable to Rousseau and to Walt Whitman; he expressed a generous and tender sensibility, rebelling against sophistication, and preferring daily sights and sounds, and a vague but indomitable faith in fortune, to any settled intellectual tradition calling itself science or philosophy.

A prophet is not without honour save in his own country; and until the return wave of James's reputation reached America from Europe, his pupils and friends were hardly aware that he was such a distinguished man. Everybody liked him, and delighted in him for his generous, gullible nature and brilliant sallies. He was a sort of Irishman among the Brahmins, and seemed hardly imposing enough for a great man. They laughed at his erratic views and his undisguised limitations. Of course a conscientious professor ought to know everything he professes to know, but then, they thought, a dignified professor ought to seem to know everything. The precise theologians and panoplied idealists, who exist even in America, shook their heads. What sound philosophy, said they to themselves, could be expected from an irresponsible doctor, who was not even a college graduate, a crude empiricist, and vivisector of frogs? On the other hand, the solid men of business were not entirely reassured concerning a teacher of youth who seemed to have no system in particular—the ignorant rather demand that the learned should have a system in store, to be applied at a pinch; and they could not quite swallow a private gentleman who dabbled in hypnotism, frequented mediums, didn't talk like a book, and didn't write like a book, except like one of his own. Even his pupils, attached as they invariably were to his person, felt some doubts about the profundity of one who was so very natural, and who after some interruption during a lecture—and he said life was a series of interruptions—would slap his forehead and ask the man in the front row 'What *was* I talking about?' Perhaps in the first years of his teaching he felt a little in the professor's chair as a military man might feel when obliged to read the prayers at a funeral. He probably conceived what he said more deeply than a more scholastic mind might have conceived it; yet he would have been more comfortable if some one else had said it for him. He liked to open the window, and look out for a moment. I think he was glad when the bell rang, and he could be himself again until the next day. But in the midst of this routine of the class-room the spirit would sometimes come upon him, and, leaning his head on his hand, he would let fall golden words, picturesque, fresh from the heart, full of the knowledge of good and evil. Incidentally there would crop up some humourous characterisation, some candid confession of doubt or of instinctive preference, some pungent scrap of learning; radicalisms plunging sometimes into the sub-soil of all human philosophies; and, on occasion, thoughts of simple wisdom and wistful piety, the most unfeigned and manly that anybody ever had.

HUGO MÜNSTERBERG

(1863–1916)

By the time James met Hugo Münsterberg at the First International Congress of Physiological Psychology held in Paris in 1889, James had read the younger man's *Die Willenshandlung* and called it 'much the most original and vigorous thing on the will with which I am acquainted.'[1] He wrote to his brother Henry later that Münsterberg was 'the ablest experimental psychologist in Germany . . . he is in fact the Rudyard Kipling of psychology.'[2] Münsterberg, trained as a physician, was inspired by a summer class taught by Wilhelm Wundt to enter the new field of experimental psychology. At the time that he and James met, he was teaching at the University of Leipzig.

James was most impressed by Münsterberg's 'indefatigable love of experimental labor' and his talents as a teacher. These strengths—and the fact that a German psychologist would be an asset to Harvard's psychology department—led him to recommend Münsterberg to direct Harvard's psychological laboratory beginning in the fall of 1892 (for a trial period of three years), lifting from James a responsibility that he did not want. For his part, Münsterberg, hoping for an appointment at a prestigious German university, saw Harvard both as an exciting professional opportunity and as a bargaining chip to use in advancing his career at home. Although he felt some doubts about his ability to learn English well enough to teach in America, Münsterberg accepted Harvard's offer.

During the 1892–93 academic year, James was on sabbatical and getting news of the department from his colleagues. 'Münsterberg is an immense success,' Royce wrote. 'His English is charming. The students love it as a mother her babe's first prattle. He fears them not, and they revere his wisdom the more, the more his speech seems shattered.'[3] In fact, Münsterberg's command of English improved so rapidly that he began to publish in his adopted tongue, with articles in the *Psychological Review* and many popular magazines. He forged strong friendships with his new colleagues, took great pleasure in his work as director of the laboratory, and, as James noticed, remained 'very enthusiastic about America.'[4] Münsterberg returned to Germany in 1895, and was then invited to return to Harvard as Professor of Experimental Psychology. For two years he vacillated; finally, in 1897, he agreed to return to Harvard permanently. His colleagues, including James, were delighted.

But beginning in 1898, Münsterberg's relationship with James appears to have changed. In the spring of 1899, James complained to his friend Théodore Flournoy that Münsterberg was 'becoming more of a metaphysician and less of an experimentalist—not altogether, as it seems to me to his benefit or to that of the higher philosophy. I don't know whether you have seen his recent volume of essays called "Psychology and Life." They do not impress me very favorably.'[5]

James was offended by Münsterberg's scorn of his interest in psychical research. According to Münsterberg, James wrote to F. C. S. Schiller, 'Real life excludes psychical research, because it offers phenomena in time and the real life is timeless. Science excludes them because they are mystical. So there is no place for them in God's great universe at all. Happy M. to be the owner of so convenient a philosophy!'[6]

James's criticism of Münsterberg was mitigated somewhat by Münsterberg's dedication of his *Grundzüge der Psychologie* to James in 1900. Although James admitted to being 'deeply flattered' by Münsterberg's homage to him, he warned Münsterberg that he was likely to find in James 'one of [the book's] worst enemies'[7] because of his objection to Münsterberg's superficial schematization of human behavior.

Besides his derision of his colleague's work, James objected to Münsterberg's attempts at dominating the profession. At the dedication of Harvard's Emerson Hall, the new home of the Philosophy Department, James was so irritated at the number of speeches that Münsterberg delivered that he complained to President Eliot. When Münsterberg discovered the complaint, he promptly resigned—forcing James to apologize, at least partially: 'I much regret to have wounded Münsterberg's feelings,' he wrote to Eliot, 'but it did seem to me well that he should get a reflection of what is being said of our department. His zeal and good intent are admirable, but in public utterances he does not strike the right quiet note.'[8]

The relatively few references to James in Margaret Münsterberg's biography of her father suggest that their relationship had deteriorated to estrangement by the time James died.

NOTES

1. WJ, *Principles of Psychology,* vol.3 (Cambridge: Harvard University Press, 1981), 1556n.

2. WJ to Henry James. *Correspondence* 2:217 (11 April 1892).

3. Josiah Royce to WJ. *The Letters of Josiah Royce,* ed. John Clendenning (Chicago: University of Chicago Press, 1970), 299 (17 October 1892).

4. WJ to Théodore Flournoy. *The Letters of William James and Théodore Flournoy,* ed. Robert Le Clair (Madison: University of Wisconsin, 1966), 31 (21 December 1893).

5. WJ to Théodore Flournoy. *The Letters of William James and Théodore Flournoy,* 78 (30 May 1899).

6. WJ to F. C. S. Schiller. Scott, 186–87 (19 May 1899).

7. WJ to Hugo Münsterberg. Perry, 148 (18 June 1900).

8. WJ to Charles Eliot. Scott, 389–90 (28 December 1905).

Professor James as a Psychologist

Every mid-year when I begin my large introductory course in psychology, I stand before a particular difficulty. A fair course ought to bring a fine combination of dryness and enthusiasm, of tiresomeness and brilliancy, and it seems natural that the text-book should furnish that necessary dullness, while the lectures brighten it up by giving a vivid comment. But in my course the text-book is the 'Psychology' of William James. That sparkles and scintillates, is brilliant and fascinating on every page, and if the lecturer still wants to secure the right mixture for the course, he has no other choice than to provide for his part all the necessary dryness and tiresomeness. William James himself, of course, would never be able to play the dull lecturer, as whatever he says is picturesque and striking; and therefore it was that as soon as he had published his book, he ceased lecturing in psychology and left it to others to supply the dullness. Yet his successors have at least the one sincere pleasure of seeing a student class peruse a text-book with the eagerness with which they might enjoy the latest novel.

Our Harvard class-room, however, shows only the same pleasure and satisfaction which a hundred psychological classes present all over the country, and all these regular students only lead the way in which hundred thousands [of] men and women, from all walks of life, have followed. They all felt it as an inspiration that such an abstract science could speak with the vivid temperament of the reformer, with the intimate warmth of a friend, with the charm of a perfect artist.

Yet the unique style which has made William James the most popular psychologist, is only the fit and natural form for the prevailing method of his work. He studies the psychological facts first of all through a most intense self-observation, and the vividness and freshness with which he brings to life the most manifold inner experiences, is the deepest cause of his wonderful success. Through them he disentangles the most complex states of mind and is able to describe the subtlest tints and shades of consciousness, the most fugitive moods and fancies. Of course such delightful intimacy and warmth may sometimes antagonize the bloodless abstract theories towards which each science after all must tend; and this freshness of the changing experiences may make it sometimes difficult to overcome the capriciouness of life by stiff consistent principles. The psychology of James is thus more descriptive than explanatory, rather emphasizes the rich varieties of the inner world than reduces them to simple formulae. And yet how often, after all, does he illuminate a whole large field—for instance, that of emotion—by one far-flashing, lightning stroke of genius.

But no genius even can be of real service to the progress of a science if he does not master the full details of its technical scholarship. Modern psychology is an experimental science with deep roots in physics and physiology. James would never have reached his controlled influence in our psychological thought if he had not been also pioneer and leader in all the painstaking labor of the physiological laboratory and of the psychophysical workshop. As early as 1877 he started experimental research in the Lawrence Scientific School, stimulating psychological interest in most various directions, and this work grew till he opened, in 1890, the large psychological laboratory in Dane Hall, where it remained till Emerson Hall was built last year. The complete fusion of these thorough scientific studies with brilliant self-observation, made his 'Principles of Psychology' invincible.

Some years ago he left the psychological field to turn towards philosophy. But now he has solemnly declared that he has given his last philosophical lecture course. That must mean, of course, that he wants to return to his first love, and that he will give in the future again only psychological lectures. William James is too good a psychologist not to see that we, his admirers, could never be satisfied with any other interpretation of his plans.

EDMUND BURKE DELABARRE

(1863–1945)

In 1896, when James wrote to Charles Eliot recommending a replacement for Hugo Münsterberg as director of Harvard's psychology laboratory for the next academic year, he could think of no better candidate than Edmund Burke Delabarre, who at the time was teaching psychology at Brown University. 'He is the best man for the purpose any of us can think of,' James told Eliot, '—very solid, already with a good reputation, and a pupil both of Münsterberg and myself.'[1] Delabarre's year at Harvard was a success, but not so outstanding that he was considered for a permanent position. Early in 1897, when James was asked to suggest possible new members for the department, he conceded that 'Delabarre seems to be the one with fewest *minuses,* though I fear he will be inferior in point of productive energy to some of the others.'[2] Delabarre returned to Brown, where he taught until his retirement in 1932.

James's assessment of Delabarre's career proved correct. Although Delabarre was a fine teacher and tireless experimenter, he had little interest in publishing the results of his work. As a colleague recalled, 'He once said to me with the modest and friendly smile that so characterized him that, after he had found the answer to a question, he sometimes found it unprofitable to write out the results of his investigations for the journals.'[3] Because he so rarely published, he exerted only minor influence in the field of psychology. James believed his work on visual sensation so important, however, that he incorporated Delabarre's findings directly into his *Principles of Psychology.*[4]

Delabarre, a native of Maine, was educated at Brown University and Amherst College (B.A. 1886). He attended the University of Berlin for one year (1887–88) and Harvard for two (1888–90). During this latter period, while James was at work on his *Principles,* he often would read chapters to his students and ask for their responses. Such discussions continued outside the classroom when, like many other graduate students, Delabarre was invited to dinner at James's home. Because Delabarre was interested in experimental psychology, James suggested that he continue graduate work in Germany, and especially recommended that he study with Münsterberg at the University of Freiburg; Delabarre earned a doctorate there in 1891.

Much of Delabarre's early work focused on optics, and his experiments attracted interest as much for their use of innovative apparatus as for their results. To measure muscular eye movements, for example, Delabarre designed a special plaster of Paris cup that fit over an anesthetized eye. The cup contained a small metal loop attached to a thread that, in turn, was attached to a stylus that traced impressions on long tapes of paper. This device enabled him to record minute movements for many hours. Two of his early articles, 'On the Seat of Optical After Images' and 'Colored Shadows,' reflect this area of inquiry.[5] Delabarre also conducted experiments on muscular sensation and used himself as a subject to test the sensory and emotional effects of *cannibis indica.*

In addition to his interest in experimental psychology, Delabarre was an enthusiastic naturalist. He was the recorder for a Brown-Harvard expedition to Labrador in 1900 and published studies of historical inscriptions on rocks in Narragansett Bay. His *Dighton Rock; a study of the written rocks of New England* (1928) proved to be a significant work both of analysis and historiography.

NOTES

1. WJ to Charles Eliot. Scott, 142 (22 February 1896).

2. WJ to Charles Eliot. Scott, 151–52 (21 February 1897).

3. Leonard Carmichael, 'Edmund Burke Delabarre,' *American Journal of Psychology* 43, no.3 (July 1945): 407.

4. WJ, *Principles of Psychology* 2: 662–74.

5. Both articles appeared in the *American Journal of Psychology,* vol.2. 'On the Seat of Optical After-Images,' February 1889, 326–28; 'Colored Shadows,' August 1889, 636–43.

A Student's Impressions of James in the Late '80s

It is hardly possible to say briefly anything newly significant about Professor James; but let me record some of the impressions he made on me while I was under his instruction, as I recall them now after the lapse of more than fifty years.

During the academic years 1888–90, I was a graduate student at Harvard, taking courses under James and Royce. According to Perry's account of his *Thought and character*, James was then in one of his periods of better health, feeling 'uncommonly hearty,' and writing of the year's work that lay before him that 'I expect to enjoy it hugely.' It was therefore a propitious time for study with him. He had nearly finished his *Principles*, and read many of its chapters to his class of graduate students during its sessions at his home. As young students, we were too inexperienced and had too little background to judge of his originality of thought, or of many others of his many-sided traits. But we were deeply impressed with his thorough mastery of his subject, his profound knowledge of all that had been written on all of its many phases, his judgment in arriving at such conclusions as were warranted by the evidence at hand. Yet he clearly realized that requisite evidence is rarely fully assembled and he was perfectly and admirably frank in admitting his many uncertainties and doubts. It was stimulating to realize his innate modesty and open-mindedness, and to feel that he was inciting us to think out his problems with him. We appreciated fully his remarkable genius for felicitous, clear and picturesque expression; although occasionally this led to complete misunderstanding of his meaning,—as when he said, in expounding his famous theory of emotions, that 'we are sorry because we cry, afraid because we run,' not the other way around. Evidently, we can be sorry without crying, afraid without running. The illustration was striking yet unfortunate, but it does not alter the fact that *some* bodily reaction precedes and is the sensory source of the emotion that we feel, which is the essence of his well justified theory.

No one could escape feeling the deep charm of James' personality, his empathic interest in everyone about him, his constant friendliness. The times when we were invited individually to meals at his home were occasions of happy sociability and of the joyous give-and-take of congenial conversation.

During those years James conducted no formal laboratory class. He was essentially an experimentalist at heart, in the sense that he sought factual knowledge and aimed to base his beliefs upon observational experience, although in a vastly broader field than the confines of a laboratory. He had a personal disinclination for laboratory work, and was distrustful of 'certain crudities of reasoning which are extremely common in men of the laboratory pure and simple.' Yet he felt strongly the importance and necessity of developing psychological knowledge by experimentation of the laboratory type as well as by accurate observation of wider personal experience. These are the reasons why, some two years later, he secured the appointment of Münsterberg to a chair of experimental psychology at Harvard. In spite of all this, he did not altogether neglect laboratory procedure himself. To me, at least, he assigned several tasks of research, such as dissection of sheep's brains, some problems in vision, and a study of the effect of noise upon mental and bodily activities. At the end of my two years at Harvard, he recommended to me and some other graduate students that we go to Freiburg to continue our studies under Münsterberg, with whose published experimental investigations and announcement of a programme for further research he had been much impressed.

Of other current incidents I can mention but a few. It was at that time that Wiedersheim's denial of the inheritance of acquired characters was first announced. As I recall it, his first impression of the new view was that, if commonly accepted, it would remove certain deterrents to immoral conduct, as when an inebriate parent need no longer fear that he may pass on a taint to his offspring. Browning's ill-bred old-age outburst against critics of his wife led James to remark that he had utterly lost all respect for the poet that he had ever felt.

Certain criticisms of the atmosphere of Harvard were then current, and James, somewhat disturbed by them, induced me to form a committee of graduate students who had come from other colleges, to compare, by means of a questionnaire, conditions at Harvard with those at their other colleges, with the result that a pamphlet was published by the Committee, almost wholly favorable to 'The Tone and Tendencies of Harvard University.'

James' interest in psychical research was evident. The medium, Mrs. Piper, was then flourishing in Boston. I had one or two sittings with her, puzzling as to how she could possibly have been able to mention so many facts concerning my private life, but otherwise not remarkable except that she ventured some prophecies which never were fulfilled. James, I think, regarded her as honest and worthy of study, although he was never fully convinced that her performances, or those of any other person, gave complete assurance of the existence of genuinely supernormal powers.

Professor Royce, soon after James' death, classed him, together with Jonathan Edwards and Ralph Waldo Emerson, as one of the three representative American Philosophers. These three men most typically had made novel and notable contributions to general philosophy, and each had uttered 'philosophical ideas characteristic of some stage and aspect of the spiritual life of his people.' The extraordinary number of fields in which James made such novel and notable contributions and his enduring potent influence in all of them, surely justify such an estimate of him as a philosopher and psychologist.

HENRY JAMES III

(1879–1947)

'My domestic catastrophe is now a week old,' James wrote to his brother Robertson on 26 May 1879. 'Babe and Mar both doing very well indeed. The former has a rich orange complexion, a black head of hair, weighs 8½ lbs keeps his eyes tight shut on the wicked world and is of a musical, but not too musical disposition. . . . I find I have a strong affection for the little animal—and tho' I say it who should not, he has a very lovely and benignant little expression on his face.'[1]

With the birth of 'little Embry,' James became a father at the age of thirty-seven. Carrying the name of his grandfather and uncle, Henry James III (known as Harry to the family) grew to favor his uncle in disposition. If he had been 'musical' as an infant, he quieted as he grew older. He did not have his father's aggressive high spirits; and, after James's second son, William, was born, it seemed to James that little Harry's needs might not be met because he was so undemanding. 'About Harry especially do I feel responsible,' he wrote to his wife, when Harry was five, 'Willyam somehow seems to me more likely to take care of himself.'[2] James need not have worried: Harry seemed to blossom once he started school. He was 'a model of schoolboy vigor,' James wrote to his cousin Katharine Prince, and at the age of eight already was reading *Pilgrim's Progress,* the *Iliad,* and the *Odyssey.*[3]

Steady, reliable, and serious, Harry was a cherished companion of his uncle on many visits during Henry James's last years. After William James's death, Alice James seemed to look upon her eldest son as head of the family. Harry excelled in his undergraduate studies at Harvard and went on to become a lawyer. Although he was a partner in one of Boston's most prestigious firms, he practiced only a few years before turning to other interests: administration (as manager of the Rockefeller Institute, member of the Board of Overseers of Harvard, and trustee of the American Academy in Rome, among many positions) and writing. Besides collecting some of his father's essays and a two-volume edition of his letters, he wrote biographies of Richard Olney, Secretary of State under Grover Cleveland, and of Charles William Eliot.

Harry was married twice: to Olivia Cutting, a New York heiress, and, eight years after his divorce from her, to Dorothea Draper. He had no children.

NOTES

1. WJ to Robertson James. ALS: Private. Will appear in *Correspondence,* vol.5.
2. WJ to Alice James. Quoted in Myers, *William James,* 40 (24 December 1882).
3. WJ to Katharine Prince. Scott, 43 (3 Feb 1887).

A Firm, Light Step

Almost anyone who was at Harvard in the nineties can recall him as he went back and forth in Kirkland Street between the College and his Irving Street house, and can in memory see again that erect figure walking with a step that was somehow firm and light without being particularly rapid, two or three thick volumes and a note-book under one arm, and on his face a look of abstraction that used suddenly to give way to an expression of delighted and friendly curiosity. Sometimes it was an acquaintance who caught his eye and received a cordial word; sometimes it was an occurrence in the street that arrested him; sometimes the terrier dog, who had been roving along unwatched and forgotten, embroiled himself in an adventure or a fight and brought James out of his thoughts. One day he would have worn the Norfolk jacket that he usually worked in at home to his lecture-room; the next, he would have forgotten to change the black coat that he had put on for a formal occasion. At twenty minutes before nine in the morning he could usually be seen going to the College Chapel for the fifteen-minute service with which the College day began. If he was returning home for lunch, he was likely to be hurrying; for he had probably let himself be detained after a lecture to discuss some question with a few of his class. He was apt then to have some student with him whom he was bringing home to lunch and to finish the discussion at the family table, or merely for the purpose of establishing more personal relations than were possible in the class-room. At the end of the afternoon, or in the early evening, he would frequently be bicycling or walking again. He would then have been working until his head was tired, and would have laid his spectacles down on his desk and have started out again to get a breath of air and perhaps to drop in on a Cambridge neighbor.

In his own house it seemed as if he was always at work; all the more, perhaps, because it was obvious that he possessed no instinct for arranging his day and protecting himself from interruptions. He managed reasonably well to keep his mornings clear; or rather he allowed his wife to stand guard over them with fair success. But soon after he had taken an essential after-lunch nap, he was pretty sure to be 'caught' by callers and visitors. From six o'clock on, he usually had one or two of the children sitting, more or less subdued, in the library, while he himself read or dashed off letters, or (if his eyes were tired) dictated them to Mrs. James. He always had letters and post-cards to write. At any odd time—with his overcoat on and during a last moment before hurrying off to an appointment or a train—he would sit down at his desk and do one more note or card—always in the beautiful and flowing hand that hardly changed between his eighteenth and his sixty-eighth years. He seemed to feel no need of solitude except when he was reading technical literature or writing philosophy. If other members of the household were talking and laughing in the room that adjoined his study, he used to keep the door open and occasionally pop in for a word, or to talk for a quarter of an hour. It was with the greatest difficulty that Mrs. James finally persuaded him to let the door be closed up. He never struck an equilibrium between wishing to see his students and neighbors freely and often, and wishing not to be interrupted by even the most agreeable reminder of the existence of anyone or anything outside the matter in which he was absorbed.

It was customary for each member of the Harvard Faculty to announce in the college catalogue at what hour of the day he could be consulted by students. Year after year James assigned the hour of his evening meal for such calls. Sometimes he left the table to deal with the caller in private; sometimes a student, who had pretty certainly eaten already and was visibly abashed at finding himself walking in on a second dinner, would be brought into the dining-room and made to talk about other things than his business.

He allowed his conscience to be constantly burdened with a sense of obligation to all sorts of people. The list of neighbors, students, strangers visiting Cambridge, to whom he and Mrs. James felt responsible for civilities, was never closed, and the cordiality which animated his intentions kept him reminded of every one on it.

And yet, whenever his wife wisely prepared for a suitable time and made engagements for some sort of hospitality otherwise than by hap-hazard, it was perversely likely to be the case, when the appointed hour arrived, that James was 'going on his nerves' and in no mood for 'being entertaining.' The most comradely of men, nothing galled him like *having to be* sociable.

The 'hollow mockery of our social conventions' would then be described in furious and lurid speech. Luckily the guests were not yet there to hear him. But they did not always get away without catching a glimpse of his state of mind. On one such occasion,—an evening reception for his graduate class had been arranged,—Mrs. James encountered a young man in the hall whose expression was so perturbed that she asked him what had happened to him. 'I've come in again,' he replied, 'to get my hat. I was trying to find my way to the dining-room when Mr. James swooped at me and said, "Here, Smith, you want to get out of this *Hell,* don't you? I'll show you how. There!" And before I could answer, he'd popped me out through a back-door. But, really, I do not want to go!'

The dinners of a club to which allusions will occur in this volume, (in letters to Henry L. Higginson, T. S. Perry, and John C. Gray) were occasions apart from all others; for James could go to them at the last moment, without any sense of responsibility and knowing that he would find congenial company and old friends. So he continued to go to these dinners, even after he had stopped accepting all invitations to dine. The Club (for it never had any name) had been started in 1870. James had been one of the original group who agreed to dine together once a month during the winter. Among the other early members had been his brother Henry, W. D. Howells, O. W. Holmes, Jr., John Fiske, John C. Gray, Henry Adams, T. S. Perry, John C. Ropes, A. G. Sedgwick, and F. Parkman. The more faithful diners, who constituted the nucleus of the Club during the later years, included Henry L. Higginson, Sturgis Bigelow, John C. Ropes, John T. Morse, Charles Grinnell, James Ford Rhodes, Moorfield Storey, James W. Crafts, and H. P. Walcott.

Every little while James's sleep would 'go to pieces,' and he would go off to Newport, the Adirondacks, or elsewhere, for a few days. This happened both summer and winter. It was not the effect of the place or climate in which he was living, but simply that his dangerously high average of nervous tension had been momentarily raised to the snapping point. Writing was almost certain to bring on this result. When he had an essay or a lecture to prepare, he could not do it by bits. In order to begin such a task, he tried to seize upon a free day—more often a Sunday than any other. Then he would shut himself into his library, or disappear into a room at the top of the house, and remain hidden all day. If things went well, twenty or thirty sheets of much-corrected manuscript (about twenty-five hundred words in his free hand) might result from such a day. As many more would have gone into the waste-basket. Two or three successive days of such writing 'took it out of him' visibly.

Short holidays, or intervals in college lecturing, were often employed for writing in this way, the longer vacations of the latter nineties being filled, as has been said, with traveling and lecture engagements. In the intervals there would be a few days, or sometimes two or three whole weeks, at Chocorua. Or, one evening, all the windows of the deserted Irving Street house would suddenly be wide open to the night air, and passers on the sidewalk could see James sitting in his shirt-sleeves within the circle of the bright light that stood on his library table. He was writing letters, making notes, and skirmishing through the piles of journals and pamphlets that had accumulated during an absence.

DICKINSON SARGEANT MILLER

(1868–1963)

In this memoir Dickinson Miller recalls James as a teacher.[1] But their relationship was more complex than that of mentor and student, and endured longer than the two years that Miller attended Harvard to earn a master's degree (1890–92). A graduate of the University of Pennsylvania (1889), Miller also had studied for a year with G. Stanley Hall at Clark University before attending Harvard, and subsequently earned a Ph.D. at the University of Halle (1893).

Referring to Miller as his 'disciple,' James recommended him for a position at Bryn Mawr, where Miller taught from 1893 to 1898. 'I am glad you like Miller who is certainly great, and ever growing greater,' James wrote to Martha Carey Thomas, president of Bryn Mawr. 'A *satisfactory* creature to have dealings with!'[2] But Miller's professional success was undermined by his health: according to his biographer, Miller 'suffered from what he called "crippling neurasthenia" ' throughout his life.[3]

This emotional instability did not diminish James's esteem of the man he regarded as his 'most penetrating critic and intimate enemy.'[4] James recommended Miller as his sabbatical replacement at Harvard in 1899, and even left his eldest son, Henry, in Miller's care while he was gone. James was effusive in his praise: 'Miller's intellect and character are both of distinguished quality, and Palmer writes that his teaching is a success,' he wrote to Charles Eliot in support of offering Miller a position at Harvard.[5] And to his young colleague Ralph Barton Perry, James wrote: 'Miller is a perfect hero for magnanimity of disposition, that you ought to be bosom friends, and I hate to think of your being rivals, for there probably would not be room for both of you so soon.'[6]

In this prediction James proved correct. In the spring of 1904, needing to cut the budget of the Philosophy Department, Eliot decided not to renew Miller's contract. Although James protested, ultimately he failed in his efforts to retain his friend on the faculty. Fortunately Miller found a position immediately at Columbia University, where he taught until 1919. Journalist Max Eastman, one of his assistants there, remembered Miller as

> an odd-looking philosopher, with rather babylike features, a fine forehead, and the manners, diction, habits, and haircut of an Episcopal prelate. His health was poor, and the doctor had prescribed fresh air and mild exercise. He had decided to take these strange medicines in a canoe on the Hudson River, and to make them palatable, he conceived the idea of having me in the business end of the canoe and mixing them with intellectual conversation. . . . Miller, impeccably clad for the sport, would climb into the boat with exquisite care and sit down facing me, bolt upright, balancing himself dexterously, yet as out of his element as a pope on a roller coaster.[7]

Despite Miller's personal eccentricities, James took his criticisms seriously. For several years James kept a notebook in which he responded to Miller's objections to the *Principles of Psychology*. He tried valiantly to argue against Miller's understanding of 'The Will to Believe.'[8] As Miller saw it, James ignored the underlying motive for willing to believe: 'a desire for a certain state of things. . . . The desire, is not directed toward believing, but toward the reality of the thing or the things in question.' Miller was disturbed by James's assertion that one could both decide to believe and, at the same time, recognize that this belief could be merely a hypothesis.[9]

In defense of his position, James asserted that 'when an hypothesis *is* once a live one, one *risks* something in one's practical relations towards truth and error, *whichever* of the three positions (affirmation, doubt, or negation) one may take up towards it.' But, James surmised, it was likely that for Miller the hypothesis was *not* lively, but 'so dead, that the risk of error in espousing it now far outweighs for you the chance of truth, so you simply stake your money on the field as against it.'[10] While James thought no evidence supported the idea of a God, Miller passionately disagreed: 'I do not accept the view that theism . . . is a subject in which one has no evidence and can get none.'[11]

Indeed, Miller suffered none of James's doubts about religious belief. In 1908 he was ordained as a deacon of the Episcopal Church; in 1911 he became a 'special preacher' at the Episcopal Cathedral in Morningside Heights, New York City. And in 1935 he was ordained a priest and served as rector of St. George's Church in Maynard, Massachusetts.

NOTES

1. The memoir, written as a letter to Henry James III in 1917, was published, with a few omissions, in *Letters* 2:11–17.

2. WJ to Martha Carey Thomas. Scott, 125 (12 February 1895).

3. Loyd D. Easton, introduction to Dickinson Miller, *Philosophical Analysis and Human Welfare* (Dordrecht, Holland: D. Reidel, 1975), 3.

4. WJ to Dickinson Miller. *Letters* 2:48 (30 August 1896).

5. WJ to Charles Eliot. Scott, 208 (20 December 1899).

6. WJ to Ralph Barton Perry. Scott, 229 (16 May 1900).

7. Max Eastman, *Enjoyment of Living* (New York: Harpers, 1948), 269–70.

8. 'The Will to Believe and the Duty to Doubt,' *International Journal of Ethics* 9 (1898–90): 169–95; review of *Religion in the Philosophy of William James* by Julius Seelye Bixler (Boston: Marshall Jones, 1926) in *Journal of Philosophy*, April 1927, 203–10.

9. Review of *Religion in the Philosophy of William James*, 208–9.

10. WJ to Dickinson Miller. *Letters* 2:49 (30 August 1896).

11. Dickinson Miller to C. J. Ducasse, n.d., published in Peter H. Hare and Edward H. Madden, 'William James, Dickinson Miller and C. J. Ducasse on the Ethics of Belief,' *Transactions of the Charles S. Peirce Society* 4, no.3 (1968), 123.

A Memory of William James

I have a vivid recollection of your father's lecture, class conferences, seminars, laboratory interests, and the side that students saw of him generally. He was in a marked degree unpretending, unconventional, human and direct. The one thing apparently impossible to him was to speak in an *ex cathedra* tone from heights of scientific erudition and attainment. There were not a few 'if's' and 'maybe's' in his remarks. Moreover he seldom followed for long an orderly system of argument or unfolding of a theory but was always apt to puncture such systematic pretensions when in the midst of them with some entirely unaffected doubt or question that put the matter upon a basis of common sense at once. He had drawn from his laboratory experience in chemistry and his study of medicine a keen sense that the imposing formulas of science that impress laymen are not so 'exact' as they sound. He was not given in my time at least to regular lectures. I can well remember the first meeting of the course in psychology in a ground-floor room of the old Lawrence Scientific School. He took a considerable part of the hour by reading extracts from Henry Sidgwick's Lecture against Lecturing, proceeding to explain that we should use as a textbook his own Principles of Psychology, appearing for the first time that very week from the press, and should spend the hours in conference, in which we should discuss and ask questions, on both sides. So during the year's course we read the two volumes through with some amount of running commentary and controversy. There were four or five men of previous psychological training in a class of (I think) between twenty and thirty, two of whom were disposed to take up the cudgels for the British associational psychology and were particularly troubled by the repeated doctrine of the Principles that a state of consciousness had no parts or elements but was one indivisible fact. He bore questions which really were criticisms with inexhaustible patience and what I may call (the subject invites the word often) *human* attention; invited written questions as well and would often return them with a reply pencilled on the back when he thought the discussion of too special an interest to be pursued before the class. Moreover he bore with students with never a sign of impatience if we lingered after class and even walked up Kirkland Street with him on his way home. Yet he was really not argumentative, not inclined to dialectic or pertinacious debate of any sort. It must always have required an effort of self-control to put up with it. He almost never even in private conversation contended for his own opinion. He had a way of often falling back on the language of perception, insight, sensibility, vision of possibilities. I recall how on one occasion after class as I parted with him at the gate of the Memorial Hall triangle his last words were something like these: 'Well, Miller, that theory is not a warm reality to me yet—still a cold conception,' and the charm of the comradely smile with which he said it. The disinclination to formal logical system and the more prolonged purely intellectual analyses was felt by some men as a lack in his classroom work though they were invariably charmed by him personally and recognised that these analyses were present in the 'Psychology.' On the other hand the very tendency to feel ideas lent a kind of emotional or aesthetic colour which greatly deepened the interest.

In the course of the year he asked the men each to write some word of suggestion, if he were so inclined, for improvement in the method with which the course was conducted and if I remember rightly there were not a few respectful suggestions that too much time was allowed to the few wrangling disputants. In a pretty full and varied experience of lecture-rooms at home and abroad I cannot recall another where the class was asked to criticize the methods of the lecturer.

Another class of twelve or fourteen in the same year on Descartes, Spinoza and Leibnitz met in one of the 'tower rooms' of Sever Hall, sitting round a table. Here we had to do mostly with pure metaphysics. And more striking still was the prominence of humanity and sensibility in his way of taking philosophic problems. I can see him now sitting at the head of that heavy table of light-coloured wood near the bow-window that formed the end of the room. My brother, a visitor at Cambridge, dropping in for an hour and seeing him with his vigorous air, bronzed and sanguine complexion, and his brown tweeds said, 'He looks more like a sportsman than a professor.' I think that the sporting men in college always felt a certain affinity to themselves on one side in the freshness and manhood that distinguished him in mind, appearance and diction. It was in this latter course that I first heard some of the phrases now identified with him. There was a great deal about the monistic and pluralistic views of the universe. The world of the monist was described as a 'block-universe' and the monist himself as 'wallowing in a sense of unbridled unity' or something of the sort. He always wanted the men to write one or two 'theses' in the course of the year and to get to work early on them. Another point of which he made a great deal was bibliography. He would say, 'I am no man for editions and references, no exact bibliographer.' But none the less he would put upon the blackboard full lists of books, English, French, German and Italian, on our subject. His own reading was immense and systematic. No one has ever done justice to it, partly because he spoke with unaffected modesty of that side of his equipment.

Of course this knowledge came to the foreground in his 'seminar.' In my second year I was with him in one of his graduate classes for both terms, the first half year studying the psychology of pleasure and pain, and the second mental pathology. Here each of us of course undertook a special topic, our readings of course suggested by him. The students were an interesting group, including Professor Santayana, then an instructor, Dr. Herbert Nichols, a remarkably gifted and original man, of boundless energy, Messrs. Mezes now President of the City College, New York, Pierce, Professor at Smith College, Angell, President of the Carnegie Foundation, Bakewell, Professor at Yale, Alfred Hodder, who became instructor at Bryn Mawr College, then abandoned academic life for literature and politics and became private secretary for Mr. Jerome, then district attorney for New York City. The last was later author of a brilliant book, 'The Adversaries of the Skeptic' and a novel 'The New Americans'—dying before he came to the maturity of his powers.

To some readers and hearers Professor James appeared at times an impulsive and hasty thinker but especially in this seminar I was deeply impressed by his judicious and often judicial quality. His range of intellectual experience, his profound cultivation in literature, in science and in art (has there been in our generation a more cultivated man?), his absolutely unfettered and untrammelled mind, ready to do sympathetic justice to the most unaccredited, audacious, or despised hypotheses, yet always keeping his own sense of proportion and the balance of evidence—merely to know these qualities, as we sat about that council-board, was to receive, so far as we were capable of absorbing it,—in a heightened sense of the good old adjective—'a liberal education.' Of all the services he did us in this seminar perhaps the greatest was his running commentary on the reports respecting such authors as [Cesare] Lombroso and [Max] Nordau and all theories of degeneracy and morbid human types. His thought was that there is no sharp line to be drawn between 'healthy' and 'unhealthy' minds, that all have something of both. Once when we were returning from visits to two insane asylums at one of which we had seen a dangerous, almost naked maniac, I remember his saying, 'President Eliot would not like to admit that no sharp line could be drawn between himself and the men we have just seen, but it is true.'[1] He would emphasize that people who had great nervous burdens to carry, hereditary perhaps, could order their lives fruitfully and perhaps even derive some advantages from the 'degenerate' sensitiveness, whatever it might be. The doctrine is set forth with regard to religion in an early chapter of his 'Varieties of Religious Experience' but for us it was applied to life at large.

It will be seen that his most striking trait was tolerance and appreciation in regard to doctrines, men and things. I believe this profoundly and perhaps in a measure unconsciously affected the whole 'department of philosophy' at Harvard. There was for this special subject a most varied faculty, James, Charles Carroll Everett in the Divinity School, Palmer, Royce, Santayana, and later Münsterberg. Some of their philosophies were as widely as possible opposed and each was set forth with the freest affirmation in spite of the presence of the others on the premises. And yet the temper of that little wing of the university was large, humourous, and indulgent, in that sense at least truly philosophical. I remember the remark of a visitor from Oxford on the singular tolerance of the place. It is not always recognized that Professor James in some considerable measure created the department. With the exception of Professors Everett and Palmer, his seniors in service, he had a decisive influence on the coming or staying of all the group I have mentioned, notably of Royce and of Münsterberg.[2] The importation of the latter who was then an *ausserordentlicher* professor at one of the smaller German universities and whose '*Beiträger sure experimentellen Psychologie*' had excited his admiration, was his own suggestion and work. It was through friends of his that money was raised for it. It was explicable enough that

1. In Miller's manuscript, the words 'President Eliot' are crossed out and 'a prominent man of the most regulated, sober and successful type' is hand-written in.—*Ed.*

2. In Miller's manuscript, 'notably of Royce and of Münsterberg' is crossed out.—*Ed.*

his tone should have influence throughout the department though I think that tone was natural to the other members of it.

In private conversation he usually had a mastery of words, a voice, a vigor, a freedom, a dignity, and therefore what one might almost call an authority, at least on all ordinary topics. Yet brilliant man as he was, he never quite outgrew a perceptible shyness or diffidence which showed sometimes in a heightened colour in the lecture room. Going to lecture at one of the last courses that he ever gave at Harvard he said to a colleague whom he met on the way, 'I have lectured so and so many years and yet here am I in trepidation on the way to my class.'

Professor Royce's style of exposition was continuous, even, unfailing, composed. Professor James was more conversational, varied, broken, at times struggling for expression—in spite of what has been mentioned as his mastery of words. This was natural, for the one was deeply and comfortably installed in a theory (to be sure, a great theory) and the other was peering out in quest of something greater which he did not distinctly see. The latter's method making more use of intuition, he gave us in the classroom more of his own investigation and discovery. He worked at first hand before us there.

Royce in lecturing sat immovable. James would rise with a peculiar suddenness and make bold and rapid strokes for a diagram on the black-board. I can remember his abstracted air as he wrestled with some idea, standing by his chair with one foot upon it, his elbow on his knee and his hand to his chin. A friend has described a scene at a little class that, in a still earlier year, met in James's own study in his house. In the effort to illustrate something he brought out a blackboard. He stood it on a chair and in various other positions but could not at once write upon it, hold it steady, and keep it in the class's vision. Entirely bent on what he was doing his efforts resulted at last in his standing it on the floor, perhaps against the wall, while he lay down at full length on the floor holding it with one hand, drawing with the other, and continuing the flow of his commentary. I can myself remember how after one of his lectures on Pragmatism in the Horace Mann Auditorium in New York being assailed with questions by people who came up to the edge of the low platform, he ended by sitting on that edge himself, all in his frock-coat as he was, with his feet hanging down, with his usual complete concentration on the subject and the look of human and mellow consideration which distinguished him at such moments, meeting the thoughts of the inquirers, whose attention also was entirely riveted. If this suggests a lack of dignity it is misleading, for dignity absolutely never forsook him, such was the inherent strength of his words and air. In one respect these particular lectures (afterwards published as his book on Pragmatism) stand alone in my recollection. An audience may very well be large the first time, but if there is any change it usually falls away more or less on the subsequent occasions. These lectures were announced for a moderate sized hall, a larger lecture-room. This was so overcrowded before the lecture began, some not being able to gain admittance, that the audience had to be asked to move to the large auditorium I have mentioned. But here day by day the numbers still grew until on the last it presented much the same appearance as the lecture-room at the beginning.

JAMES ROWLAND ANGELL

(1869–1949)

James Angell came to Harvard in 1891 after earning a master's degree at the University of Michigan, where he had studied with John Dewey and used as text James's *Principles of Psychology*. That book, he said, had a profound influence on him. 'The great inrush of provocative observation, the wealth of pertinent facts, the ingenious manipulation of data, the wide knowledge of relevant literature, and above all the irresistibly fascinating literary style swept me off my feet.'[1] Angell served as James's research assistant during his year at Harvard, helping him sort through documents gathered from the American Society for Psychical Research, including personal testimony from people who claimed to have experienced hallucinations. That material, Angell recalled, 'not only gave me a first-hand sense of the character of the evidence underlying belief in these phenomena, but it also put me in contact with one of the most inspiring and spiritually beautiful human beings I have ever known.'[2]

The admiration was reciprocated: Angell, James wrote to Münsterberg, 'is young, but *exceedingly* clear headed and practical, and made a more favorable impression on me last year than any student I have ever had, from the experimental point of view.'[3] After earning a master's degree at Harvard, Angell decided to go to Germany to study with Wilhelm Wundt. Finding no professional openings in Wundt's psychology laboratory, he took classes instead at the universities of Berlin and Halle. He was writing his doctoral thesis when he received two teaching offers from America: one paying $1500 from the University of Minnesota and another for a smaller salary from Harvard. He went to Minnesota—and never completed his work for a doctorate.

At Minnesota he found the laboratory conditions so poor that after one year, when Dewey invited him to join his department at the University of

Chicago and direct the well-endowed psychology laboratory, Angell readily accepted. The University of Chicago became the center of his intellectual life for more than a decade.

Although Angell chafed at being categorized as a 'functionalist,' nevertheless he was glad to distinguish himself from other psychological schools. Functionalist psychology, Angell explained, allowed researchers to move beyond the merely descriptive (or structuralist) experiments that had characterized past research in most college laboratories. Instead of documenting what happened and how it happened, functionalists concerned themselves with cause and context, seeing 'mental activity as part of the larger stream of biological forces which are constantly at work.'[4]

Angell's *Relations of Structural and Functional Psychology to Philosophy* (1903) seemed to James 'clear and illuminating. . . . You have developed a full coat of mature philosophical feathers around your psychological core,' James wrote to Angell, urging him to write a psychology textbook around 'functional lines.'[5] That textbook appeared in 1904, to wide acclaim.

Although Angell's affection for James never diminished, he found himself puzzled by James's *Pragmatism,* particularly James's ideas about truth and reality. Like many of James's critics, Angell believed that there was something essential about an event or a phenomenon 'with which no interpretation of ours can do away,' as he explained it.[6] 'Truth is, if you please, made. But what you *can* make and still have it true, is subject to limitations set by something which we may loosely call "events." It is this fact that I feel you slur. We are in other words not wholly foot-free in the interpretations which we make.'[7] Although James tried to defend his ideas, Angell insisted that James's theory of truth left 'a sort of ghost-world as a reality,'[8] a world in which Angell preferred not to live.

Early in the century, Angell was one of the most respected psychologists in the country, elected president of the American Psychological Association in 1906 (the same year that James was president of the American Philosophical Association). Later, Angell moved into academic administration at Chicago and then at Yale, where he was appointed the university's president in 1921.

NOTES

1. James Angell, 'James Rowland Angell,' in Carl Murchison, *The History of Psychology in Autobiography,* (Worcester, Mass: Clark University Press, 1936), 3:22.

2. Murchison, *History of Psychology in Autobiography,* 7.
3. WJ to Hugo Münsterberg. Scott, 85 (9 August 1892).
4. Murchison, *History,* 28.
5. WJ to James Angell, Scott, 316 (9 August [1903]).
6. James Angell to WJ, 25 December 1907. Houghton.
7. James Angell to WJ, 16 January 1908. Houghton.
8. James Angell to WJ, 4 January 1908. Houghton.

William James

No one who knew William James can ever write of him in a wholly objective and dispassionate spirit. Nor can one cherish any hope of transfusing into words the abundant richness of his wonderful nature. Any just estimate of the man would require for its accomplishment a soul as pure and fine and brave as his own. The final valuation of his work must be confided to another generation. These lines are devoted to a few brief reminiscences, and particularly to such as may remind us of the profound changes in our psychological thought and practice for which we are primarily indebted to him.

To be sure at the time of his death, James was generally regarded as a philosopher rather than as a psychologist. And a philosopher he was in the best sense of the word, a devoted and courageous seeker after the deepest truths of life. But he was also a psychologist, easily first among his countrymen, and to emphasize this fact is the peculiar privilege of this REVIEW, with the first number of which his name was associated as an editor.

We may begin our reminiscences with the publication of 'The Principles of Psychology' in 1890. Prior to that James had been writing occasional brilliant articles and essays, some of which appeared later in modified form as chapters in the book, still others coming to life again in the volume entitled *The Will to Believe.* But until the appearance of The Principles his influence was on the whole secondary and local. With the publication of this great work, which the writer believes to be altogether his most valuable and lasting monument (it has in it most distinctly the seeds of all his later philosophical development) a profound and radical change came over the scene.

Who does not remember the sense of glowing delight with which we first read the pages of the big, cumbrous, ill-bound and rather ill-printed volumes? It was like inhaling a rare, pungent mountain air, vital, bracing and almost intoxicating. To many of us of the younger generation the book was assigned as a text. We read it as one reads the most fascinating tale of a master—spell-bound and transported and yet withal feeling ourselves acquiring new powers, and gaining command of pregnant thoughts. Scores of other readers fared as did we and so it came to pass that almost over night James became the recognized fountain head of the most original and most vigorous psychological thinking in our country. To get the perspective one must recall the conditions of our literature at that time.

In 1887 Ladd published his treatise on *Physiological Psychology* and Dewey his text-book on *General Psychology.* Two years later came Baldwin's *Senses and Intellect.* Signs were therefore not wanting of an intellectual ferment at work. But Ladd's volume was too technical to attract general attention, and the other two books, although favorably received, suffered under the suspicion of being philosophy rather than pure psychology, added to which both were addressed to the needs of college students and followed rather rigid lines of exposition. Prior to the appearance of these works, American students had been nurtured almost exclusively on Porter, McCosh, Hickok, Wayland, Haven, Hopkins, and their various followers. Not that all these authors deserve in any sense to be classed together, but simply that they represented in various degrees scientifically archaic and outworn methods in psychology, which were nevertheless still current in our colleges. At such a critical period appeared the epoch-making *Principles.*

It is difficult to appreciate how much that is now familiar and commonplace in psychological writing was introduced by James. But the simplest process of comparing the authors last mentioned with the writings of today abundantly exhibits the transition which has occurred and for which James more than any other one man is directly responsible.

Perhaps the most fundamental of all the doctrines he introduced and popularized was the physiological conception of habit as the basal principle of mental organization. He not only made this pivotal in his account of the associative processes of the intellect, but he exhibited it as the central feature in the development of the will. When a decade later he published his *Talks to Teachers,* he took it up again and made it cardinal for educational practice.

If the principle of habit may in certain ways be regarded as the most important interpretative principle running through his work and the one which enlisted the widest and most immediate interest—and general assent—it must in other ways share the honor with its complementary principle, the cerebralistic hypothesis of the conditions of thought.

This hypothesis is of course in no sense an invention of William James.

Indeed, in many ways it simply formulates facts well known to the veriest way-farer. But no previous English writer on psychology since Hartley's day had espoused this view so explicitly and at the same time made such constant practical use of it. James turns to it at every point for the explanation of mental phenomena, a practice which caused him to be branded by the orthodox as a dangerous materialist.

He shared with Lange the honor of revolutionizing the current view of emotion. The exposition of his theory rescued the subject at a stroke from the dull routine of purely descriptive psychology and, notwithstanding a constant fire of acute criticism, his position has substantially held its own up to the present day.

Following closely in the footsteps of Darwin, he made instinct an essential part of the study of the human mind in a way no other psychologist had done. He took a large, flexible, dynamic view of instinct which gave it a place in the very forefront of human life and so of human psychology, instead of relegating it to the limbo of 'left-overs' from our animal ancestry for which apologies must be made and moralizing indulged.

He wrote perhaps the only thoroughly entertaining account of reasoning that we have in the English language and yet managed to make clear much of what is technically most essential to know, if one would understand the actual workings of the mind. Despite their admirable analytic fidelity to detail, one has only to compare with James' chapter on 'Reasoning' in the *Principles,* certain of the contemporary German analyses of the process, to feel that he is in reality closer to the pith of the matter than they.

His account of space perception established the subject on a level which it had never before reached in modern English writings and thereby rendered a service of lasting value. It still remains, twenty years after it was written, one of the most valuable of store-houses for all the fundamental phases of the subject.

James made a conscious and systematic struggle for the recognition of the vague, the fugitive, the transitory, in consciousness, as over against the 'block-house' scheme of mental organization. This tendency appeared most clearly perhaps in his celebrated chapter on the Stream of Consciousness, and more especially in his doctrine of 'Feelings of Relation' in which we have the first adequate insistence in contemporary writing on this aspect of consciousness.

His conception of the self as a hierarchy made a deep impression, not so much perhaps for its intrinsic novelty, as by reason of the peculiar picturesqueness and force of his description and his pungent sallies at the expense of popular complacencies.

He made much wider use than had any previous English-speaking psychologist of materials drawn from the pathological side of mental life. This was in part no doubt a reflex of his medical training, in part was due to his intrinsic interest in the unusual. This trait appears very strikingly in the selection of material for his great work on religious experience.

No one thing so radically divided professional opinion of James as his support of the Psychical Research Movement. In England the society began its career under auspices in many respects most favorable and in all respects scientifically respectable, not to say, eminent. But in this country, James for years stood almost alone among men of high intellectual repute, and although he was eminently conservative in his estimate of the results of the work of the society, he nevertheless committed himself to belief in certain mediumistic phenomena in a way which seriously offended many of his professional colleagues. At best, they regarded him as a man whose judgment could not be trusted, at worst as an unwitting backer of quackery and fraud.

His position on the issue was all of a piece with his insistent and never failing protestantism, his passion for fair play, and a just hearing for all sides of every question. He was never afraid to make a mistake if only it were honest, and he started off on a new tack when he found himself in error, as though fallacy were a regular part of the day's work. He had a wholesome contempt, which I have heard him more than once express with characteristic vigor, for the pose of infallibility and essential omniscience assumed by certain distinguished scholars. It seemed to him at once petty and contemptible.

Whether or not we agree with his view of psychic research, it will be a thousand pities if James' attitude in the matter should fail to teach us of the younger generation the high rewards of honest independence and the insidious dangers of moral stultification which lurk in a lethargic or a cowardly intellectual conformity to ruling creed, whether of church or of science.

In this matter, as in the others to which we have referred, we may gratefully look for his most enduring contributions not so much in the specific doctrines which he taught and defended, as in his splendid spirit of eagerness for the truth, his open-minded willingness to find this truth in humble and out of the way places, and his dauntless courage in proclaiming his faith in whatsoever he found worthy.

With few men could an inventory of his accomplishments, however impressive, be so entirely and grotesquely inadequate as with James. It has been a favorite comment upon his writing that in his case the 'style is the man' in an extraordinary measure. And the saying is true, but what it leaves unsaid is more than what it utters. His personality was fascinating and magnetic to a degree which his writings hardly indicate. This was perhaps in part due to the wonderful play of light in his eyes, in part to the singularly sweet and resonant tones of his voice, to say nothing of the racy picturesqueness of his words. But inwardly no doubt it sprang from the unsounded wells of sympathy in his nature which made every human creature a thing of at least passing interest to him.

As a teacher he was especially sympathetic and stimulating. He overestimated the capacities of many of his students most seriously, or at least, appeared to do so, but this only put them on their mettle to make good his estimate. What he did in this way to encourage his own pupils, he did more widely for struggling talent wherever he chanced to note it. No brochure so obscure, no writer so unknown, but that if James detected any spark of promise, he sent a word of appreciation. How much such encouragement meant to many a young scholar toiling for recognition, no one will ever know. But the sum must be large beyond belief.

William James was that rarest of human beings—a great man who was also simple, kindly, brave and true. His memory will always be with us as an inspiration and a benediction.

F. C. S. SCHILLER

(1864–1937)

James admired, and even envied, the school of philosophy centered around the work of John Dewey that had emerged from the University of Chicago. 'At Harvard,' he wrote to Canning Schiller, 'we have plenty of thought but not school.'[1] For a time, the two men, who felt closely allied philosophically and who were perceived by other philosophers as being 'of the same gang,'[2] imagined that they could join forces to propagate their ideas. 'If only we might get you here!' James wrote to Schiller in 1897 when Schiller was about to leave his position at Cornell University. 'You and I could then found a regular school of pluralism and sweep the country.'[3]

F. C. S. Schiller was born in Germany and studied at Oxford. In 1893 he came to the United States to continue his education at Cornell, where he also served as an instructor in philosophy. Schiller was not happy at Cornell, and the department did not urge him to stay. In 1897, when he sought a new position, James enthusiastically wrote letters of recommendation for him in the hope that he would stay in the United States. But Schiller decided to return to Oxford, where he taught for the rest of his career. Beginning in 1926 he spent part of each year at the University of Southern California.

Schiller consistently applauded James's ideas and wanted to help publicize them, but he believed it unfortunate that James attached the confusing name *pragmatism* to his ideas about verifying truth. Instead, Schiller proposed the name *humanism* to describe his and James's philosophy. The term, said Schiller, seemed 'significant and apt, and was not encumbered with old senses likely to interfere and to be confused with its philosophic use.'[4] At first James rejected the term, but his own frustration over the response of colleagues to the concept of pragmatism gradually won him over to Schiller's proposal. In his review of Schiller's *Humanism: Philosophical Essays*, James conceded that '"Humanism" is perhaps too "whole-hearted" for the use of philosophers, who are a bloodless breed; but, save for that objection, one might back it, for it expresses the essence of the new way of thought, which is, that it is impossible to strip the human element out from even our most abstract theorizing.'[5]

James's colleagues, however, considered the problem with pragmatism not so much in the name but in the idea that individuals can establish their own authority for judging truth. When such thinkers as Arthur Lovejoy criticized James's formulation of pragmatism as being so poorly circumscribed that it could encompass thirteen definitions, Schiller responded that thirteen was, in fact, too few. 'For it was an essential feature of "pragmatism,"' he argued, 'to be recalcitrant to the scientific fiction which depersonalizes truth. If every "truth" originates with an individual thinker facing an actual problem and choosing the best solution that presents itself to his mind, and framing the best judgment for containing it that he can conceive, and succeeding in winning the assent of others to the goodness of his judgment, it surely follows that its depersonalization is a fiction.'[6]

Schiller saw, as many of James's colleagues did not, that pragmatism, or humanism, was a philosophy intended to serve as a basis for social life in a democracy. It allowed many diverse voices to be heard and considered, and assumed that a consensus would emerge from those diverse voices to affirm a collective sense of reality. 'By admitting that every centre of experience should be heard from, because it may yield a contribution to the common store,' Schiller wrote, humanism, 'grants universal suffrage in the realm of thought, though it does *not* imply equality of value.'[7] The problem of equality of value proved more disturbing to James's critics than it did to Schiller.

James's friendship with Schiller is reflected in a hefty amount of correspondence: at times Schiller apparently wrote to James every day. But in the end James found himself annoyed by Schiller's style, which he thought undermined the force of his ideas. In letters and even in reviews, he urged Schiller to 'tone down a little the exuberance of his polemic wit.'[8] Schiller, as this essay reveals, did not retreat from his enthusiastic celebration of the man he considered one of the two greatest human beings of his time.

NOTES

1. WJ to F. C. S. Schiller. Perry, 501 (15 November 1903).
2. WJ to F. C. S. Schiller. Scott, 280 (24 April 1902).

3. WJ to F. C. S. Schiller. Scott, 154 (6 March 1897).

4. F. C. S. Schiller, *Must Philosophers Disagree?* (London: Macmillan, 1939), 101.

5. WJ, *Essays, Comments, and Reviews,* 551–52.

6. Schiller, *Must Philosophers Disagree?* 104.

7. Schiller, *Must Philosophers Disagree?* 105.

8. WJ, *Essays, Comments, and Reviews,* 541.

William James

The history of philosophy is by no means rich in new ideas and picturesque personalities. I once set myself to enumerate the really important and novel ideas that had occurred to philosophers, and found that I could not get beyond nine.[1] Nor would it be very much easier to count up as many great personalities among philosophers, and even these seem to get not commoner but scarcer as time goes on. They are to be found, almost exclusively, among the philosophers of antiquity, whose biographies we may suspect to have been inflated by a strong infusion of myth. If we can believe the traditions that have come down to us, and whether we can or not will depend on our native and acquired credulity, Thales, Pythagoras, Heraclitus, Protagoras, Empedocles, Parmenides, Socrates, Plato, and Plotinus may have been personally great: but since that time who is there on whom this epithet could plausibly be bestowed?

I suppose, therefore, that I ought to regard it as a singular piece of good fortune that the only two human beings who ever at once made upon me an impression of personal greatness should both have been philosophers: the one was Arthur Balfour, the other was the subject of this article, William James.

James, moreover, was not only personally great, but also the effective promulgator of a great idea, the bearer of a great message, the last indeed in my list of the nine great ideas which have cropped up in philosophy, and of the only great idea which has so far taken birth in America, Pragmatism. So you see how great is my responsibility in endeavouring to give you, in the short space of one hour, some idea of a great man and a great idea, of William James and of Pragmatism!

A Los Angeles Public Library Lecture, 1930.

1. Cp. p.94.

First, let me try to give you some idea of James's personality. I was not privileged to sit at the feet of James while he was still teaching at Harvard University; but when, nearly forty years ago, I set out on my first voyage to discover America, I was told that James was one of the few men in America I must not fail to meet, and was equipped with a letter of introduction to him from James Bryce, the famous historian and British Ambassador at Washington. It so happened that I had no opportunity of presenting myself to James for several years, but when the auspicious moment came, the effect was instantaneous and electrical. Within five minutes of first meeting James, I found myself talking to him as if I had known him all my life! That was one of the effects of James's personality on people. He had a marvellous gift of psychological sympathy in dealing with nearly every one, and inspired confidence as well as admiration. The one exception to this rule that I observed was the case of a philosopher and a colleague, George Santayana. He and James seem to have been naturally antagonistic and antipathetic to each other, I don't know why, and you should bear this in mind when you read what Santayana has to say of James. A more typical display of the real James I witnessed years later when James first came to Oxford.

He had never met G. F. Stout, who was then endeavouring to instil a little psychology into the medieval Oxford mind, and was anxious to make his acquaintance. So I took him round to the Stouts' to tea. It was a Sunday afternoon, and we had hardly begun to talk when an undergraduate called. Stout imprudently told James that the young man was suffering from a curious obsession, and this at once aroused James's sympathy. The result was that James and Stout spent the rest of the afternoon talking to the young man about his troubles, while Mrs. Stout and I were left disconsolate, to lament the great psychologist's excessive sympathy with the distresses of the human soul! You will find abundant evidence of his catholic sympathies with every sort and condition of human nature, throughout his incomparable *Letters,* so skilfully edited by his son, Henry, which I hope I may suppose many of you have read. If not, may I recommend you to take an early opportunity of filling in this gap in your education? You will thoroughly enjoy the process, and it will give you some idea of the great range of James's interests. He is equally charming in condoling with a little son on the loss of a milk tooth, in acknowledging the gift of an azalea from an appreciative class of Radcliffe College girls, in discussing the psychology of Shakespeare's genius, and in refusing an invitation to a formal gathering of professional philosophers.

It was in virtue of his psychological sympathy that James had such a fascination for all sorts of cranks, not only philosophic, with the sole exception of the hard-bitten shrivelled pedant. Now cranks are people who in general are not accustomed to encounter much sympathy: the world treats them coldly and severely. So when James received them with an open mind and ear, and listened to them and took an interest in their struggles to express themselves, and soothed them and treated them as though they might really have become, by some divine chance, the vehicles for some unsuspected revelation, they promptly fell in love with him, and became his devoted adherents. James treated them tenderly and spent enormous amounts of time and trouble on them and not a little money. I remember in the nineties of the last century he had on his hands a little self-educated Polish Jew cobbler in New York, who had a philosophic soul (not sole) for ever urging him beyond his last, and a firm conviction that he had discovered the Secret of the Universe. Said James: 'What if this little fellow should turn out to be a second Spinoza?' and in the end got up a subscription among his friends, but mainly I suspect out of his own pocket, to enable him to get his revelation off his chest. I still have a copy of the resulting publication. It is called *The Disclosure of the Universal Mysteries;* but I have never heard that it has appealed to the patriotism of Jewish philosophers like Spinoza's *Ethic* or to the philosophic pride of shoemakers, like the works of Jacob Böhme.

James, however, did not merely lavish precious balms of human sympathy on his cranks: he also exploited them. Whenever he wanted to say anything particularly neat and scathing about a philosophic doctrine he was upsetting, he could always mobilize one of his pet cranks, whom he appeared to have kept up his sleeve for this very emergency. He would then quote from him some vivid and outrageously apt dictum, with crushing effect. Thus, who that has met them can ever forget the 'unlettered carpenter' of James's acquaintance who so neatly laid down the principle, *and the limits,* of democracy in the memorable saying, 'There is very little difference between one man and another; but what little there is is very important,' or the old lady of Boston who was wont to divide philosophies into the *thick* and the *thin,* or the gorgeous pictorial phrases James extracted from his 'pluralistic mystic,' Benjamin P. Blood?

On James's death some of his cranks tried to attach themselves to me; but I, alas, was not equal to the occasion nor able to retain their allegiance. I suppose I was too distant, either spiritually or geographically. In particular I remember one who wrote under the name 'Salvarona' and had evolved what he called a metaphysic of Hunger, and used to send me pamphlets about the nervous system of Jesus. I am afraid I was too much of a logician and not enough of a psychologist to appreciate his work, but James would, I am sure, have made good use of him and have immortalized him by quotation.

But I must not spend all my time on James the man, for I know you will want me to speak about James the philosopher. The first thing I would beg you to note about him is that he was not, strictly speaking, a professional philosopher at all. He was really one of the great succession of amateurs who have stirred philosophy and stimulated thought, in line with Descartes, Spinoza, Leibniz, Berkeley, Hume, Schopenhauer, Mill, Bentham, and Spencer. For he was brought up to be a scientist, a physiologist, and a doctor of medicine, and the first course he delivered in Harvard University was one in anatomy. James took to philosophy from the love of it, from personal interest in its problems, and not because he thought he could make a living by cataloguing the varieties of philosophic opinion, and speculating about the sense of the abstruse abstractions in which defunct philosophers have hidden away their esoteric doctrines.

He told me once that the first philosophic lecture he had ever listened to was when he began to lecture on philosophy himself! This unphilosophic past shows, I think, in James's work, not indeed in any lack of grip of the essential problems, which, as professional philosophers should never be allowed to forget, are the common problems of human life, but in his elevation above the sordid squabbles of philosophy, in his freedom from the 'genteel tradition' with its transparent insincerity, and in the vigour and originality of his thought. His exemption from what, I fear, is too often the dull mechanical routine of academic philosophy largely accounts for the virgin freshness with which James's mind approached the problems of philosophy. It gave him all the advantages which the amateur has over the professional, and enabled him to discover, like Plato before him, that philosophy is *love* of wisdom and that in matters of the spirit love is not always blind, but a source of insight and penetrating perception, and that valuable truth is least likely to reward the nerveless and half-hearted efforts of 'dispassionate' research.

Secondly, I would have you note that there was a great deal of the *artist* in James's composition, and that his literary genius was largely hereditary. He thought at one time of making painting his profession, as two of his sons have since done; and both his father and his brother, the novelist, have amply shown that power over words was an heirloom in the family.

At the same time I would not have you think that James's style, which is so delightfully different from that of most philosophers, and makes anything he writes such a joy to read, was a sheer gift of the gods or of fortune, and required no cultivation. I believe that his way of writing was part of a fully considered policy, part of a deliberate protest against the paralysing Germanism which he saw creeping into American academic life, together with German scholarship and ideals of research, desiccating the professor and alienating him from the people. James felt strongly, and it seems to me rightly, that philosophy could have no future, and could never hope to grapple with its problems, or to impress the world with the value of its findings, unless it could manage to express itself in intelligible and attractive language. He saw that the carelessness and illiteracy of Kant had done as much irredeemably to *spoil* German thought, and to render it *incapable* of precision and lucidity, and even of knowing its own mind, as the literary genius of Plato had for ever made the fortune of Greek philosophy; so he wished American philosophy not to abandon the better models British philosophy had provided in Locke, Berkeley, Hume, and Mill.

He himself surpassed his models. His own writings read more easily than anything else in philosophic literature. Of all his works only the big *Psychology* can be called technical in style, and even this is mainly due to the great chunks of quotations from other psychologists which it embodies. The rest are popular and intelligible, to all except some philosophy professors. For James reads so easily that many of his philosophic colleagues, unaccustomed to such light and palatable fare, have tortured themselves to find hidden meanings in what he says, and so have often missed his points.

But, as you probably know, easy reading does not usually mean easy writing. And so it appears to have been with James. Whenever he was engaged upon any considerable piece of literary composition his letters to his friends grew full of groanings over the slowness and arduousness of his progress. He assures them that working all day and rewriting half a dozen times has only yielded him a page and a half of manuscript, and envies them their facility and rapidity of composition. Yet I was often tempted to take these complaints with a grain of salt. No doubt they were justified at times, but at others James must have written easily. His letters, for example, must often have been dashed off at full speed, as the handwriting and the erasures show. And what is most remarkable, their style is no whit inferior to that of the most finished compositions. Thus there is no trace in the finished product of the labour that sometimes went to its production. The quality is alike exquisite, whether the writing was difficult or easy, rewritten half a dozen times or just dashed off on a casual postcard. The letters are a complete proof that James could write just as well on the spur of the moment as in his most laborious works. It was all a question of getting out his intrinsic quality, and this was sometimes easy, sometimes harder.

In coming finally to the philosophic achievements proper of James I shall have to confine myself to a few capital points. The first is that he broke down for good and all the hard and fast divisions which false abstractions had introduced into the treatment of philosophic problems. For example, it was long the custom of those who did not understand the significance of his work to regard him as a psychologist who had strayed beyond his tether and taken to theory of knowledge and even metaphysics. But what James had actually done was to shatter the classification which put psychology in one compartment and shut off metaphysics and theory of knowledge in separate partitions. As a matter of fact the whole of James's philosophy is part of one endeavour. It is contained already in his big *Psychology* published in 1890. If you want chapter and verse, read H. V. Knox's little study of James which is largely composed of quotations selected by preference from the *Psychology*. This point was also proved by John Dewey's feat in extracting his Instrumentalism from the *Psychology* without any further help from James. But the other philosophers were too dull to perceive this. They thought that as his philosophy appeared in a work called 'Psychology' it did not concern them. They praised it as psychology, for it was such good reading; but that a good psychologist could also be, nay, could for that very reason be, a great philosopher, never entered their heads. When James proceeded to draw out the implications of his new psychology and to set down its applications to their disputes, they were genuinely shocked to find that a mere reform of psychology portended a revolution in philosophy.

The reform in psychology which James initiated, and which is my second point, had all the simplicity of genius. It consisted in the overthrow of the psychological atomism known as associationism, and the substitution therefor of a description of psychic process as a continuum. As soon as it was done, it became obvious that the new description was much simpler and easier and that associationism had been based on quite outrageous fictions.

Yet there were reasons for these fictions. British philosophy had quite naïvely started from common-sense and taken as indisputable fact the analysis of reality which has been found sufficient for its purposes. This analysis broke up the real into a world of distinct interacting things and persons, all immersed in the continua of space and time. Now actually this is far from being either complete analysis or complete atomism. For space and time and causal connexions suffice to weld together the many into a world. But it is possible to mistake the aim of common-sense procedure. If it is assumed that the aim of common-sense is to provide not an effective platform for action, but a logically complete analysis of the continuous into discrete atoms, and if it is taken as self-evident that every distinguishable impression or idea is a distinct existence, it is clear that common-sense analysis does not go nearly far enough, and stops far short of its logical conclusion. So Hume said, let us be logical, insisted on going the whole hog, and triumphantly reduced the world to an atomic dust-heap of sensations. Space and time were alleged to be atomic in their composition, causation was reduced to succession, floundering in a mire of unwarranted expectation, while of the self which held together and remembered its experiences, Hume frankly and openly despaired. He gave up the problem how such feats were possible for what could *ex hypothesi* be nothing but a series of flashes of sensation.

But the result of Hume's radical consistency was chaos and scepticism, and subsequent philosophy had to find a way out of the *impasse* into which he had led it.

Unfortunately the philosophers all started on the wrong track. They did not retrace their steps sufficiently far, nor go back behind the work of common-sense. Under the leadership of Kant it seemed clear to them that, inasmuch as Hume had destroyed causation and the other connecting principles, what was needed was to resuscitate a new and more impressive set of 'synthetic' categories, to stitch Humpty-Dumpty together again.

So Kant set himself to manufacture them, in great profusion, and to decorate them with the title of 'pure *a priori*,' without which no German philosopher can now think his thought decently arrayed. All his successors followed Kant like sheep. No one raised the prior question, whether after all philosophic reflexion ought not to have started further back, with really crude experience, as it is given *before* any intellectual work is done upon it and it is analysed at all, and arranged in a practically manageable order by the categories of common-sense. Had the question been raised why and how the common-sense world was constructed, it would have been evident that a world of interacting things was by no means what the mind originally encountered in the beginning of knowing. The real datum for the nascent mind was a big buzzing confusion as James said, *i.e.* a chaotic continuum. If now one started from that, one clearly never needed any principles of *synthesis*. One needed rather justifications for *analysis*, clues for the practice of breaking up the flux, in thought, and slicing it up into separate entities. This was the great discovery in psychology and epistemology made by James, and almost simultaneously by Bergson in France.

It completely transformed the situation and side-tracked as wholly irrelevant and superfluous the problems put by Hume and Kant and their successors. All that was now needed was motives and means for breaking up the flux. These were easily forthcoming in the shape of psychological observations on the selectiveness of attention and the variations of interest. James was fully entitled to declare that the real way to a truly critical philosophy led not *through* Kant but *round* him, and that the Kantian formulation of the problem of knowing with all its endless and fruitless intricacies could, and should, be short-circuited altogether. Moreover, by discarding the false premisses which British empiricism had shared with, and foisted upon, German apriorism a new, more radical and more tenable empiricism had become conceivable.

It was this that led, thirdly, to the development of Pragmatism, than which no novelty of thought has ever been more grotesquely and stupidly misinterpreted. Really, however, it was a very simple affair. It was merely a revolt against a number of pernicious abstractions which had long blocked the path of philosophic progress. Thus it had been assumed as a matter of course that there was no connexion between the canons of right thinking and the actual procedures of our thought; or in other words, between logic and psychology. Nor yet was there any connexion between right thinking and right doing, and between theory and practice, nor any doubt about where the line between them should be drawn. By denying this dichotomy and showing how even our highest 'theoretical' abstractions were derived from, and relative to practical needs, were intended for use upon the problems of life and drew their significance from this relation, Pragmatism reinstated *life in its integrity* as the supreme aim of philosophic thought. By refusing to take meaning, use, and value as three unrelated notions which had nothing to do with one another, pragmatism for the first time rendered the nature of truth intelligible, and enabled philosophers to understand the process by which truths are in real life actually established, developed, and if need be, modified, and scrapped. This process proved to be identical with the procedure which had long been practised by the sciences spontaneously and with signal success. It is not too much to say that on one side Pragmatism means the discovery by Philosophy of the method of Science. But the method of science, rightly understood, is the method also of all knowing and all living, and the scientists themselves, misled by the false formal logic of intellectualist philosophy, had not understood it. They had only practised it, instinctively, and without theoretic sanction from the current logic, like every one else who had problems to solve and knowledge to acquire. Now that the new pragmatic logic has exposed the inanity and malignity of the old logic, and explained the procedures of actual knowing, we may expect logic to act as a stimulus, and no longer as an obstruction, to the growth of knowledge.

Thus Pragmatism has restored to Philosophy its contact with everyday life and with the working sciences. Philosophy is no longer doomed to be an idle game of 'contemplation,' juggling with verbal counters, whose sole use is to minister to the superiority-complex of its adepts, and to inculcate contempt for the activities, pursuits, and values of the vulgar. It has been emancipated from the dead hand of Pedantry which withers what it touches and kills what it lives on; but so long as any society breeds pedants and promotes them to professorships, *this* achievement will never quite be forgiven William James.

Similarly his famous doctrine of the Will to Believe, which opens out such vast fields to the cultivation of a verifiable and progressive religious life, and has done so much to found a new science of the psychology of religion, will never be acceptable to those who are openly or secretly antireligious. But it is best understood as a further plea for a recognition of the integrity of human nature, and of the profound irrationality of relying on an elegant extract called 'pure reason' in order to grapple with the riddles of the Sphinx. With a masterly but loving hand James traced out the real complexity of human belief, and the subtle relations between belief and action, and for ever disposed of the pretensions of those of faint heart and little faith to have a monopoly of philosophic elevation, logical security, and scientific rectitude.

Let me finally say a word of warning about the Americanism of James's philosophy. I am not in general in favour of introducing nationalism into the discussion of philosophic and scientific questions, which I think prosper best when there is the freest intercourse and completest co-operation between those who are devoted to their elucidation. The nationalist excesses of the learned in all countries were among the most shameful revelations of the decline in civilization occasioned by the late war. Like the churches, the universities nowhere upheld the universality of human values, but were tempted to play the jackal to the wolves of war. Moreover, it seems to me to be very unsound and dangerous to argue from the character of a people to that of a philosopher belonging to that people. For every people is so mixed in its composition that any individual may inherit from his actual ancestors qualities very unusual and rare in the people at large. Also the philosopher may be a genius, and is pretty sure to be at least an eccentric, who departs in various ways from the norm of his people. And if in addition he is also a professor, it is well to remember that he belongs to a very highly selected class, leading a very peculiar and specialized life, and tempted in various ways to dissent from the current opinions popular in his time and country. We should therefore expect the professor as such to develop everywhere a strong and even excessive bias in favour of the theoretic life, that is, in favour of the life he leads.

I do not of course deny that the social life and the social valuations which surround him may have an influence on even the most opinionated professor. I merely want to point out that his reaction to popular standards is quite as likely to be dissent and violent aversion as accommodation. Hence to account for Pragmatism it is not enough merely to point to the pragmatic activities of American life. After all, if all that was necessary for the discovery of Pragmatism was just comprehension of American life and of the salient features of American civilization, any one of hundreds or thousands of American philosophy professors might have discovered Pragmatism long before James.

Actually Pragmatism was a great and difficult discovery. You can take this from me, because I had myself taken several steps on the way to it, before James blazed a trail that all could follow. But great discoveries have a knack of seeming very simple after they are made, like the egg of Columbus and natural selection and Newtonian gravitation, though thousands of apples have for ages fallen on uncomprehending heads. Pragmatism is no exception to this rule. American civilization, resting as it did on the physical conquest of a continent and the applications of science to life, no doubt pointed to Pragmatism as the theory of its practice; but after all the same has more or less been true of human life and activity always and everywhere. Actual human life and actual knowing are everywhere pragmatic.

The civilizations of the valleys of the Euphrates and the Nile were from the first based upon the practical control of those powers of nature; what the early Egyptians achieved in the case of the Nile the modern Americans have not yet surpassed in the case of the Mississippi. Moreover, always and everywhere, a genius has been needed to discover the meaning of human activity, and with it the truth of Pragmatism. In the Greece of the fifth century B.C. the genius was Protagoras, and it cost him his life; in the China of the Ming dynasty it was Wang-yang-min, and it cost him four centuries of oblivion, till he was unearthed again by an American scholar; in the America of the nineteenth century the genius who revealed to the American people the meaning of their doings, and so enabled them to go on doing them more intelligently and harmoniously, was William James.

ARTHUR ONCKEN LOVEJOY

(1873–1962)

When Arthur Lovejoy entered Harvard as a graduate student in 1895, he was acting against the wishes of his father, a physician who had given up medicine to enter the Episcopal ministry and who feared that Harvard's philosophy department would turn his son away from the church. But Lovejoy felt strongly motivated to pursue the study of philosophy: partly because he had been inspired by George Holmes Howison, with whom he had studied as an undergraduate at Berkeley; partly to exert his independence from his overbearing father; and partly to achieve what he considered to be 'the chief end of man': self-consciousness.[1]

Lovejoy's impression of James was less enthusiastic than that of some other graduate students. He wrote to his father that James was a disappointing lecturer, but better in 'the independent exposition of his own highly suggestive notions and enthusiasm.'[2] Lovejoy also studied with Royce, Palmer, Münsterberg, and Santayana, earning a master's degree in 1897. He did not continue for a doctorate, explaining to David Starr Jordan of Stanford University, when he was being considered for a position, that 'I am personally very indifferent about it and regard it as unwise for a man to go at all out of the way of his own philosophical interests in order to conform to the requirements of this exercise.'[3] Just a few days before, Royce had sent Jordan a letter of strong support for Lovejoy, commending him as 'an admirable man,—growing, learned, resolute, ingenious, and sensible . . . He is a man of admirable moral fibre.'[4]

Lovejoy got the position at Stanford, where he taught from 1899 to 1901; he resigned to support a colleague who was being harangued for political views. He quickly received an offer from Washington University in St. Louis, Missouri, where he taught until 1908, and then spent most of his career as Professor of Philosophy at Johns Hopkins University.

George Boas, his colleague at Johns Hopkins, describes him as a man 'who was supposed to be terrifying, but he was not terrifying at all.' He was, however, exacting. 'It is true,' Boas admitted, 'that he has never tolerated gross exaggeration, vagueness, dogmatism in conversation, and I have heard him arrest a sentence in mid-passage when a term or idea was to his way of thinking too loose a foundation for continued discussion.'[5] This uncompromising demand for clarity and logic undermined his relationship with James.

Although Lovejoy's warm memoir of James hints at a close friendship, in fact the two men were at odds, philosophically and temperamentally. Lovejoy enjoyed puzzling out detective stories, memorizing the vital statistics of baseball games, and studying Civil War battle strategy; in short, he took pleasure in applying logical systems to human experience. James, on the other hand, was anecdotal, impressionistic, and intellectually acrobatic.

Their differences are evident in an exchange of letters focusing on Lovejoy's critique of James's *Pragmatism*.[6] In 'The Thirteen Pragmatisms,' Lovejoy identified thirteen sometimes contradictory propositions encompassed in the idea of pragmatism, and tried to distinguish between 'pragmatism as a theory of meaning and pragmatism as a theory of truth.' Lovejoy complained that pragmatism could not posit a theory of knowledge that transcended concrete experience because pragmatism was oriented toward the future and demanded that the validity of a proposition must be judged by its effects.

After James read 'The Thirteen Pragmatisms' in galley form, he commented that he felt 'somewhat disappointed ere the end' by Lovejoy's distinctions. 'They all fit into and build out the general pragmatist scheme for which you show no sympathy and (it seems to me) little understanding. . . . That scheme is to establish a completely concrete account of what men mean by "truth." . . . You give an impression (certainly not intended) of arguing as if, because so many things go into the natural history of live truth, they must cancel each other, and the learner *must* have to fall back on "intellectualism," with its unexplicated term "agreement."'[7]

Irritated by Lovejoy's insistence on abstraction, James complained about the criticism to his friends Schiller ('I'm getting tired of being treated as ½ idiot, ½ scoundrel') and Kallen ('Lovejoy also is writing very well, tho' fearfully off the track in parts').[8] But Lovejoy persisted in his belief that James was anti-intellectual and illogical. James, Lovejoy wrote, 'was himself prone, in his enthusiasm for the point which he was at the moment expounding, to forget the qualifying considerations which he elsewhere plainly enough acknowledged or even emphatically affirmed. It cannot, I suppose, be denied that he was likely sometimes to overstate the truth immediately before his mind, especially if it seemed to him a truth that had been shabbily treated, a deserving philosophical waif that had been arrogantly turned away from the doors of all the respectable and established doctrines.'[9] Lovejoy was not susceptible to such sentimentality.

NOTES

1. William Pepperell Montague, 'My Friend Lovejoy,' *Journal of the History of Ideas,* 1948, 424.
2. Arthur Lovejoy to Wallace Lovejoy, 8 November 1896. Quoted in Daniel Wilson, *Arthur O. Lovejoy and the Quest for Intelligibility* (Chapel Hill: University of North Carolina Press, 1980), 21.
3. Arthur Lovejoy to David Starr Jordan. Wilson, 26 (19 May 1899).
4. Josiah Royce to David Starr Jordan. *The Letters of Josiah Royce,* ed. Clendenning, 389 (1 May 1899).
5. George Boas, 'A. O. Lovejoy: Reason-in-Action,' *The American Scholar,* 1960, 537.
6. 'The Thirteen Pragmatisms,' *The Journal of Philosophy* 5 (1908): 1–12, 29–39; 'Pragmatism and Theology,' *The American Journal of Theology* 12 (1908): 116–43.
7. WJ to Arthur Lovejoy. Perry 2:482–83 (22 December 1907).
8. WJ to F. C. S. Schiller. Scott, 465 [17 January 1908]; WJ to Horace Kallen. Scott, 473 (12 February 1908).
9. Arthur Lovejoy, 'William James as Philosopher,' *The Thirteen Pragmatisms* (Baltimore: Johns Hopkins University Press, 1963), 92.

William James as Philosopher

James's genius lay chiefly in this, that he had by nature, and retained undiminished to the end of his life, an extraordinary immunity to the deadening influence of those intellectual processes of classification and generalization in which, in one form or another, scientific and philosophical reasoning largely consist. He kept an unweakened sense for the particularity of the particular—a sense which the occupations of the philosophical system-builder ordinarily tend to atrophy. Thus he was always prepared to see in each individual person, each separate fact, each immediately present aspect of experience, even in each distinct logical category, something unique, unshared, irreducible, ineffably individuated. And toward each new, not-yet-fully-examined fact he always maintained an attitude of liberal expectancy; because it was enough like certain other facts to be classified with them was no reason for assuming that it might not, if given a fair chance, develop wholly novel and admirable qualities and potencies of its own. Uniformities were to be recognized so far as they actually exhibited themselves; but they were not to be allowed wholly to prejudice the case of 'the unclassified residuum'; and it was in the unclassified residuum that James's greater interest lay. He was thus predestined by the possession of what may be called a particularist mind to be a pluralistic philosopher.

Here, no doubt, more nearly than in any other single point of view, lies the center of William James's personal vision. The temper of mind which I have tried to indicate appeared in his character as a social being as plainly as in his tendencies as a philosopher, as truly in his attitude toward his fellows as in his attitude toward the universe. The most largehearted and tenderhearted of men, he showed the characteristic quality of his generosity not so much in his bestowal of material kindnesses, large and constant and delicately considerate though those were, as in his unquenchable *interest* in all sorts and conditions of individuals, his wholehearted appreciation of other men's qualities, and his indefatigable encouragement of their work. This interest in others was not at all the generalized and regularized benevolence of the philosophical 'altruist,' loving mankind in the abstract upon principle; it was not the interest of the moralist, sedulous to edify and to improve; it was only in part the interest of the sympathetic hedonist, rejoicing in the spectacle of the happiness of others or pained at their griefs. It was essentially the interest of a lover of human nature in the concrete and of the richness of its individual manifestations—especially of the diversity of its intellectual-emotional reactions upon the common data of experience. James's capacity for admiration of the intellectual performances of others was astonishing in its range and in its heartiness; not only his old pupils, but utter strangers, neglected Spinozas of the ghetto or Hegels budding unobserved in provincial newspapers, were likely at any moment to receive a letter, or one of his characteristic post cards, with a few, or sometimes many, words of heartening applause—applause often too liberal, but not undiscriminating—evoked by the reading of some piece of work that seemed to him to have in it something of freshness or individuality. The least sign of the emergence in American philosophy, or, indeed, 'anywhere, of a mind having a quality of its own, possessing novel or distinctive and strongly-marked powers, caused in him a joy like that of a man who had found the pearl of great price. I can even recall once hearing him exclaim with admiring wonder over some examination papers of Harvard undergraduates which he had been reading. It was not that those productions as a rule betrayed any extraordinary familiarity on the part of their authors with the subjects with which they were supposed to deal. But the ready ingenuity of these American youth who could, upon so slender a basis of actual acquaintance with the matter in hand, fill so many pages of blue book with stuff so plausible—and often conveying such surprising novelties even of misapprehension—that, to James, was after all a delightful and not altogether unadmirable manifestation of the possibilities of the human mind. All this generosity in appreciation, no doubt, sometimes led him into extravagances; originality was, to him, a mantle that sometimes covered completely a rather great multitude of sins. But this 'characteristic excess' of James's was not only the excess characteristic of a singularly magnanimous mind; it was also the excess of a mind singularly alert to the real differences, the personal and unique traits of the reactions upon life of other minds. Even where he could not share or directly sympathize with those reactions, they had, if honest and serious and not illiberal, scarcely less value in his eyes.

It is, of course, a natural consequence of this that one of the two traits by which James's more directly ethical writings are chiefly distinguished is an exceptionally vivid feeling for the underived and intrinsic value of almost all distinctive and spontaneous manifestations of human nature, the indefeasible validity of each personal point of view not itself merely negative and destructive of others, the inner significance *for itself*, when lived simply and heartily, of every separate pulse of vital experience. This gospel had been, in a different fashion, powerfully preached before James preached it, by Whitman and by Stevenson—two lay moralists who, by reason of natural affinity of mind, seem to have influenced him not a little. In the domain of practical ethics the most characteristic thing, as it seems to me, that James ever wrote is the essay 'On a Certain Blindness in Human Beings,' the kernel of which consists in certain very happily chosen passages from those writers. But to him, since he was not simply a lay moralist but a philosopher, the teachings of that essay were merely one practical application of a more general way of thinking. He himself took pains in the preface to the volume containing the essay to insist upon the larger implications of the ideas expressed in it:

> The address 'On a Certain Blindness in Human Beings' . . . is more than the mere piece of sentimentalism which it may seem to some readers. It connects itself with a definite view of the world and of our moral relations to the same, . . . I mean the pluralistic or individualistic philosophy. According to that philosophy, the truth is too great for any one actual mind, even though that mind be dubbed 'the Absolute,' to know the whole of it. . . . There is no point of view absolutely public and universal. Private and incommunicable perceptions always remain over, and the worst of it is that those who look at them only from the outside never know *where*.

In this passage is manifest the very process of transition in James's thought from the intense feeling for the individual and the particular characteristic of the innermost temper of his mind to the generalization and formulation of that feeling in a metaphysical doctrine. On the practical side—to dwell for a moment longer upon that aspect of the pluralistic spirit—the outcome of this characteristic of James's was that, whenever occasion arose, he always stood as the champion of a 'democratic respect for the sacredness of individuality' and of 'the outward tolerance of whatever is not itself intolerant.' To these phrases, now become somewhat empty and ineffective through much vain repetition, he sought to restore 'a passionate inner meaning.' It was almost inevitable that one of this temper, in facing the especially difficult contemporary casuistical problem of the treatment of the backward by the 'civilized' races, should be a stout anti-imperialist. He once exclaimed in a certain amazed impatience over the inability of most 'Anglo-Saxons' to see that these 'new-caught, sullen peoples' 'really had insides of their own.' The consideration from which he could himself never escape was that all manner of individuated entities—races, persons, ideas, types of religious experience—have 'insides of their own' never wholly to be identified with any aspect which they may present on the outside; that 'no one elementary bit of reality is eclipsed from the next bit's point of view, if only we take reality sensibly and in small enough pulses.'

There are, however, it is worth-while to note, certain tendencies in modern thought, two or three different phases of individualism, to which these pluralistic preconceptions of James's might seem to point, but into which they did not in fact carry him. The special differentiae of his own sort of 'individualistic philosophy' ought not to be overlooked. One familiar type of pluralism in recent philosophy, for example, has been the monadism, or 'multi-personal idealism,' represented by such writers as Renouvier, Thomas Davidson, Mr. Sturt, Professor Howison, and, in his earlier phase, Mr. E. D. Fawcett. These men, too, may be said to have developed the spirit of democracy into a metaphysics; for them also there is no single center of reality that is 'absolutely public and universal,' and 'the facts and truths of life need many cognizers to take them in.' But the metaphysics of James can hardly be described as a monadology. The motives which lead to that sort of pluralism he did not, for the most part, strongly feel; and the pluralistic inclinations which he did feel did not seem to him to lead to just that sort of pluralism. The independence of the action of each human self from all external causation, its 'cut-off' character and its consequent personal responsibility, an idea which has, for example, presented itself to Howison very forcibly, was to James hardly a congenial idea. This was partly because his pluralism was combined in his mind with another tendency yet to be mentioned, his 'temporalism.' He was, if I may so put it, even more essentially a 'length-wise' than a 'cross-wise' pluralist; it was primarily and more frequently the uniqueness and the creative efficacy of the passing phases in each flowing stream of consciousness that he had in mind, rather than the timeless discreteness and inaccessibility to external influences of any windowless monads.[1] Discreteness, indeed, was not a category under which it was easy for his mind to represent any concrete entity; though he was, as has been said, peculiarly ready to recognize qualitative diversity and a certain incommensurability in things, he was also prone to think of them as imperceptibly passing into one another and in constant interplay with one another, as somehow immersed, though never dissolved, in a larger stream of being from which a constant endosmosis takes place. How far this combination of a special sensitiveness to the unique individuating differences of things with a disposition (shown in a predilection for metaphors drawn from the properties of fluids) to think in terms of a continuum, led to actual contradiction in James's philosophy, I do not here wish to discuss; but it was, I think, the combination distinctive of his personal type of pluralism.

Just this combination, however, might perhaps have been expected to produce certain other tendencies of thought in James, to which, once more, he did not in any exceptional degree incline. On the side of his appreciative attitudes, for example, his moral and aesthetic likings and dislikings, it might have led to that exaggeration of catholicity in sympathy and admiration which, as it showed itself in a Whitman, amounted to virtual indifferentism, to the professed feeling that each aspect and fragment of reality, as it happens to turn up, is as good as any other—and a bit better; or that, if any choice at all is to be made, the preference must always go to mere bigness or mere intensity of emotion. This 'democratic' spirit toward the diverse elements of human life, as they are manifested in one's self or in others, this doctrine of the intrinsic equality of all the phases of existence is, unless offset by other tendencies, hardly likely to promote the fighter's temper or the reformer's zeal. But from this large, loose, and sprawling attitude of unselective acceptance of things, James was delivered by certain complementary features of his temperament. He had, indeed, as has been sufficiently remarked, an extraordinarily wide capacity for appreciation and sympathy; his first impulse, in the presence of a novel type of fact or person, was to seek to understand and to admire. But he had also a somewhat choleric nature. He had not many, but he had a few strong, temperamental aversions and disgusts; Plato's 'spirited part of the soul' was well-developed in him. His tolerance—as a phrase I have already quoted from him intimates—did not extend to the toleration of intolerance; anything that

1. It is perhaps proper to mention that, in a letter to the writer, James himself once adopted his antithesis: 'I would also call myself a length-wise pluralist.'

savored of cruelty, overbearance, narrowness, awoke in him a hot indignation; for soft and relaxed ways of thinking and ways of living he had a keen dislike; and for overblown intellectual pretense and the spiritual emptiness of a great part of the world's respectabilities he had a penetrating vision and a humorous contempt. Various and intense as was his response to the manifold interestingness of existence, great as was his power to find value in things commonly unconsidered or despised, life presented itself to him, in the last analysis, in a dualistic, a Manichaean, guise—as a field of combat rather than as merely a source for the promiscuous enrichment of experience or an object of undiscriminating aesthetic appreciation. With all the exceptional breadth and geniality of his nature, there remained a touch of Puritan austerity in him. He had a temperamental need of a certain hardness and opposition in his environment. The world he found a place in which a man is imperatively called upon to take sides.

Nor is there in this any real incongruity with that catholic sense for the distinctive quality of each particular phase of reality which was his dominant characteristic. The dualistic aspect, the fighting edge in James's view of life was rather an evidence of his power of recognizing real differences. For the very essence of the inwardness of certain items of existence is their antagonism to certain other items. To accept and affirm all reality and call it good is after all to deny some parts of it, for the inner meaning of some parts lies in their negations. To sympathize equally with powers bent upon the destruction of one another, to be on the side of both Ormuzd and Ahriman, to be one with the red slayer and the slain is in reality to fail to understand the 'inside' aspect of either. The attempt to harmonize such opposites can commend itself only to minds whose vision for the inner distinctiveness of other individual existences has become at least a little blurred through the habit of thinking of things in lumps, who rise so easily to 'higher points of view' that they quite forget that the higher point never truly reveals the observed object's situation as it appears at the object's own level. James's position with respect to the problem of evil was thus a manifestation of that same trait of his nature which was also the source of his pluralistic tendencies. At least some evils—the sufferings of animals, for example, or certain monstrosities of moral perversion—seemed to him simply intrinsically and irreducibly bad. They may be triumphed over, they may even be made instrumental to good; but the badness that was in them can never be *aufgehoben,* nullified, or even perfectly compensated. Readers of *The Varieties of Religious Experience* must recall the nightmare-like horror of a passage in which James's extraordinary sense for the reality of the individual is turned upon this aspect of the world:

> Our civilization is founded upon the shambles, and every individual existence goes out in a lonely spasm of helpless agony. If you protest, my friend, wait until you arrive there yourself! To believe in the carnivorous reptiles of geologic time is hard for our imaginations,—they seem too much like mere museum specimens. Yet there is no tooth in any one of those museum-skulls that did not daily through long years of the foretime hold fast to the body struggling in despair of some living victim. Forms of horror just as dreadful to their victims, if on a smaller spatial scale, fill the world about us today. Here on our hearths and in our gardens the infernal cat plays with the panting mouse, or holds the hot bird fluttering in her jaws. Crocodiles and rattlesnakes and pythons are at this moment vessels of life as real as we are; their loathsome existence fills every minute of every day that drags its length along; and whenever they or other wild beasts clutch their living prey, the deadly horror which an agitated melancholiac feels is the literally right reaction on the situation.

This, as a reading of animal psychology, is perhaps somewhat overdrawn; but the passage is singularly typical of the vividness in James of what a psychologist might call the ejective imagination. When things of this sort are once seen as palpitating, individuated facts there is nothing to be done, James wrote in one of his early essays, but to cry out against all such aspects of reality Carlyle's 'Everlasting No.' James has sometimes been compared to Emerson, chiefly for the reason that the two have been the most influential American writers on philosophical themes, and the only two who have had a wide international hearing. But in one important respect James is the antithesis to Emerson. That bland disregard for 'those unconcerning things, matters of fact,' which has been said to be the root of Emerson's optimism, was impossible to a man with James's type of vision. And since this pleasant Emersonian nearsightedness has become in certain quarters a contagious and a noxious spiritual disease, it is fortunate that from the original center of that infection so potent a corrective has of late been dispensed. James was, to be sure, no pessimist; and the sort of utterance that I have last quoted was never the last word with him. But it expressed a side of the real world which he was convinced was not to be denied nor rationalized away. And the universe could therefore never appear to him, in any final reckoning, as wholly good or as rational through-and-through, but rather as of a mixed character, and above all, of a character largely yet to be formed. That process of formation involved, to his mind, purgation and elimination as well as enlargement and enrichment. And both results depended for their realization in great, perhaps in a decisive, measure upon the present and future loyalty of human agents to the not-yet-attained ideals which they mysteriously find within themselves, to 'the demands which the self of one day makes on the self of another,' to the 'imperative goods' whose 'nature it is to be cruel to their rivals.'

These last considerations, however, already bring to mind a second (not wholly separate) characteristic trait of James's personal mode of apprehension of reality—the only other such characteristic which it will be possible to consider here.[2] He was one of those in our day who have most fully and clearly realized that the primary peculiarity of conscious experience is its flowing temporally successive character; that this ('time of inner experience') is a unique *quality* of existence, not to be reduced to anything else nor described in terms of anything else; and that no philosophy can be adequate which virtually ignores (as most of the historic philosophers have ignored)

2. It would have been worth-while, if space had permitted, to note the influence of James's 'particularistic' sort of intellectual vision in some of his more special and technical metaphysical doctrines, especially in his earlier view (which, for reasons briefly indicated later in this paper, he eventually abandoned) of the impossibility of 'compounding' states of consciousness, and in his logical theory of the 'externality of relations' which seems to have had an important part in the development of the 'new realism.' There was a third strain in James's thought—less potent, yet significant—which should at least be mentioned: the nominalistic and simplifying temper, the desire to translate abstractions into 'concrete particulars of somebody's experience,' the demand for the rigorous elimination of all obscure and redundant notions. On one side of him, James continued the succession of the great British nominalistic empiricists, the prophets of the law of intellectual parsimony, such as William of Ockham, Berkeley, Hume. In certain moods of his reflection he became, incongruously, very much what the French call an *esprit simpliste.* Thus he seeks to reduce the concepts of 'God,' 'freedom' and 'immortality' to their 'positive experienceable operation' and so finds that 'they all mean the same thing, *viz.*, the presence of "promise" in the world.' This trait is not strictly contradictory to James's dominant characteristic; it is rather the negative side of the same sense for concrete, particularized reality. Yet it tended, unquestionably, to work against the pluralistic spirit; for it naturally predisposes to the nullification of real differences and the too speedy reduction of multiplicity to unity. James's 'particularism' gave birth to two children, the pluralistic and the nominalistic tendency; and these two sometimes came to be at variance in his mind.

the primacy of the temporal quality of experience as a starting point for the interpretation of the nature of reality and the meaning of truth. Readers of James's earliest philosophical essays must already have seen what aspect of human existence, what sort of moment in life, presented itself to him as the central and illuminating fact, the point at which we have reason to suppose that the inner nature of reality is most directly revealed to us. This is the moment in which a man looks before and after, faces the future *as* future, and knows that that future, as yet a field of alternative possibilities, is to be defined and shaped, that certain of those alternatives are to be forever shut out from real existence by the decision now in process of forming itself in his mind. Now, just as the dominant methods and preoccupations of both science and philosophy have tended to lead thought away from the particular to the generalized, so they have tended to lead thought away from the truly temporal—from the uniqueness of the unprecedented and unrepeatable single moment in the time-flow—to fix it upon the eternal or the immutable or the identically recurrent. Logic has been interested in changeless concepts, metaphysics in the absolute and eternal, science in unvarying laws, in qualitatively immutable 'primary' properties of bodies, in quantitatively constant sums of matter and energy, in 'causes' conceived as capable of presenting themselves as the 'same' over and over again in perfect indifference to mere diversities of date as such. Except by certain idealistic metaphysicians, the 'reality' of time has not been denied; but most that makes up the actual temporality of time and its significance in our inner experience has been commonly disregarded not only by philosophy and science, but even by theology and religion. James's vision of the distinctiveness and the validity of the 'particular' point of view was complemented by—or rather implied—an equally keen sense of the validity and the distinctiveness of the temporal point of view. And his task as a philosopher was that of stirring up his contemporaries to do justice to these two primary yet neglected aspects of existence.

EDWIN DILLER STARBUCK

(1866–1947)

Edwin Starbuck was born in Bridgeport, Indiana, attended Indiana University (1890–93), Harvard University (1893–94), and in 1895 earned a master's degree from the Harvard Divinity School. He continued graduate work at Clark University, earning a doctorate in 1897. His first position was as assistant professor of education at Stanford, where he taught from 1897 to 1904, followed by a year of study in Zurich, Switzerland. He later taught philosophy at the State University of Iowa and the University of Southern California.

Starbuck's interest in the experience of conversion led him to devise a questionnaire about religious practices that he circulated throughout the Harvard community. At first James was skeptical about the project, believing, he wrote, that the 'question-circular method of collecting information had already, in America, reached the proportions of an incipient nuisance in psychological and pedagogical matters.' He suspected, furthermore, that the responses would 'show a purely conventional content' rather than sincerity or originality.[1] James soon discovered, however, that Starbuck's method produced fascinating results.

From 'a barrelful and two large cartons of raw data,' Starbuck drew material for his first book, *The Psychology of Religion: An Empirical Study of the Growth of Religious Consciousness* (1899), for which James wrote a preface. He then lent to James this prodigious collection of data for use in writing the Gifford Lectures, later published as *The Varieties of Religious Experience.* Starbuck's sources provided a generous number of anecdotes for James, who cites this material frequently throughout his text.

Although focusing on similar questions, the two men had distinctly different goals. Starbuck, as James put it, aimed 'to disengage the general from the specific and local . . . , and to reduce the reports to their most universal psychological value.'[2] According to James, Starbuck concluded that conversion 'is in its essence a normal adolescent phenomenon, incidental to the passage from the child's small universe to the wider intellectual and spiritual life of maturity.'[3] James, on the other hand, wanted to expand the boundaries of the ways in which we define religious experiences by presenting countless quirky, idiosyncratic testimonies rather than focusing on conversions of 'very commonplace persons, kept true to a pre-appointed type by instruction, appeal, and example.'[4] James found Starbuck's approach too 'schematic,' because it did not explore more imaginatively subconscious forces and mystical experiences.[5]

When James's book was published in 1903, Starbuck, predictably, deemed it hyperbolic: James, he believed, emphasized extreme examples of religious practices. While Starbuck asked how religion fulfilled rational needs, James allowed for the existence of potent mystical forces. 'I think,' James wrote to Starbuck, 'that the fixed point with me is the conviction that our "rational" consciousness touches but a portion of the real universe and that our life is fed by the "mystical" region as well. I have no mystical experience of my own,' he admitted, 'but just enough of the germ of mysticism in me to recognize the region from which their voice comes when I hear it.'[6]

Although James acknowledged that other readers also took exception to the kinds of cases he reported in *Varieties*, he insisted that 'it would never do to study the passion of love on examples of ordinary liking or friendly affection, or that of homicidal pugnacity on examples of our ordinary impatiences with our kind. So here it must be that the extreme examples let us more deeply into the secrets of the religious life, explain why the tamer ones value their religion so much, tame though it be, because it is so continuous with a so much acuter ideal.'[7]

Although James publicly praised Starbuck for his application of scientific method to questions of religion, privately he voiced reservations. Writing to his friend James Cattell in 1903, James admitted, 'Starbuck I can't place—I think his book on conversion to be an excellent contribution to the science of human nature, but it is not homogeneous enough with other men's work to be comparable.'[8] Certainly Starbuck's book, with its thirty-two tables and fourteen graphs, is not homogenous with any study of religion by William James.

NOTES

1. Preface to Starbuck's *Psychology of Religion*, repr. in James, *Essays in Religion and Morality*, ed. McDermott, 102.
2. WJ, *Essays in Religion and Morality*, 103.
3. WJ, *The Varieties of Religious Experience*, 165.
4. WJ, *The Varieties of Religious Experience*, 165.
5. WJ, *The Varieties of Religious Experience*, 172.
6. WJ to Edwin Starbuck. *Letters* 2:210 (24 August 1904).
7. WJ to Edwin Starbuck. *Letters* 2:209 (24 August 1904).
8. WJ to James Cattell. Scott, 313 (10 June 1903).

A Student's Impressions of James in the Middle '90s

Three of the lures for my selection of Harvard University for graduate study were C. C. Everett, Dean of the Divinity School, who was lecturing on the Philosophy of Religion; William James, who wrote and lived a psychology surcharged with cultural and spiritual fineness; and Hugo Münsterberg, the highly trained experimental psychologist whom James had induced Harvard to steal from Freiburg. My work, I knew, was to be in the empirical, including the experimental, approach to the study of religion. I had collected bulletins and written letters all about the scholastic landscape to find the right place to camp for advanced study. What an array! The catalogue from P—University said, in effect, 'this course is to show that the Christian Religion is and all other religions are not capable of psychological justification'!

On the occasion of the opening lecture period of the first semester, Professor James appeared, almost late, moved smoothly and unobtrusively up the middle aisle to the slightly elevated platform, placed a small bundle of books from his arm on the desk, paused, gave the class a split second of a friendly glance, lifted the index finger of his right hand above the forehead as if it were the symbol of a new idea and remarked, 'Oh, excuse me, I forgot something.' A minute or two following the time signal he returned, seated himself serenely at his desk and began, not lecturing to us or at us, but discussing *with* us, some of the men and movements in psychology. He showed two or three significant recent books; we should help decide if we wished to use a text and, if so, which it should be.

His 'lectures' were always vitalizing. No studied rhetoric. Always happy turns of intriguing phrases, a glow of warmth and meaning. Never a moment wasted on shop-made humor. We were always thinking *together.*

One day he ventured a diagram on the blackboard to clear up some notions we had stumbled into about relations existing between 'selfhood,' 'cognition,' 'feeling of value,' 'affectors' and 'effectors.' There were circles or lines symbolizing each of these and other states and processes. In going back over some of it he got a little ensnared in the entanglements. He backed away, cocked his head to one side and remarked, 'What the deuce have we got here anyhow!' With friendly smiles and a chuckle the members of the group helped to disentangle the snarl and moved together for several strides along the psychological highway, having a good time at a bit of road building into the bargain. That sort of 'teaching' made us like the subject and love the instructor.

James' friendly informality was rooted in his inherent tactfulness. Absorbing the social formalities and conventions into a congenial mental weather, he would, for instance, make an appointment with a student for a personal conference over some 'problem' at his house at, say, eleven or five o'clock, and make that device a way of inveigling him into participating in the gracious hospitality of a perfect home. He was the consummate artist at living.

James had an uncanny way of coming to know us individually. One day before class he whispered to me the inquiry whether I would mind stopping for a minute after the recitation. After the decks were cleared, he pulled from his inner pocket a questionnaire sheet that had come into his hands, printed closely front and back, asking with much incisiveness about religious upbringing, beliefs and attitudes, how the person got that way, the lines of growth from childhood to maturity, the what and when of periodicities, if any, and other items. 'This sheet,' he said, 'bears your signature. Did you perpetrate it?' 'Guilty,' I confessed. 'But this is New England,' he observed, 'and people here will not reply to an inquisitional document of that sort.' 'But they are already doing so,' I replied. 'How do you capture or captivate them?' he persisted. 'I wheedle them; I explain that this is the beginning of a new science in the world—the psychology of religion, and we must have the *facts*. Failing in this approach, my favorite technique, since I am a husky, is to throw the victim flat on the floor or lawn, sit on his chest and extort a solemn promise to confess everything.' James graciously responded with merriment to the cheap humor and remarked that he would like, if he might keep the document, to suggest a more effective way of obtaining the desired data.

Three or four days later we were approaching on opposite sides of the wide street near Sanders Theatre. I saluted. He waved. We met exactly on the street-car lines in the middle of the street. He pulled from his pocket that self-same questionnaire, subscribed with the legend: 'This study is done with the approval of C. C. Everett, Dean of the School of Religion of Harvard University, Alexander MacKenzie, Pastor of the First Congregational Church of Cambridge, Mass., and William James, Professor of Psychology, Harvard University.' I braced myself and stood the shock, while hunting vainly for fitting words of appreciation. 'But you mayn't do that,' I protested; 'this is freak stuff and you have a reputation to defend.' He waved the objection aside playfully. That was a chronic attitude of James toward every student.

This attempt to unearth the raw data of the inner life caused repercussions both favorably and vexatiously at home and abroad. Professor J. Estlin Carpenter of Oxford, amongst a few others, tried to render assistance by securing confessions in England. Professor Burton of Smith College sought to collect religious life histories from his students. One of them sent the document to her father who was a member of the faculty at Yale. He wrote, 'If my daughter is to be exposed to that kind of spiritual vivisection, I shall immediately take her from the College.' In fighting the way through the barrage of religious transcendentalisms and negativisms, it was James' influence and continual thoughtfulness that helped most of all.

James was always more than fair-minded. A half dozen years after the inquisitional episodes hinted above he wrote me at Stanford University, where, as a member of the faculty under the tutelage of another omnivorous mind, I was carrying on in the study of religious experiences. He had been invited to give the Gifford Lectures at Edinburgh and was tempted to call the series, 'The Varieties of Religious Experience.' Had I any unused data from which he might draw? It was one of the most genuine pleasures of my life to be able to express to him a barrelful and two large cartons of raw data. He made use of many a skit and, contrary to specific instructions but true to his nature, he never failed to make acknowledgments.

James was faithful to significant fact in its minuteness as well as to widening Truth with its reach. He is a blind psychologist who is not something of a philosopher and a fatuous philosopher who is not infinitely circumspect about the concrete data of experience; it must never be forgotten that James set up the first psychological laboratory in America at Harvard, although in choosing between the specificities and the humanities of psychology he later abandoned it.

William James, a name of sacred memory to us all. James, humanly responsive and spiritually sensitive. The friend of perhaps every pupil who came under his tutelage. It is a sober and cherished privilege today to hold in tender recollection William James, in whose presence the haughty were reduced to simplicity, the hungry were fed, and the eager and earnest enjoyed constantly deeper integrations and more alluring vistas.

JOSEPHINE CLARA GOLDMARK

(1877–1950)

Josephine Goldmark and her sister Pauline (1874–1962) met James in the summer of 1895, when their friend Dickinson S. Miller brought him to their summer home in Keene Valley, where James had come to hike. At the time James was fifty-three; Pauline, twenty-one, was about to enter her senior year at Bryn Mawr College, where Josephine also attended. Pauline Goldmark was a spirited, intelligent young woman, and James was captivated by her. A few years later, when Pauline and her other sister Susan were about to embark on a trip to Europe, James wrote to his Oxford friend F. C. S. Schiller to ask him to direct the two travelers to interesting sites. He gave a brief description of Pauline: 'Pauline is a biologist, has done practical philanthropy work among the poor in N. Y., is athletic, a tramper and camper, and lover of nature such as one rarely meets, and withal a perfectly simple, good girl, with a beautiful face—and I fairly dote upon her, and were I younger and "unattached" should probably be deep in love.'[1]

James's letters to Goldmark suggest that he was deep in love. Yet his passion did not threaten his marriage (although Alice James was notably cool toward Pauline), but buoyed his spirits.[2] Pauline's liveliness, her love of nature, and her independence and self-possession made her enormously appealing to James. He thought she would make 'the best wife of any girl I know,'[3] and he wished she could be in Cambridge to serve as a model for his twenty-one-year-old daughter. 'For Peggy's sake I wish you could be "around,"' he wrote to Pauline. 'She is changed beyond all recognition, feels alone in the Universe and needs some model of feminine character to show her in which direction to aspire, Model,—or models! For she will certainly make her own choice. I wish she might choose to be like you.'[4]

In the eighty-five letters to Pauline that have survived, James reported on his work, commented about politics, and cautioned her about her own overwork. But Pauline's commitments would not be moderated. Beginning in her college days and throughout her career, Goldmark was energetically involved in social and political reform, a fact not surprising when one considers her heritage. Her father, Joseph Goldmark, a physician and chemist, was a leading figure in Austria's Revolution of 1848. Forced to flee the country when he was convicted of high treason and complicity in the murder of the Minister of War, he was sentenced to death. Once in the United States Goldmark married Regina Wehle, the daughter of a Prague businessman who had emigrated with his family because of the anti-Semitism and intractable economic problems that followed the incendiary revolutions of 1848 throughout eastern Europe. Among the Goldmarks' ten children, the eldest daughter, Helen, married Felix Adler, founder of the Ethical Culture Society and professor of political and social ethics at Columbia; another daughter, Alice, married jurist Louis Brandeis; the eldest son, Henry, an engineer appointed to the Isthmian Canal Commission in 1906, spent eight years designing and supervising the building of the Panama Canal.

Pauline Goldmark served as secretary of the National Consumers' League, and later was assistant director in the Bureau of Social Research of the Russell Sage Foundation, where she trained investigators and supervised publication of such books as *West Side Studies*, about the youth in the slums of Manhattan, and *The Longshoremen*. In 1907 she initiated the first investigation of canneries in New York State. From 1912 to 1914 she worked with the New York State Factory Investigating Commission to produce reports on labor laws affecting women and on sanitation in factories. During the First World War she served as executive secretary of the Committee on Women in Industry, a part of the Council of National Defense.

Josephine, too, was involved in social reform, as publications secretary of the National Consumers' League and in gathering information for legal briefs for Louis Brandeis in his cases concerning social legislation. Among Josephine's books were *Child Labor Legislation Handbook* (1907), *Fatigue and Efficiency* (1912), and *Impatient Crusader* (published posthumously in 1953), a life of her associate Florence Kelley.

NOTES

1. WJ to F. C. S. Schiller. Scott, 187 (19 May 1899).
2. Saul Rosenzweig offers an interesting examination of James's relationship with Pauline Goldmark in *Freud, Jung, and Hall the King-Maker* (Kirkland, Washington: Hogrefe & Huber, 1992) 182–95.
3. WJ to F. C. S. Schiller. Scott, 198 (11 October 1899).
4. WJ to Pauline Goldmark, 1 August 1902. Houghton.

An Adirondack Friendship

I

'What most horrifies me in life is our brutal ignorance of one another,' once wrote William James to a young correspondent whom he had recently met in the Adirondack woods and with whom he was to continue a friendship never far removed, either in actuality or in retrospect, from that region of virgin forest.

> You will receive this week a little volume from my pen [he continues], of which you are familiar with most of the contents already, so that you need not read them. There is, however, one Essay 'On a Certain Blindness etc.' which I do want you to read, because I care very much indeed for the truth it so inadequately tries, by dint of innumerable quotations, to express, and I like to imagine that you care for it, or will care for it too.

The essay, thus sent to Pauline Goldmark, quotes Whitman, Tolstoy, Jefferies, Wordsworth, Hudson. And the 'truth,' so effectively illustrated, is the preciousness, to each one of us, of our own, particular, inner satisfactions and resources.

Central in the essay and at the heart of this friendship was William James's feeling, passion almost, for the 'peculiar sources of joy' in living close to nature in the literal American sense. Echoes of camping and of what he calls in a later letter the 'truths so communicable under these conditions' fill the beautiful article which he commended to his young friend.

> We of the highly educated classes (so-called) have most of us got far, far away from Nature. . . . We are stuffed with abstract conceptions, and glib verbalities and verbosities; and in the culture of these higher functions, the

peculiar sources of joy connected with our simpler functions often dry up. . . .
The remedy under such conditions is to descend to a more profound and primitive level. . . . Living in the open air and on the ground, the lop-sided beam of the balance slowly rises to the level line. The good of all the artificial schemes and fevers fades and pales; and that of seeing, smelling, tasting, sleeping, and daring and doing with one's body grows and grows. . . .
I am sorry for the boy or girl, or man or woman, who has never been touched by the spell of this mysterious sensorial life with its irrationality, if so you like to call it, but its vigilance and its supreme felicity.

Such supreme felicity, such rejuvenating powers of wild nature, William James had long since found in Keene Valley, in the heart of the Adirondack Mountains, when in 1895 he first met Pauline Goldmark there. The Valley is, indeed, not infrequently mentioned in his published Letters. To his brother Henry, for instance, he writes in 1906:—

You missed it, when here, in not getting to Keene Valley, where I have just been, and of which the sylvan beauty, especially by moonlight, is probably unlike aught that Europe has to show. Imperishable freshness! . . .

Even earlier he writes to Mrs. Henry Whitman, in the inimitable style which flashes in the shortest note or postcard, excusing himself from a proposed visit to her at Beverly:—

Just reviving from the addled and corrupted condition in which the Cambridge year has left me; just at the portals of that Adirondack wilderness for the breath of which I have sighed for years, unable to escape the cares of domesticity and get there; just about to get a little health into me, a little simplification and solidification and purification and sanification—things that will never come again if this one chance be lost; just filled to satiety with all the simpering conventions and vacuous excitements of so-called civilization; hungering for their opposite, the smell of the spruce, the feel of the moss, the sound of the cataract, the bath in its waters, the divine outlook from the cliff or hill-top over the unbroken forest—oh, Madam, Madam! do you know what medicinal things you ask me to give up? . . . I wish that you also aspired to the wilderness. There are some nooks and summits in that Adirondack region where one can really 'recline on one's divine composure' and, as long as one stays up there, seem for a while to enjoy one's birth-right of freedom and relief from every fever and falsity.

It was natural that in writing to Pauline Goldmark—whom, especially in the early years, it pleased him to identify with the vigor of youth and the mountain tops—Keene Valley, 'the blessed spot,' should be more often mentioned than to other correspondents. She was at the time a girl of twenty-one, in her last year at Bryn Mawr. Her summers since early childhood had been spent in the woods and mountains of that Adirondack region. The primeval forest, uncut, uncleared; its pristine freshness; delight in these wild aspects of nature as compared with the trimmer and mellower European landscapes of other summers—all this was implicit in their friendship.

The theme is rarely elaborated, taken for granted rather, often caught in a phrase or a paragraph, a persistent and deep-lying sentiment. She was, as it were, the symbol of a mood, a region, a way of life.

'But you, my dear young friend,' he writes early in their friendship, 'are such an up-at-sunrise, out-of-door, and mountain-top kind of a girl, that (knowing you in no other capacity and ignorant of all the hidden selfishnesses and sinister recesses of your character indoors) I give you credit for every conceivable sort of magnanimity, generosity and freedom. Ah, Pauline, don't ever let me be disappointed!'

Indeed, there is scarcely a letter written to her from any place during the fifteen years until his death in 1910 which does not have some reference to the Valley or the out-of-doors. 'Rather than be writing of Edinburgh,' he ends an exquisite account of the old city, 'I would be sitting or lying on any summit whatever in the neighborhood of K.V., communing with your adjacent soul.' Or again in a note from the Harvard Club in New York:—

> I go back to Boston in an hour, having been here 48 hours on *other* business and not seen you. I expected to when *I* left, if only for a minute, but I'm so 'rushed' and breathless that I'm ashamed to appear in your presence. You probably find those interviews unsatisfactory yourself.
>
> Ach, könni' ich mich neiderlegen
> Weit in den tiefsten Wald
>
> for about 6 hours of steady talk, with the world faded to immeasurable distance—'t would be different. As it is, I must wait.

Or on another occasion, near the end of his life:—

> Your piece of cardboard, dearest Pauline, which arrived at noon, when your full presence was looked for, was a sad substitute. But no matter, I'm re-

signed in these days to everything! I long to see you, but not cooped up in a room, on a hill or in a forest rather.

The Keene Valley of these letters is a narrow valley some six miles long, lying about twenty-five miles west of Lake Champlain in the northern part of New York State. The special grace of the Adirondacks derives from their long geologic past. Among the oldest mountains of the whole earth, they have been worn down through time into the lovely curves and graceful outlines which give them their special character.

Viewed from the little hill clearing at the southern end of Keene Valley, long known as 'Beede's,' low converging ranges of blue distance hem in the Valley to the north; on the east rises the Giant-of-the-Valley, broad-based and broad of summit, whose steep spruce and balsam heights are scarred by broad rock slides. The other high peaks mentioned in the letters—Gothics, Haystack, Marcy, and others—are clustered to the southwest, forming a sky line, seen from any eminence, of majestic grace. A large area has here been preserved as virgin forest to this day.

II

It was in the late summer of 1895 that our common friend Dickinson Miller first brought Mr. James to our summer home at 'Beede's,' a half mile from the Putnam-Bowditch shanty of which Mr. James was part owner. Mr. James's own acquaintance with this region was of an earlier date, during the late seventies. His son, Henry James, has described his father's first connection with the Valley.

Where the Ausable Club's picturesque golf-course is now laid out, the fields of Smith Beede's farm then surrounded his primitive, white-painted hotel. Half a mile to the eastward, in a patch of rocky pasture beside Giant Brook, stood the original Beede farmhouse, and this Henry P. Bowditch, Charles and James Putnam, and William James had bought for a few hundred dollars (subject to Beede's cautious proviso in the deed that 'the purchasers are to keep no boarders'). They had adapted the little story-and-a-half dwelling to their own purposes and converted its surrounding sheds and pens into habitable shanties of the simplest kind. So they established a sort of camp, with the mountains for their climbing, the brook to bathe in, and the primeval forest fragrant about them.

William James's love of the outdoors was compounded of many strains. Mountain climbing itself—its sheer exhilaration, the conquest of summits and the outlook from great heights—had for him its thrilling appeal.

'To these youngsters, as to me long ago, and to you to-day, the rapture of the connexion with these hills is partly made of the sense of future power over them and their like,' he wrote to Pauline in 1907, when he was obliged to confine his walking to the lower ranges.

In a memorial sketch of his life, Dr. James Putnam recalls Mr. James's unusual grace and lightness of foot in climbing.

> As a walker, he used to be among the foremost, in the earlier years, and it was a pleasure to watch his lithe and graceful figure as he moved rapidly up the steep trails or stretched himself on the slope of a rock, his arms under his head, for resting. He had the peculiarity, in climbing, of raising himself largely with the foot that was lowermost, instead of planting the other and drawing himself up by it, as is so common. This is a slight thing, but it was an element counting for elasticity and grace.
>
> There were periods when he took the longest walks and climbs, but after a time he felt that very vigorous exertion did not agree with him; and this belief, combined with his love of talk with some congenial person on some congenial subject, usually kept him back from the vanguard and rather at the rear of the long line, where he could walk slowly if he liked and find the chance to pause from time to time in order to enjoy and characterize in rich terms the splendid beauty of the steep forest-clad slopes, with the sun streaming through the thick foliage and into the islets between the tall trees.

In such surroundings, the thing most treasured was not only the escape of the scholar and teacher from the winter's routine, nor even the greater simplification of living such as that, for instance, which Mr. James enjoyed during his spring on a California campus and celebrated in letters home. It was something, as has been intimated, which satisfied a deeper, primal need. It was something which comes from life in the wilderness, sleeping upon the ground, close to nature and all earth forces; from the joy of the senses in sun and shade, water and wind, smell of wood smoke and forest air; a return to more primitive reactions and responses of our human nature; upwellings from the great Unconscious on which our lives are based.

> Whoso walks in solitude
> And inhabiteth the wood,

Choosing light, wave, rock and bird . . .
Into that forester shall pass,
From these companions power and grace.
Clean shall he be, without, within,

wrote Emerson, who himself had known and camped on a lakeside in the Adirondacks, in his day.

On him the light of star and moon
Shall fall with purer radiance down.

An 'organic-feeling need' is the phrase repeatedly used by William James of his deep-seated longing for the woods, as when, for instance, he writes from Nauheim to Miss Fanny Morse, in July 1901:—

> What I *crave* most is some wild American country. It is a curious organic-feeling need. One's social relations with European landscape are entirely different, everything being so fenced or planted that you can't lie down and sprawl. . . . Thank heaven that our nature is so much less 'redeemed'!

In another letter from Europe, when ill and in exile, he touches on this deep undercurrent of feeling for the spiritual values in nature:—

> Scenery seems to wear in one's consciousness better than any other element in life. In this year of much solemn and idle meditation, I have often been surprised to find what a predominant part in my own spiritual experience it has played, and how it stands out as almost the only thing the memory of which I should like to carry over with me beyond the veil, unamended and unaltered. From the midst of everything else, almost, *surgit amari aliquid;* but From the midst of everything else, almost, *surgit amari aliquid;* but from the days in the open air, never any bitter whiff, save that they are gone forever.

III

Even more significant and intense was the spiritual import of a night spent under the stars of which Mr. James left a unique account. It was a night spent near the summit of Mount Marcy, highest of the Adirondack peaks. He had bidden Pauline and a small party with her to meet him there, himself ascending from the Adirondack Lodge, a large log house isolated in the forest on the other side of the mountain.

From the Lodge, in June 1896, he writes to Pauline:—

> This place is a regular sanctuary. I came up fearfully tired cerebrally, but have never felt such a sense of peace and of safety since I was born.
>
> I assume that you are not in Europe and I hope that you are not at Woods Hole. I have been here for four days past; and basking in the moon's rays on the Observatory last night, the brilliant idea struck me of writing to ask whether you do not think it would be the extremity of 'niceness' before the said moon has entirely ceased, to 'organize a party,' including the fair Josephine, and come up to the Marcy Camp, where I should meet you, and, after passing the night, all of us descend hither for as long as might seem pleasant, you and your sister being my guests, and then go out to Keene Valley by the trail, or rather by the lumber road which I am sorry to hear has been put through. Are not your brothers with you? F. Adler I suppose to be in Europe. But can't Waldo come? Or is he in examination agonies as my poor Billy is? Bring anyone you can!

The meeting place thus set was known as 'Panther Gorge,' where a small Adirondack camp of rough-hewn logs had been built, open in front, and carpeted with balsam boughs on which perhaps a half-dozen persons might stretch out for the night. A little brook flowed down beside the camp, which overlooked the densely wooded gorge. But Mr. James could not spend the night under even this slight cover. In one of the most beautiful characterizations of places or moods from his pen, he subsequently described to Mrs. James what he calls 'one of the most memorable of all my memorable experiences.'

> The guide had got a magnificent provision of firewood, the sky swept itself clear of every trace of cloud or vapor, the wind entirely ceased, so that the fire-smoke rose straight up to heaven. The temperature was perfect either inside or outside the cabin, the moon rose and hung above the scene before midnight, leaving only a few of the larger stars visible, and I got into a state of spiritual alertness of the most vital description. The influences of Nature, the wholesomeness of the people around me, especially the good Pauline, the thought of you and the children, dear Harry on the wave, the problem of the Edinburgh lectures, all fermented within me till it became a regular *Walpurgis*

> *Nacht.* I spent a good deal of it in the woods; where the streaming moonlight lit up things in a magical checkered play, and it seemed as if the Gods of all the nature-mythologies were holding an indescribable meeting in my breast with the moral Gods of the inner life. . . . The intense significance of some sort, of the whole scene, if one could only *tell* the significance; the intense inhuman remoteness of its inner life, and yet the intense *appeal* of it; its everlasting freshness and its immemorial antiquity and decay; its utter Americanism and every sort of patriotic suggestiveness, and you and my relation to you part and parcel of it all, and beaten up with it, so that memory and sensation all whirled inexplicably together; it was indeed worth coming for, and worth repeating, year by year, if repetition could only procure what in its nature I suppose must be all unplanned for and unexpected. It was one of the happiest lonesome nights of my existence, and I understand now what a poet is.

The next day the party returned to the clearing over the summits, by what is still known as the 'Range' trail.

> We plunged down Marcy, and up Basin Mountain [continues Mr. James], led by C. Goldmark, who had, with Mr. White, blazed a trail the year before;[1] then down again, away down, and up the Gothics, not counting a third down-and-up over an interesting spur. It was the steepest sort of work, and, as one looked from the summits, seemed sheer impossible, but the girls kept up splendidly, and were all fresher than I. It was true that they had slept like logs all night, whereas I was 'on my nerves.' I lost my Norfolk jacket, at the last third of the course—high time to say goodbye to that possession—and staggered up to the Putnams' to find Hatty Shaw [the housekeeper] taking me for a tramp. Not a soul was there, but everything spotless and ready for the arrival today. I got a bath at Bowditch's bathhouse, slept in my old room and slept soundly and well, and save for the unwashable staining of my hands and a certain stiffness in my thighs, am entirely rested and well. But I don't believe in keeping it up too long, and at the Willey House will lead a comparatively sedentary life, and cultivate sleep, if I can. . . .

IV

The physical exertion of this trip proved too much for Mr. James, and resulted in a heart strain, writes his son, 'though not great enough seriously

1 That is, there was here no path to follow, only 'blazes' on the trees.—AUTHOR

to curtail his activities if he had given heed to his general condition and avoided straining himself again.'

Unfortunately, in the following June of 1899, after 'some slow walks which seemed to do me no harm at all,' he writes Pauline, he 'drifted one day up to the top of Marcy,' and then had the bad fortune to miss the short trail down, a mistake which 'converted what would have been a three-hours' downward saunter into a seven-hours' scramble. This did me no good—quite the contrary; so I have come to Nauheim just in time.'

In the two following years of enforced rest abroad, the woods hold their supremacy of charm in retrospect, as these sentences from a letter of January 1900 show:—

> Don't commiserate me or think it necessary to indulge in condolences when you write; for to such completion—if not worse—must we all come at last, and I've had a happy life of it so far. But I shall never see Keene Valley again; and all the more precious are its memories.

Sometimes during this period, it is true, the letters are in a lower key, as in a postcard from Nauheim later in the same year:—

> *Deux mots de toi m'ont fait le roi du monde,* which is as much as to say that I have profoundly enjoyed your letter with its expressions of kindness, and its breath of health and life, wafted from another world. This is only to acknowledge its reception, for I am too much 'out of it' to enthusiastically write letters nowadays, least of all to the conquering young and well, of whom you are always my chief example. 'I to the night of time decline, you rise into the morn!' I've actually taken to a bath chair! I always used to think, when I met anyone in a bath chair, that they were born so and did it by nature. I now know better.

And again, the same month, on receipt of a balsam pillow sent to him from the Valley, in the same vein:—

> Bad Nauheim, Sept. 29, 1900
>
> Last night a notice came of a package from 'Goldmark' awaiting me at the Custom House.—'What do you suppose it can be?' said A. H. J. 'I bet it's a balsam pillow,' replied I, and such, sure enough, it proved to be, when she went for it this morning. The Custom House people thought at first it might

be a way of smuggling tea. Then they were doubtful whether to enter it under the class 'pillows,' or the class 'perfumery.' At last 'pillows' was chosen, and a duty paid of 25 pfennigs. What a happy thought it was of yours, and what a delicious reminder of other scenes of happiness! I take for granted that your own hands culled the needles. I wish I could make some analogous return, but such things have no analogue.

And a few days later:—

Nauheim, Oct. 2 (1900)

It is pleasant to know where the balsam came from and to think I got remembered on the Gothics. . . . The delicious golden weather continues—'sublime in the sky swings the sun of September,' and the paths of this exquisite park, which I wish you were here to admire, are strewn with yellow leaves. . . . I have recommenced to write Gifford lectures at the rate of one ms. page a day, and now that October has begun, I feel as if next summer and home were not so distant. I like to hear of you at Seneca Lake and my dying advice to you is don't give up your capacity for taking vacations! Adieu. W. J.

Even upon his return from abroad, Mr. James's vigor had not yet returned. From New Hampshire he writes to Pauline, in September 1901:—

How good to think of you as the same old loveress of woods and skies and waters, and of your Bryn Mawr friends. May none of the lot of you ever grow insufficient or forsake each other! The sight of you sporting in Nature's bosom once lifted me into a sympathetic region, and made a better boy of me in ways which it would probably amuse and surprise you to learn of, so strangely are characters useful to each other, and so subtly are destinies intermixed. But with you on the mountain-tops of existence still, and me apparently destined to remain grubbing in the cellar, we seem far enough apart at present and may have to remain so. Alas! how brief is life's glory, at the best. I can't get to Keene Valley this year, and [may] possibly never get there. Give a kindly thought, my friend, to the spectre who once for a few times trudged by your side, and who would do so again if he could. I'm a 'motor,' and morally ill-adapted to the game of patience. I have reached home in pretty poor case, but I think it's mainly 'nerves' at present, and therefore remediable; so I live on the future, but keep my expectations modest.

V

This hope was, happily, borne out. And early in the new year he begins to look forward with all the old buoyancy:—

95 Irving Street, March 26th, 1902

My Dear Pauline,

The weeks and months fly by without our hearing from you or of you, so I think I might well break the silence by letting you hear from me. I hope that your news is as good as mine. Mine is better than I deserve—my health, which had begun to mend seriously already when you were here, has gone on steadily improving, so that during the past month I have been feeling quite like old times again, and am counting on Keene Valley once more in September, with who knows how much capacity for walking thrown in—Is n't it nice? . . . Enough of ourselves. I wish I could frame a distincter imagination than I am able to, of what *your* life is like. We ought to be neighbors! But the original chaos out of which this world grew has been but imperfectly mended, and I live in Cambridge and you live in New York! This summer you will tell me more about it. We shall be back early in July.

I trust that your Mother has had a well winter and that all the rest of you are well. This is just a word, dear Pauline, to check the process of oblivescence which I fear has been going on in your youthful soul-righteous oblivescence of such a decrepit old party as I have been. But phœnixes arise from ashes—and I at any rate don't oblivesce!

Ever affectionately yours,

Wm. James

I take it for granted that you are all going to Keene Valley again.

The high peaks Mr. James did not thereafter climb. But he returned to the Valley almost every summer and still enjoyed all that the woods afforded on the lower ranges. Trails to little lakes, lying hidden on the mountain side, encircled with blue gentian, sundew, and sphagnum moss; or to far outlooks from high rock ledges; or to one of the many waterfalls, crystal clear, which distinguish the Adirondack forest—these were still within his reach. To such lessened outings he refers in the course of a later letter:—

St. Huberts, Sept. 14, '07

Dear Pauline,

Hurrah! hurrah! that communication should be at last re-established! Your dear letter of the 11th came yesterday with its implied prospect of more, and with its breath of your camping days, which maltreated you less rainily than I had been a-fearing. If I could only go camping with you again, even for 48 hours, I think the truths so communicable under those conditions would conduce to much appeasement. . . . No 'camping' for me this side the grave!

A party of 14 left here yesterday for Panther Gorge, meaning to return by the 'Range,' as they call your 'summit trail.' Apparently it is easier than when on that to me memorable day we took it, for Carly Putnam swears he has done it in 5½ hours. I don't well understand the difference, except that they don't reach Haystack over Marcy as we did, and there is now a good trail. . . .

By going slowly and alone, I find I can compass such things as the Giant's Washbowl, Beaver Meadow Falls, etc., and they make me feel very good. I have even been dallying with the temptation to visit Cameron Forbes at Manila; but I have put it behind me for this year at least. I think I shall probably give some more lectures (of a much less 'popular' sort) at Columbia next winter—so you see there's life in the old dog yet. Nevertheless, how different from the life that courses through *your* arteries and capillaries! Today is the first honestly fine day there has been since I arrived here on the 2nd. (They must have been heavily rained on at Panther Gorge yesterday evening.) After writing a couple more letters I will take a book and repair to 'Mosso's Ledge' for the enjoyment of the prospect. If you write to me again (which I by no means feel sure of!) pray explain your activities, and give me a scheme of your future peregrinations and addresses.

Ever your friend W.J.

But it was the Range trip or trail over the summits which remained in his mind ever after, as a kind of landmark. He wrote in remembrance:—

That summer, when we walked over the 'Range' and I went to California to 'talk to teachers,' marked my completest union with my native land.

In William James there was always the 'double pull,' the *Zwiespalt,* with which his letters were filled on his return from his frequent journeys to Europe. He was at once lover of the American wilds and also, fundamentally, the cosmopolitan, the lover of Europe, the restless traveler, the keen and sympathetic observer. It was an essential characteristic of his own individualism and insistence upon the unique quality of every individual life that he should turn upon each nation, each country, each person he met, that humane yet penetrating eye.

The joys of foreign travel Mr. James often encouraged his young correspondent, Pauline Goldmark, to seek—Alpine heights, the English countryside, or, it might be, the satisfaction of the historic sense, so difficult to capture in the abstract, so vivid in the presence of ancient beauty. He compared impressions, and in a phrase or a page evoked the foreign scene and its particular flavor.

Thus, for instance, in some consecutive letters of 1908 written from abroad:—

Mariemont, Edgbaston, May 31, '08

Paolina Mia—

Yesterday morning, coming down stairs at Oxford, I found your letter from Athens and the steamer lying on the hall table and have had it all to myself. Beautiful letter, showing how you too have felt 'the wonder that was Greece.' How many different ways of being wondrous in this world! In some respects the Athenians were like Iroquois, in some like Parisians of today, in others like their sole selves—you can't escape them. They are at the heart of all our European culture, but you must see their country to imagine them. How I wish I might have been with you there for 24 hours! You don't tell me where you lodged, or by what route you are making for Naples, or any other sordid detail. No matter—I don't deserve to know so much. I am glad you're going to Rome, which of all places in Europe is the one I'd rather spend a winter in again. Stay there as long as the (probable) heat will let you, and drink deep draughts of the wide horizontal perspectives, topographic, moral and historic. Read Machiavelli's *Prince* and *Life of Castracani* to give you the spirit of the Renaissance. I am spending 36 hours with Oliver Lodge, Alice being at Harrow. Tomorrow to London and back to Oxford on Tuesday for another week of unspeakable social fatigue. I have got thru my lectures, and love Oxford, both place, people, and institutions: but I started on my last legs and am tired as I have seldom been, with the unceasing 'sociability' required. I long for the country. I've grown fearfully old in the past year, except 'philosophically,' where I still keep young, but I can't keep pace with your strong young life at all any more, and you do well to drop me out of your calculations. I'm out of the running in so many ways that I can only figure as a valetudinarian in the eyes of people like yourself, God bless you. But, ironically enough, I am more and more of an 'authority'!! We go in 10 days to the Cotswold hills and on the 23rd to Durham for another honorary degree—drat it all. If my extreme fatigue continues I shall make tracks for home to get my back under a pine tree with no social complications, and recover.

Keep us informed of your movements. Harry arrived 3 days ago, Peg arrives about July 1st.

The beauty and wholesomeness of this England are immense, and Oxford, now that I have been part of the machine for a month, seems familiar and democratic. Goodbye! Heaven bless you, dear Pauline—Your affectionate W. J.

Ullswater Hotel, Patterdale July 2, '08.

Your letter, beloved Pauline, greeted me on my arrival here three hours ago, just as I had settled again into the unhealthy conviction that to communicate with me was more trouble to you than it seemed worth. Pardon the injurious thought. This letter, earthquake, photograph and all show you to be writing *con amore* and I thank you from my heart. All I really *needed* was to know your whereabouts, present, and future so far as that was fixed. I supposed the Rome address, which was all you had given me, to be long since obsolete, on account of heat; but how mistaken I was, since you are returning thither, and D. S. M. is actually installed there! So I send this also to Rome with some confidence that it will get you. Surely one has to stay indoors most of the day in Rome at this season, which will account for Miller's doing so much 'work.' Moreover when you are as old as M. and me, you will probably find that a bit of the habitual work daily—*reading* is enough—gives you a better moral digestion for all the sightseeing and lying waste. How I *do wish* that I could be in Italy alongside of you now, now or any time! You could do me so much good, and your ardor of enjoyment of the country, the town, and the folk would warm up my cold soul. I might even learn to speak Italian by conversing in that tongue with you. But I fear that you'd find me betraying the coldness of my soul by complaining of the heat of my body—a most unworthy attitude to strike. Dear Paolina, never, never think of whether your body is hot or cold, live in the *objective* world, above such miserable considerations. . . .

I have been riding about on stage coaches for five days past, but the hills are so tree-less that one gets little shade, and the sun's glare is tremendous. It is a lovely country, however, for pedestrianizing in cooler weather. Mountains and valleys compressed together as in the Adirondacks, great reaches of pink and green hillside and lovely lakes, the higher parts quite fully Alpine in character but for the fact that no snow mountains form the distant background. A strong and noble region, well worthy of one's life-long devotion, if you were a Briton. And on the whole what a magnificent land and race is this Britain. Every thing about them is of better quality than the corresponding thing in the U. S.—with but few exceptions, I imagine. And the equilibrium is so well achieved, and the human tone so cheery, blythe and manly! And the manners so delightfully good. Not one *unwholesome* looking man or woman does one meet for 250 that one meets in America. Yet I believe (or suspect) that ours is eventually the bigger destiny, if we can only succeed in living up to it, and thou in 22nd St and I in Irving St must do our respective strokes, which after 1000 years will help to have made the glorious collective resultant. Meanwhile, as my brother H. once wrote, thank God for a world that holds so rich an England, so rare an Italy! . . . A breeze has risen on the Lake which is spread out before the 'Smoking room' window at which I write, and is very grateful. The lake much resembles Lake George. Your ever grateful and loving W. J.

Ullswater Hotel, Patterdale. July 3, '08, 9:30 A.M.

Dear Pauline,

My pen ran off yesterday upon Anglicanism and other abstractions without deigning to deal with your dear concrete letter, which gives me such an impression of your active healthy nature and susceptibility to happiness. . . .

You ask about Casentino and the Val Verna: I forget all names, but imagine that you mean the country about Assisi with wh. St. F. had so much to do. I have been there, and been immensely impressed, both with the landscape and the unique legendary history. The strange thing was the quick *success* of the good F.'s enterprise.

But how can *our* ideas of strangeness be applied to a time when the earth and the sky were all mixed up together, and we ourselves, God, Christ, the devil and the angels formed one vividly and immediately present little family circle? Vivid as a camera picture, and nothing in it more than a mile off, or a year away! I was particularly struck with that little private sanctuary of F., away up on the mountain side, with everything so tiny and its little bed of penance hollowed in the rock. The lair of the wild beast, indeed, and that beast the Saint!

I hope that on your way from Siena to Rome you will have stopped at Orvieto, if you have n't been there already, as you probably have. Not only the church but the town 'took' me immensely when I was there 3 years ago. The fierce little poor people's houses, with their outside stairs, and the masonry binding things with such style in its irregularity. Was that your own photo of the Greek goatherd? If so, I applaud; and wish you may have snapped off some of the little dwellings on the hill slopes at Orvieto.

Here, the heat continues and a misty glare envelops the mountains. I shall pass a quiet day. Unfortunately I've already been recognized by some Durham people, but as they have a 'motor,' I shall perhaps get some compensation. How I wish that you might have been of our party at Durham. Both the Cathedral and castle were so impressive. As for Oxford, the beauty is endless. One must live there a month to fathom its uniqueness. There never ought to be a second one attempted in this world.

Ah Pauline, Pauline. God bless you! Your W. J.

Ullswater Hotel, July 5th, 9:30 A.M.

Dear Pauline,

Well! I have got off three successive letters to you anyhow, and *that* part of my life at least can't be undone! Here goes for a fourth, and tho' I fear that you may flinch from the persecution, it makes me feel temporarily quite young again,—not more than 34 years old, or 34 and a half, to find that I can keep it up so well. A cool and rainy day, with the mountains mostly hid by clouds. Not unbecoming to the region, more so in fact than the cloudless heat glare. The friendly Squances took me out again yesterday afternoon for a 40 miles ride in their automobile which he drives very skilfully down the steep hills—Ullswater, Keswick, Grasmere, Ambleside—in fact the cream of the district, unrolling itself successively under the becoming cloudy sky.

Great uplifted moorlands and almost tropically embowered roadsides alternated in this drive, and the richest thing in the latter way was 'Fox Howe,' the house which Dr. Arnold (of Rugby) built on a bit of land selected by 'Mr.' Wordsworth (and well selected) for the view, and died almost immediately after. His children have lived there more or less ever since, and the septuagenarian Miss Arnold, who received us, proved a very jolly old girl—a friend of Miss Squance. How I should have liked you to see the country, so much of it at once! It is really a wonderful little country for strength and compressed variety—the hills all look much higher than they really are. England has nice things, natural as well as human, within her limits. . . .

If you want some good Italian reading, try to get Settembrini's memoirs, a Neapolitan of the revolutionary time, with the most extraordinary Italian grace of nature piercing through his horrible recital of suffering. Massimo d'Azeglio's memoirs I suppose you know—they exist in English. . . .

I suppose that you are tempted towards Tyrol, to do some mountain scaling. The Salters enjoyed their walking in the Austrian Tyrol more than any part of their year abroad, and after Rome *you* must long to get the breath of the Scipio's sepulchres out of your lungs. . . .

If I could obey my real impulse, I would go home this month and spend the rest of my summer at the Putnams'. Goodbye, Pauline, goodbye. Your W. J.

Atmosphere, light, perspective never more subtly reproduced than in a single paragraph in a letter from Edinburgh, engage the artist who was never lost in William James. (Had he not studied painting under Hunt in his youth before turning to the study of medicine?)

I think your party did n't come to Scotland [he writes]. Edinburgh and the country round about are *grossartig,* as noble and strong as any city in the world, I fancy. Today is sunny (for a wonder), and Alice, Harry and Peggy have gone to the Trossachs. The atmospheric effects in the town are extraordinary, vistas receding in plane after plane of aerial perspective, in an air full of delicate aqueous vapour, silvery brown smoke, and ancient decayed sunshine held in solution in it, so that it figures as a bodily object of the most exquisite sort. But let me not Ruskinize!

VI

Circumstances had early made of William James a citizen of the world, who had lived much abroad. Yet such were his constitutional restlessness and what has been called 'the perversity which was a fascinating trait in his character' that he was seldom content to settle down for long. In spite of regularly recurring visits to Europe, he came to feel that a long sojourn there uprooted him from America and American life. That difficulty of readjustment which we must all experience in greater or less degree on returning from the older order of civilization, with all its wealth of historic association, was particularly marked in Mr. James. In his later years it was aggravated by his illness and necessary relinquishments of activity. Yet as early as 1894 he was writing to Carl Stumpf:—

One should not be a cosmopolitan, one's soul becomes 'disintegrated,' as Janet would say. Parts of it remain in different places, and the whole of it nowhere. One's native land seems foreign. It is not wholly a good thing, and I think I suffer from it.

His brother Henry had by this time made a different choice and had settled for the rest of his life in England. But William remained, with whatever reservations, rooted in America. He was, indeed, to stand out in the course of time as a 'typical' American.

To you [he writes to his brother], who now have real practical relations and a place in the old world, I should think there was no necessity of ever coming back again. But Europe has been made what it is by men staying in their homes and fighting stubbornly generation after generation for all the beauty, comfort and order that they have got—we must abide and do the same.

To Pauline he repeatedly expresses a similar sentiment, as in the course of the following letter early in their acquaintance. The opening sentence refers to an invitation for her to come for a visit to Cambridge:—

C/o Edmund Tweedy, Esq., Newport, R.I., April 18, '99.

Alas, my dear Pauline, what a letter from you is this that Mrs. James sends me from home this morning? I *did* make bold to hope that you might come. Is there no one to take your place on the Consumers' League? Or can't you come—*after* the first of May? Mrs. Brandeis—that charming being—whom I recently saw at Mrs. Evans', told me of your summer plan, but said you were to leave early in May. Is the date such as to make a visit quite impossible? I should so 'admire' to see you playing the part of a member of our family.

What a winter of estrangement it has been! With no lectures given or heard, no pups offered and ignored or contemptuously rejected by telegraph, no snatches at conversation in the midst of crowds, no baskings on the lawn at Bryn Mawr, no nothing at all, in short; and yet all sorts of real things to talk about, accumulating on my side of the fence. You may say 'why, since you have a week of holiday, don't you run down here, and come and see me and talk them over?' Well! that sounds natural; but . . . there are a number of reasons too long and subtle to be put down on paper why I must say here at Newport and not go to New York during this April recess. So if you can't come to us in May, I must even waft you with this a quasi-eternal farewell. I am glad on the whole to hear of your determination to go abroad only for the summer and to spend most, if not all, of your time in the British Isles. . . . The *ideal* use to be made of Europe, in my opinion (at any rate when one is of my age), is to go there in the spring, and spend 3 months of irresponsible travel, and then come home. Not settle down anywhere for the winter. You get an extraordinary refreshment from the sight of the beauty and the novelty; and when that mood wears off, you had better get back to your own work again. It would be nice, all the same, to meet you in Europe next winter—no matter where. . . .

Now this is a long letter and a good one, and says nothing about pups, so I am disposed to demand an immediate reply. Pray write to me *here* and tell me whether you can possibly come after the 1st of May. . . .

And in any and every case, believe me—with friendliest regards to your mother and sisters,

Your sincere friend

Wm. James

VII

A decade later the note of sadness, the *Zwiespalt* between 'incompatible allegiances,' is uppermost in a letter written from New Hampshire during the Indian summer season.

At Salter's 'Hill Top,' Thursday, Oct. 22nd, '08.

Dear Pauline, You see where I am. We reached Boston last Friday after a stormy passage, and I took the train on Saturday morning straight up here. I go down this afternoon to attend poor Charles Norton's funeral. He was 82, and has had on the whole a fortunate life, having coöperated with most of the better things that were going in his time, and having given great help and encouragement to individuals by his appreciative sympathy and recommendations, when as yet they were unknown. Verily a good way in which to be remembered.

How I wish I had had you near me these last days to compare the way in which the exchange of continents had affected us severally. I think that to some extent, at any rate, our impressions would have been the same. One gets so quickly attuned to the beauty, solidity and tidyness of Europe that it makes one's own country seem strange, and in my case the effect is enhanced by the fact that I can bear no practical part in improving the face of nature now-a-days, and the excellent way in which Europe takes care of you instead of appealing to you to take care of her exactly suits my complaint. Here, everything is *to be done*. . . . When I came up here it was heart-breaking. Two souls in my breast. The ancient American beauty of the season, unutterably sentimental in its femininity and *dearth*, and the robust fullness of all that I had left in England. The two schemes of being are so discrepant that one should draw no comparisons. But the total result, anchored as I am to America, is to fill me with pathos and pangs. . . . I know that you too feel the double pull also, and I would give anything to have you near, so as to compare notes. How jolly, but how short that meeting was in London. . . .

Goodbye!

Your always affectionate

W. J.

This was, however, a passing mood. The autumn splendor, as a rule, awoke in him a spiritual no less than a physical response, and fortified his essential Americanism. On another occasion he writes from New Hampshire:—

About to leave these sylvan glories, what is more natural than to write a word to you, and express my sorrow that you had to return to town before they had developed? I have been fortunate enough to wait till yellow is beginning to be the prevailing colour, but the whole preceding month has been a spectacle of jewelry, as if the world were rubies and gold, and emerald and topaz. The thing has been at once violently sensational and exquisitely spiritual. I never saw so much of it, or such warm Americanism in the atmosphere, and I wish that you could have enjoyed it with me. It makes one patriotic!

I have been thinking of Keene Valley and East Hill the past few days, for I have been writing, at Professor Knight's solicitation (a Saint Andrews professor—editor of Wordsworth), 37 pp. of reminiscence of T. Davidson, to go into a 'life' of him which K. is about to publish. When once I got started, I enjoyed the writing greatly—with D. as a subject, it became so easy to be racy. . . .

I am in fine condition, almost my own self again in spirit as indeed I ought to be, for my outward duties etc. are now 'fixed' so harmoniously. Goodbye! Have a good winter, don't over work yourself, and keep a place in your affections for your ancient but faithful friend. W. J.

Over against this flaming picture—the 'hillsides reeking, as it were, and aflame with ruby and gold and emerald and topaz,' as he puts it in the article on Thomas Davidson—may be set an ordinary American winter landscape, as seen from a railroad window and sketched in black and white in the course of a letter from the train:—

Boston, New York and Chicago Special, Feb. 24 [1904], 9 A.M.
at Syracuse, just after breakfast.

My Dear Pauline, This is just a part of my yesterday's letter. I forgot to say certain things then. For instance to express a hope that the Bryn Mawr dinner went off well—if it has gone off. What male Being or Beings did you have there? Do you make speeches (here goes the train!). And did you or Mlle. Joséphine make one? . . .

We are rocking and stumbling along through a wild northeasterly storm. The snow is over, but the horizons disappear in the blackish grey of a frozen atmospheric jelly, while the white fields receive the trees against them as if drawn in pencil, the house roofs and the car roofs when we pass them are pure white and break beautifully upon their almost black sides, altogether it is a beautiful drawing in crayon and stump; and good as summer is for the soul, I verily suspect that winter is more beautiful for the eye—*on the whole,* and I would n't spend a winter *entirely* without our wild cold and snow for anything. I saw some exquisite days, the perfection of weather, in Florida, but when I came back to Boston cold, I said, 'This is my native air and I claim it.' It is only a question of the number of weeks one shall claim it.

I go back, now, I hope, to a less interrupted half year, in which I may possibly do some of my own proper tasks; so far, it has been nothing but jobs to oblige others, to which I could n't say no. I am ashamed to say how much interested I have become in my own system of philosophy (!) since Dewey, Schiller, a Frenchman named Bergson, and some lesser lights, have, all independently of me and of one another, struck into a similar line of ideas. I am persuaded that a great new philosophic movement is in the air, and I pray to be spared to play an active part in it. Those movements seem ridiculously abstract in their original form, but they filter down into practical life through the remotest channels.

Now! there! Is n't that the best letter I ever wrote you? I pray you, make response! How has the work at the League gone? How has society gone? How has reading gone? Of course you are pro-Jap. Are n't they little Romans? This seems to me a case where one's anti-war principles have to yield before the presence of deep animal instincts. For the issue is unquestionably, 'Shall all races succumb to the white race?' And I don't believe that God meant that they should lie down just yet. However it turns out, it will make the world a worse place to live in for a long time to come. If the Japs beat, it may be one of the great turning points in human history. Certainly *they* feel that and will fight to exhaustion. And so, for that matter, ought Russia to. Goodbye, and God bless you, whoever may beat. Your W. J.

A different American scene, on the grandest scale, is reflected in a letter from the Grand Canyon of the Colorado. Here Mr. James had stopped on his way across the continent to lecture at Stanford University, California, during the second term of 1906:—

Dear Paolina,

I am breaking my journey by a day here, and it seems a good place from which to date my New Year's greeting to you. But we correspond so rarely that when it comes to the point of tracing actual words with the pen, the last impressions of the day and the more permanent interests of one's life block the way for each other. I think, however, that a word about the Canyon may fitly take precedence. It certainly is equal to the brag; and, like so many of the more stupendous freaks of nature, seems at first smaller and more manageable than one had supposed. But it grows in immensity as the eye penetrates it more intimately. It is so entirely alone in character that one has no habits of association with 'the likes' of it, and at first it seems a foreign curiosity; but already in this one day I am feeling myself grow nearer, and I can well imagine that, with greater intimacy, it might become the passion of one's life—so far as 'Nature' goes. The conditions have been unfavorable for intimate communion. Three degrees above zero, and a spring overcoat, prevent that forgetting of 'self' which is said to be indispensable to absorption in Beauty. Moreover, I have kept upon the 'rim,' seeing the Canyon from several points some miles apart. I meant to go down, having but this day; but they could n't send me or anyone today; and I confess that, with my precipice-disliking soul, I was relieved, though it very likely would have proved less uncomfortable than I have been told. (I resolved to go, in order to be worthy of being your correspondent.) As Chas. Lamb says, there is nothing so nice as doing good by stealth and being found out by accident, so I now say it is even nicer to make heroic decisions and to be prevented by 'circumstances beyond your control' from even trying to execute them. But if ever I get here in summer,

I shall go straight down and live there. I am sure that it is indispensable. But it is vain to waste descriptive words on the wondrous apparition, with its symphonies of architecture and of colour. I have just been watching its peaks blush in the setting sun, and slowly lose their fire. Night nestling in the depths. Solemn, solemn! And a unity of design that makes it seem like an individual, an animate being. Good night, old chasm! . . .

And now, dear Paolina, what of yourself? I try to think of your life and occupations, but can't do so successfully. Enlighten me. Write a good, *long*, gossipy, egotistic, tattling letter, telling me about everything, important and unimportant. Such a letter as I inwardly deserve, though I do so little outwardly to merit it. Address 'Stanford University, California.' . . . I have just taken the liberty of sending a copy of *Kipps* (first-rate!) to your sister Josephine—I hope that you have n't all read it already. Write! write! write! and lengthily! to

Yours as ever W. J.

VIII

Two late letters, written in 1909, the year before Mr. James's death, touch on a Western camping trip of Pauline's, with all the old ardor of enjoyment:—

Silver Lake, N. H., June 22d, '09

Dear Pauline,

Instead of having to stay on at Cambridge as two and a half weeks ago I thought I should, I found that I could get away, so I came up here immediately to the Salters', where I have been living in a state of high contentment and communion with nature ever since. Previous to that I was at Stockbridge and Salisbury, and am only confirmed in my old belief that with May and June doing what they *are* doing, in the country, it is sin and suicide for any free man or woman deliberately to stay in town. The simplification of life, the good smelling air, the exquisiteness of the leafage, the wild flowers and birds, the coolness (until yesterday), have all been balm to my soul, and I find that by walking slowly enough I can get about anywhere and everywhere I will. I have thought of you shut up in New York, with aching protest. My own family, too, in Cambridge, seem to me perverse. . . . I have just finally declined an invitation to the Jubilee of the University of Geneva, where I understood confidentially that I was to be made a Doctor of Theology!!!! The temptation was strong to go, so as to crow over Royce, and listen to his sarcasms in return—Irving Street would be more lively as a result! Besides, there was a possible breath of Switzerland again. But that is all dismissed, and I look forward to July and most of August at our place here (the family arriving about July 1st), with (*hoffentlich*) 3 or 4 weeks at 'the Valley' after that! Meanwhile I make myself happy reading Plutarch's *Lives*, which (strange to say) I open for the first time in my 68th year. The time for standard works is assuredly old age, so I don't *urge you* to go at Plutarch *now*, tho I'm sure you will enjoy him if you do. He's as enthralling as any modern novelist, as good a story teller, moralist, and psychologist, and more everlasting human business gets transacted in his pages than in any others I know—they are, as Emerson said, 'rammed with life.' Ah, Pauline, when shall you and I ever converse together again? I thought of you yesterday again in reading in a really charming volume called *In Tuscany* by one Carmichael. Have you seen it? If not, I must send you a copy. And don't forget to tell me whether you have the *Way of All Flesh* and *Tono Bungay*. You *must* go to the Columbia River, or wherever that western camping project was to take you. Lose no chance during all these young years to live with nature—it is the eternal normal animal thing in us, overlaid by other more important human destinies, no doubt, but holding the fort in the middle as the security of all the rest. Go! and drink your fill! and temporarily forget everything except the day that is. You will tell me all about it, when you get back to the Valley in September.

I shall go down to Cambridge again on Friday and stay till after Commencement, bringing the family up to Chocorua. I trust that you and yours are all very well and either gone already or on the point of going to the blessed spot. Believe me, dear Pauline,

Yours ever affectionately

Wm. James

Cambridge, Sept. 5, 1909.

Dear Pauline:

Your letter of July 25th reached me duly and gladdened my heart by awakening lively images of the bath in Nature's beauties and wonders which you were about to have. I hope you have *drunk deep*, for that goes to a certain spot in us that nothing else can reach, more 'serious' and 'valuable' tho' other things profess (and indeed seem) to be. Where 'Field' and 'Yoho Valley' are I have n't the least idea, but somewhere, I suppose, off the Canadian Pacific Road, which I only hope you will have enjoyed as I enjoyed it 10 years ago. The big *continental* consciousness that one gets in traversing America is an element of experience wholly unlike anything else, when one gets it for the first time—I fear, however, that the 1st time usually means the last time so far as the wondrous soul-dilating part of it goes. If you had sent me any possible address, I should have written to you—but you did n't. . . .

Write to me how it went with you this summer, dear Pauline—no very long letter if you don't feel like one, but enough to reassure your ever affectionate old friend. W. J.

The last letter, like the first and almost every one of this correspondence, returns to the out-of-doors. It was again from Nauheim, from the beautiful park which he loved there; it was near the end. But it speaks of trees, and blackbirds, and the open air.

Nauheim, May 29th, 1910

Beloved Pauline,

On this rainy lonely morning, my heart goes out in your direction and I can't help sending you a *Gruss*. I went to my bath at six this a.m. (it is now 10.30) and had the park, the trees and the blackbirds all to myself. Would thou had'st been there! This was because I am expecting a certain powerful young professor named Goldstein from Darmstadt, who is translating one of my books, and I had to get the bath out of the way. It has begun to rain, and I hope that G. won't come; for to converse in this place and not to be in the open air is altogether wrong.

Well! God bless you, Pauline. Be good and happy.

Your old friend W. J.

RALPH BARTON PERRY

(1876–1957)

Ralph Barton Perry, the precocious only son of George Perry, a schoolteacher, and his wife, Susannah, was named for Ralph Waldo Emerson because, family legend had it, his father hoped that he would someday become a Harvard professor. Perry graduated from Princeton just before his twentieth birthday and might have trained for the ministry at Princeton Theological Seminary were it not for his father's urging that he spend a year at Harvard. By 1899, he completed his doctorate in philosophy. After a year of teaching at Williams College and two years at Smith College, he returned to Harvard, rising through the department until he was named chairman in 1906 and Edgar Pierce Professor of Philosophy in 1930.

Describing his years as a graduate student at Harvard, Perry recalled his attraction to James, who, he said, 'combined the attributes of the light cruiser, the submarine, and the bombing aeroplane. . . . James proved the rallying-point for those in whom the youthful spirit of revolt was stronger than tradition and prestige.'[1] Unlike Royce, whose idealism Perry found uncongenial, James put forth a 'common-sense realism' that accounted for 'a common world, inhabited by our perceiving bodies and our neighbours, and qualified by the evidence of our senses.'[2]

Just three years older than James's eldest son, Perry enjoyed a filial relationship with his mentor; when he had professional decisions to make, he often asked James's advice. When Perry wondered if he should accept a position at Smith, James advised him to refuse, asking if his 'susceptible heart, at so inflammable an age [could] stand the exposure'[3]; and when Perry was offered a position at Stanford, James dispassionately laid out the pros and cons, adding, 'Were I at your age and the temptation to come here came to me, I think I should yield to it, in spite of some uncertainties.'[4] In neither case, however, did Perry follow James's counsel.

During his fifteen-year association with James, Perry became a close and trusted family friend. The two men hiked together in Keene Valley, and James even tried to play matchmaker between Perry and Pauline Goldmark. Early in Perry's career, James strongly endorsed him for a position at Harvard. 'I have the very highest opinion of his talents and character,' he wrote to President Eliot in 1899, 'and I am sure of his successful development.'[5] A short time later James wrote to George Herbert Palmer, assuring him that Perry was 'certainly the soundest, most normal all-round man of our recent production.'[6]

Perry's legacy as a philosopher is linked to his relationship with James. He edited two posthumous collections of James's work: James's *Essays in Radical Empiricism* (1912) and *Collected Essays and Reviews* (1920), and won a Pulitzer Prize for his two-volume biography, *The Thought and Character of William James* (1935). A prolific writer, he published more than 200 essays and more than twenty books, including *The Approach to Philosophy* (1905), *The Moral Economy* (1909), and *The New Realism* (1912), in which he defined the perspective of many of his contemporaries who rejected post-Kantian idealism. Because he believed that philosophy must account for itself in public life, he devoted some of his works to social issues: these include *The Free Man and the Soldier* (1916), *General Theory of Value* (1926), *Realms of Value* (1926), and *The Humanity of Man* (1956).

In a brief autobiographical essay written at his retirement from Harvard, Perry admitted that even though he did not train for the ministry, he never ceased being a preacher. 'I can see now,' he wrote, 'that when I became a college and university teacher instead of a Presbyterian minister I merely substituted the platform for the pulpit, the lecture or public address for the sermon, and the class or audience for the congregation.'[7] The topics of his lectures often reflected his deeply held political and social values: 'I have always felt it to be the duty of a philosopher,' he said, 'to shed what light he could on current public issues and to take his stand.'[8]

Perry's personal convictions led him into public roles. During World War I, as a major in the army, he served as executive secretary of the War Department Committee on Education and Special Training. In the 1930s he was an advocate of Roosevelt's New Deal, and, in his writings and lectures, he urged the United States to take a forceful stand against Hitler. During World War II he served as chairman of the Committee of American Defense, Harvard Group; and after the war was chairman of the Universities Committee on Post-War International Problems. He was an active supporter of the establishment of the United Nations. 'That element in my composition which inclined me in earlier years to the Christian ministry is accountable, no doubt, for my sustained interest in moral philosophy,' he wrote, explaining his 'reforming zeal.'[9] Yet he did not consider himself an iconoclast, but rather 'old-fashioned—that is to say, Christian and democratic in the historic sense of these terms. . . . Or, since Christianity and democracy were once revolutionary, and are still regarded with suspicion by the friends of tyranny and established privilege, I might describe myself as one who is revolutionary enough to remain loyal to the great revolutions of the past.'[10]

NOTES

1. Ralph Barton Perry, 'Realism in Retrospect,' in *Contemporary American Philosophy*, eds. George P. Adams and William Pepperell Montague (New York: Russell & Russell, 1940), 2:188.
2. Perry, 'Realism in Retrospect,' 189.
3. WJ to Ralph Barton Perry. Scott, 230 (17 June 1900).
4. WJ to Ralph Barton Perry. Scott, 402 (26 February 1906).
5. WJ to Charles Eliot. Scott, 207–8 (20 December 1899).
6. WJ to George Herbert Palmer. *Letters* 2:121 (2 April 1900).
7. Ralph Barton Perry, 'First Personal,' *Atlantic Monthly* October 1946, 107.
8. Ralph Barton Perry, 'Brief Biography.' Manuscript, Harvard Archives.
9. Ralph Barton Perry, 'Realism in Retrospect,' 2:201.
10. Ralph Barton Perry, 'Realism in Retrospect,' 2:208.

Professor James as a Philosopher

It is characteristic of Professor James that he should so easily have shifted the centre of his interest from psychology to philosophy. Having little respect for formal distinctions, he finds food for philosophy as well as food for psychology in the same experience. He was already a philosopher while he was a psychologist, and he is still a psychologist now that he is a philosopher. In this very general respect, as well as in various special points of doctrine, he is a lineal descendant of the English empiricists, Locke, Berkeley, Hume and Mill. Like these philosophers, he is not so much interested in the classification of problems as he is in their solution. The 'categories' and 'schematisms' which Kant and his followers have been so fond of refining are matters of book-keeping which he is glad to leave to others. Nor is this merely a matter of temperamental choice with him, for it rests upon the conviction that experience cannot permanently be consigned to 'pigeonholes' without being falsified. Professor James's critics have urged, not without warrant, that the task of philosophy is peculiarly one of systematization, and have convicted him of confusion and desultoriness. Indeed his nearest disciples would scarcely deny that his left hand does not always know what his right doeth. But this very disposition to ignore logical formalities and conventions is nevertheless one of the main sources of his power. His thought is always warm and well nourished. The highly stimulating quality of his teaching comes of his living constantly in the fresh air of experience; his characteristic gift is the conveying of experience. He is himself never satisfied with symbols and definitions, because his experience is forever outstripping them. Hence his students are often disappointed when they come to him for clear and final ideas; but they never fail to get something to *think about.*

This empiricism may be said to be the dominant idea in Professor James's thought. Indeed he prefers to call himself a 'radical empiricist,' thus emphasizing his unwillingness to force any construction whatsoever upon the universe, even the form of unity. Instead of looking to the order and necessity of nature, or to the convergence of ideals, for his working conceptions, he finds them in the casual conjunctions and the dramatic surprises which life manifests in the living. His philosophical consciousness does not reduce or transmute these, but assembles them. In philosophy as well as in his practical judgments and appreciations, he is an individualist, a lover of the unique. The object of his cosmic emotions is not the constant and abiding element in the universe, but the aggregate of many rare and incommensurable things. He has too much respect for nature to attempt to domesticate it, and too much respect for his fellows to depreciate their failure to conform.

Professor James's individualism or 'pluralism' finds expression in his rigorous criticism of monism in all its forms, whether naturalistic or idealistic. His metaphysical *bête noir* is the 'block universe' of the absolutists, the subsumption of all experience under the form of an immutable eternity. Latterly his empiricism and his pluralism, together with his sense for the vital core of experience, have assumed the form of a philosophical system in the 'pragmatic' movement, of which he is the acknowledged leader. 'Pragmatism' is primarily a theory of knowledge, but it involves a metaphysics. It consists essentially in the doctrine that knowledge is a natural process through which experience shapes and orders itself consistently with practical needs. Truth is in the making. Experience is both plastic, in that it lends itself to knowledge; active in that it knows and directs itself, and progressive in that its most orderly systematizations tend to survive and cohere. In various applications and points of detail this doctrine has already been foreshadowed in Professor James's various books and short papers; the author is at present engaged upon its constructive presentation.

No one is doing more than Professor James in forging the ideas that are to mark the present age in the history of thought. The recognition of his eminence is universal, not only among his fellow-philosophers, but also (as does not always follow) throughout the whole fraternity of thoughtful men. Furthermore, the perpetual liveliness of his mind makes it impossible that any book of his should be discounted in advance except in point of its charm and solid value. Hence his forthcoming 'Pragmatism' provokes a keener expectancy than the projected work of any English or American philosopher.

JOHN ELOF BOODIN

(1869–1950)

John Boodin was born on a farm in southern Sweden where his ancestors had lived for generations. He attended the local parish school and seemed destined to become a farmer, like his father and grandfather. 'I helped work the farm until I was fourteen,' he wrote later, 'and learned to love nature and respect the processes of nature, with its seasons of seed-time and harvest. There was not much machinery and the contact with nature was intimate. Through this training I became an empirical realist.'[1]

At the age of twelve the budding philosopher graduated from the parish school. His quick mind attracted the attention of a young minister, who recommended that he be tutored for entrance to the Fjellstedt gymnasium in Upsala. Boodin attended the school for a year and a half, but a bout of illness caused him to withdraw temporarily, and his father's sudden death made it impossible for him to return. Instead, at eighteen he emigrated to the United States. After working in Illinois as a blacksmith, he was able to save enough money to enroll in a local normal school. After a year of teaching children, he decided to return to college, entering the University of Colorado as a sophomore. His savings, however, stretched only for one year. He found a job in Minneapolis working with Swedish immigrants, and in 1893 enrolled at the University of Minnesota, where he studied with James Rowland Angell and read James's *Principles of Psychology.* He then won a scholarship to attend Brown University, where he received a bachelor's degree in 1895 and a master's in 1896. There he first met James, who had come to speak at the school's Philosophical Society. Finally, he achieved his goal of enrolling at Harvard, funded by a Hopkins scholarship, and obtained a doctorate in 1899.

Besides forging a warm friendship with James, with whom he took a seminar in psychology, he also garnered the support of Royce, whose seminar on Hegel inspired some of Boodin's own early writings. Royce, Boodin admitted, 'was the master with whom I wrestled for the salvation of my soul from 1897 to 1900. It was in his seminar especially that I developed and expressed the beginnings of my metaphysics.'[2] Royce was so impressed by Boodin's work that he recommended him to George Platt Brett, the president of Macmillan, publishers of a strong list of philosophical works. 'Professor Boodin is a rising man, with a good record and standing as a philosopher,' Royce wrote early in 1911; 'as strong a man as any of his age in the West. I have advised him to get himself into book form as soon as possible. His essays, so far, are predominantly although not extremely technical. But he is clear and wholesome, and ought to win a good hearing. I certainly should advise your taking up the questions of his proposed book.'[3]

The book in question, *Truth and Reality,* was published by Macmillan later that year and was dedicated to William James, 'Not the late but the ever living / and inspiring genius of / American philosophy.' Intending the book as an introduction to the theory of knowledge, Boodin discusses the nature of truth, the criterion of truth, and the relationship of truth to objects. While much of the book is devoted to explaining and defining pragmatism, which Boodin champions, nevertheless he admits, 'I like to visit sometimes, in the company of my friend Royce, a beautiful Greek temple built according to Plato's Idea of the Good. . . . And withal the soul is filled with such sweet harmony as to forget for the time being its limitations and its longings.'[4]

The temple which Boodin prefers to visit, however, is a work-in-progress begun by William James, 'who spent a lifetime trying to provide a framework and who is now at work on some plans for the interior. It is a place where everybody has something to do. Each one is allowed to choose his own task, make his own plan and fix his own salary. There is no supervision as yet; in fact the plan is that there shall be no supervision of the work as a whole. This,' he added wryly, 'is looked at askance by outsiders, and mutiny is prophesied.'[5]

Boodin saw his own task as simplifying and defining pragmatism. Like Lovejoy, Boodin believed that James's definition was open to confusion, and that pragmatism, as discussed by philosophers, included a wide range of doctrines and theories. According to Boodin, pragmatism was 'simply the application of the ordinary method of the scientific testing of an hypothesis to philosophic hypotheses as well.'[6]

Boodin continued to explore the problems of pragmatism and the application of scientific method to philosophy in *A Realistic Universe* (1916) and *Cosmic Evolution* (1925); he addressed metaphysical questions in *God and Creation* (1934) and *The Religion of Tomorrow* (1943). Boodin taught philosophy for four years at Grinnell College, Iowa; the University of Kansas from 1904 to 1913; Carleton College, in Minnesota, for the next fourteen years; and until he retired in 1939 at the University of California at Los Angeles.

NOTES

1. John Boodin, biographical essay in *Contemporary American Philosophy,* eds. George P. Adams and William Pepperell Montague (New York: Russell & Russell, 1930), 1:136.
2. Boodin, essay in *Contemporary American Philosophy,* 138.
3. Josiah Royce to George Brett. *The Letters of Josiah Royce,* ed. Clendenning, 552 (2 January 1911).
4. John Boodin, *Truth and Reality* (New York: Macmillan, 1911), 10.
5. Boodin, *Truth and Reality,* 12.
6. Boodin, *Truth and Reality,* 186.

William James as I Knew Him

I

I had come under the influence of William James indirectly in my Junior year, 1893–94, at the University of Minnesota as a student under Professor J. R. Angell who was fresh from Harvard and introduced us to James's books on psychology. They had a wonderful fascination for me and made me decide, as so many others have done for similar reasons, that this was the kind of thing I wanted to study. I also wanted to be near the author and made up my mind to start East to realize that ambition. I failed, however, to get a scholarship at Harvard. Instead I secured employment in Providence in connection with the church work among the Scandinavian immigrants and won a scholarship at Brown, where I studied philosophy two years under that brilliant, lovable teacher, James Seth. It was my second year at Brown, 1895–96, that James published his paper, 'Is Life Worth Living?' (*The International Journal of Ethics*, October, 1895), which aroused so much discussion. We decided to take it up for one of our evenings in the philosophical club and invited William James to be with us.

At last I was to have an opportunity to see and hear William James. There was a paper, first, giving an exposition of James's essay. Then the discussion was to follow, and James told us that he would wait until the end before saying anything. I was to lead off the discussion. Strangely enough now that I was in the presence of the man whom I wanted most of all for a friend, whether by a whim of the moment or compelled by logic, I did nothing but make fun of his theory. I pointed out that his theory provided no objective criterion of value, but made all our superstitions, day dreams and

Editor's Note [*Personalist*]: Professor Boodin of the University of California at Los Angeles has most generously consented to assist in this memorial to William James by allowing the Editor to abstract from a manuscript which was written by him at the time of the death of James in 1910.

air castles equally sacred with the best established truth, so long as they furnished a soporific for the individual's conscience; that the Moslem paradise with its dark eyed houri had as much claim upon us as Christianity, etc., etc. I brought the laugh on James; and, instead of waiting for the end as he had suggested, he got right up after my speech and said that now was the time for him 'to sail in.' He was profoundly stirred by the seeming levity of my attack and made a long and impassioned speech in defense of his position, building it out in a pragmatic way to meet the attack. We were all deeply impressed with his personality—his warmth and seriousness. While I had no chance to meet him, as he had to take a train immediately after his speech, I felt more than ever attracted to him.

What was better I had, in spite of the warmth of his rejoinder, made a permanent impression upon him. I had given him, he told my friends, just the opportunity he wanted. He inquired from my teachers into my life and plans. He nicknamed me affectionately 'the orator' and stood by me to the end of his days. When he was called upon the same year to give the annual address before the same society, he explained that he had built out his theory to meet the attack at his previous visit and gave us that famous address 'The Will to Believe,' in which he defined, in an immortal and masterly way, the claims of our emotional and volitional nature 'to adopt a believing attitude in religious matters, in spite of the fact that our merely logical intellect may not have been coerced.' Thus in a small, though capricious, way I was instrumental in bringing out one of his great masterpieces and the book which he shortly named after the essay. And what was better, I had made a friend who was to mould, as no other, my own life.

One afternoon in going to my room from the Harvard library I met William James dressed up in his best style, silk hat, patent leather shoes and evening dress. He stopped and shook hands, as I came up to him. I said: 'How fine you look.' 'Yes,' he said, 'I am going to dinner on Commonwealth Avenue. Come and walk a piece with me.' I was too glad to do it and so we walked all the way to Commonwealth Avenue, some three miles. We drifted into philosophy naturally. And he told me how he escaped being a metaphysical idealist. He told me that when Royce first came to Cambridge he was overawed by his immense intellect and felt compelled to share his idealism, but he finally had managed to break away and now had become a radical empiricist. Absolute idealism had ceased to be coercive over him, as he put it. He did not seem conscious of Henri Bergson at the time, i.e., 1897–98, though sometime after he gave Bergson credit for his emancipation. While he was sincere in both cases, he equally overrated in each case the mastery other minds had possessed over him. In his *The Meaning of Truth,* one of his last books, he was able to collect essays dating back to the beginning of his literary activity; and, though there doubtless is development, there is no apparent break. But this was his generous feeling toward those that had in some measure contributed to his insight.

He always expressed the greatest admiration for Royce, even when he made fun of Royce's Absolute, as he did in private and before his classes. As he put it on this walk:

> If there is an absolute, he must be just like Royce, a great metaphysician with a great stack of books under his arm and knowing everything,

and then he laughed.

Our talk drifted to other topics. He had just been nominated to the Gifford lectureship at Edinburgh. This came to him as a great surprise. It seemed both to please him and to amuse him. He said:

> All you have to do is to write something and get a little reputation. And then you will be made a Gifford lecturer and have a chance to make ten thousand dollars.

But what he could possibly do with it worried him. He said he must take C. C. Everett's course in the psychology of religion and get some material. Then he began to pump me as to what I had gotten out of the course of this profoundly spiritual teacher, whom his students learned to revere as a prophet and saint. Finding, however, that the course was really dialectical in character and dealt with the three ideas of the reason, he concluded that it wouldn't do after all. He must stick to experience. He had always read everything he could get hold of in biography. And while he wanted to find out from me, I soon learned that he had a mass of wealth of which I knew nothing. And it was all life, not cold generalizations. It is simply inconceivable that James could have been anything but an empiricist. He had a wonderful instinct for facts, for first things, though he had a profound admiration for other types of mind, just because they seemed like other universes, which he both felt he ought to and could not explore.

James loved to hear about my adventures in the making of an American.

He listened intently and with satisfaction to the sagas—the folk lore or local legends of my native highlands of southern Sweden, upon which my imagination had fed as a boy. And he sighed when I told him that the railroads, the public schools and the factories were now making the provincial costumes and the folk lore a thing of the past. He liked to hear about my early experiences as an immigrant, as a miner and blacksmith, about those profane and warm-hearted friends who are bent to their task under ground, about the old blacksmith who taught me the mystic formula for stopping blood; about the life of the immigrants of the city among whom I had become a missionary as a student. He liked to hear all this for it was life, first hand experience; and he was always hungry for life.

One reason why James was attracted to me was doubtless his love for the unusual, for the picturesque. And I was different—had a different background, 'a different accent like no other, foreign or native' though it seemed southern to him. I was surrounded with an air of mystery, so he said. James was frightfully afraid that civilization would level everything to one dull plain of monotony. This was one secret of his passionate appeal in favor of independence for the Philippines which accidentally came into our keeping.

James showed this love for the picturesque in his own life. Of course we all know it in his style, in those matchless descriptive metaphors everywhere. He showed it in the variety of his outlandish friends. But he showed it also in little details such as dress. I remember how amused we used to be one winter at James's appearance in coming to class. He wore a pair of tan shoes, a silk hat, cane, frock coat and red-checkered trousers. But somehow he did not seem freakish. There was a fitness about it. His appearance gave color and atmosphere to his philosophy. And he was handsome and striking with it all.

What impressed me about William James, after I came to know him intimately, was his genius for friendship even more than his brilliance of intellect. This he possessed to a greater extent than any other man I have known. It was to this gift of sympathy that he owed his marvelous insight into human nature. James's writings, like that of every great soul, are autobiographical in the deepest sense. There is a current notion of a psychologist as a cynic, a sort of Sherlock Holmes, who keeps watching people out of the corner of his eye and making them very uncomfortable by giving himself the air of seeing right through them. This caricature of the real psychologist is matched only by the attitude expressed by some professional psychologists who give themselves great credit for profundity by stating that psychology is a merely artificial study—a decomposing of psychic life into atomic elements and then describing it in terms of physiological concomitants. James could sit for neither of these definitions. He neither confused the most fascinating of sciences with asinine cynicism nor with psychological *a priorism.* He lived life first, sympathetically, genuinely and spontaneously, and then had the wit to look back upon his experiences—not for the sake of mere retrospect, but for the sake of more intelligent living. Life was always full of surprises for him. He had so much to learn from others and the world was such a fascinating place. For him experience, life among human beings, were first things. Theorizing about life was a secondary matter. It seemed he could not help but learn the human mind, just because he rang true in all situations.

This love of humanity extended to all conditions of men, so they were genuinely human. He had friends among the insane, as well as among the conventionally sane. He once brought a monomaniac friend of his to talk to his seminar in abnormal psychology. Such people would come to his home to see him and to relieve themselves by opening their hearts to him and telling him their symptoms, their fears and forebodings. No wonder that he has such splendid pathological material in his volumes, though it must have seemed uncanny to the family at times.

Then there was the Italian banana man with his stand on the corner of Oxford and Kirkland, just where Professor James had to pass on the way to and from his classes. He was much interested in him. He not only gave him friendly greeting, but when the banana man looked at him with those tender and beseeching brown eyes, he couldn't resist buying bananas as he passed. Another 'dago' friend called at his house and he bought bananas of him, too.

One day I met Professor James on the street; and he said, 'Hello, brother, I have been wanting to invite you to dinner for a long time. You must come tonight.' And of course I came. It was then his splendid wife revealed the predicament of the bananas. She said: 'You must eat lots of bananas and you must come often, because we have more bananas than we can use.' Professor James smiled that benignant soulful smile which warmed like April sunshine and said: 'Never mind, Alice, they are all our brothers.'

I must tell an incident from my own experience to illustrate the large heartedness of this great man. I had just taken my final degree in 1899 and the labors of the years had told on me pretty severely. I had gone to Rhode Island for my vacation, when on the Fourth of July I received a peremptory note from Professor James to come to Cambridge at once as he was worrying about me. Knowing his impetuous good nature, I took the next train to Cambridge. He told me that I must not work during the summer and that his friends had provided a way for me to take a sea voyage and spend the summer quietly in Europe with my mother.

He was very much disappointed when I replied that I did not think it would be right for me to receive any assistance from anybody now that I had completed my education through my own efforts. He told me I was proud and had no right to be, but insisted on taking me over to his friend and neighbor, Professor Royce, 'for him to talk to you.' Royce, himself very sensitive, rather took my side in the generous controversy. After dining and talking philosophy with my friend, I returned at night to Rhode Island and supposed the matter settled. But the next day I received a letter from James inclosing a check and telling me if I wanted to be his friend I must take the next steamer for Europe. So there was nothing to do but take the next steamer.

I returned to Harvard the following fall very much refreshed for further study and for the lectureship which I had been awarded as resident doctor and fellow. Professor Royce went to Scotland that winter for his Gifford Lectures at Aberdeen and courageously gave me his seminar as audience and critics of my theories. I naturally wrote an account to James of my summer and my year's venture. It reached him ill in Europe, where he was trying to prepare his own Gifford Lectures. The following letter to me deserves to be quoted in full to show his thoughtfulness, in the midst of his distress, of a struggling student, as well as for throwing light upon his own state of mind at the time:

Carqueiranne, France, March 16, 1900

Dear Boodin:

Your letter was a most agreeable surprise, with its good account of your condition and present happiness. I had already heard from Palmer of your prosperous vacation, and from some one else lately of the good audience at your lectures. I have still to hear of their character and ultimate success. Peg away at the *pluralistiche weltansicht.* Royce's lectures, which are the only philosophy I have read since last July, are perfectly charming, but to my mind absolutely inconclusive as *proof* of anything. My impression is that monism, like the republican party, is fattened to kill, and anyone can stick his knife into the blubber. Work out your theory in as untechnical a form as you can, even as Royce has worked out his, and it will make its mark, you may be sure.

I have been very ill indeed, but am better, and mean to be *well.* I have written but one Gifford lecture, and ought to write but very short letters—I always repent of it when I transgress. So I will just write a testimonial to enclose, and say good bye. Remember me to Savery, and the other philosophers. Is Carr in Cambridge? or where? Ever most cordially yours.

Wm. James.

William James was delightfully frank and stimulating in his class work. He was not given to formal lecturing in the class room, but rather relied on the taking up of important books, with brilliant comments and flashes of insight, and informal discussion with the students, for impressing his ideas upon their minds and bringing to light their own ideas. The undergraduate students would sometimes complain because they did not get things dictated to them in neat little formulas which they could reproduce at examinations. They sometimes found him unsystematic and unprofessional. But on looking backward they, too, could see that he had furnished them a new universe of thought and appreciation in which to live and work. In graduate work the informal method was ideal. It furnished the maturer student just that inspiration and suggestion which would spur him on in his particular field of interest.

In the meantime James himself was quite one of the students. He not only brought armfuls of books and references, which showed his own live interest in what was going on; but he was all the while taking a vital personal part in the work. He would express naive surprise and delight at a new idea or a new mode of presentation by a student and almost overwhelm such a student by the warmth of his appreciation—brag about him before the seminar, bring him home to dinner, spend a whole evening with him, talking the idea over. You would think he was the veriest freshman from the number of things he could learn from others. On the other hand, he was equally frankly bored by the mediocrity and slovenliness of other students. I remember his stopping one of the self-confident, dogmatic type in the midst of a discussion and saying to him: 'Mr. X, I can't stand your God Almighty air.' On the outside of an examination paper of a friend of mine, whom he was trying to stimulate, he wrote in handing it back: 'damn it, why don't you make yourself more clear.' My friend, while he knew he had

James's good will, got quite irate at first and burned the paper. I couldn't quite make out whether it was the small *d,* with which James had begun, or the reflection on his style which troubled him most, but he did seem to think that he deserved a big *d.* Anyway, he has long been sorry that he destroyed this valuable souvenir. He says if he had it now he would frame it and hang it on his study wall. James knew just how to treat different people so as to help them. And he knew that some people you had to hit square between the eyes to make an impression on them. He invited my friend to dinner afterwards.

James's easy fluent style has been universally and rightly praised. But if anyone thinks he could sit down and just dash off a production in the manner of the spring poet, he is very much mistaken. It was a laborious style to him. It was an artistic triumph of a brilliant mind. I remember during the year of 1897–98 how James complained that he had written and rewritten a discussion, Sundays up in his attic, but that somehow the thing wouldn't come. He did give us, however, three important lectures at the end of the year as a result of this fretting. And they were the best statement of his empirical pragmatism that I knew him to make. He made it wonderfully clear how ideas must terminate in concrete experience in order to be declared true. It is obvious to any student of James that, while he adopted the term pragmatism from C. S. Peirce, the doctrine itself is implied in all James's work from the beginning of his publications and is the lineal descendant of that empiricism which is the characteristic contribution of the English speaking race.

I pointed out to him in later years that his theory was not such a change in his point of view as he imagined. I told him that the core of his pragmatism had been beautifully stated in his essay, 'The Sentiment of Rationality.' He smiled and said he was wonderfully pleased at my high opinion of 'that little paper.' It was his virgin effort, he said, the first paper he published, dating back to 1879.

As a teacher William James stood preeminently for quality. No amount of weary plodding could secure the doctor's degree in his work. It was his business to stimulate latent genius and bring it to its fruition. Examinations, however elaborate, were merely a form to eliminate unfit mediocrity from the teaching profession. Kind hearted as James was, his conscience was rigorous in applying this standard of quality. The conflict of his tender emotions and his conscience was illustrated in a striking manner in a case in my own day at Harvard. A worthy man of fair ability had left his work and brought his family to Cambridge in order to earn a degree in philosophy. It became apparent after some time that the man could not meet the qualitative test; and it became necessary to warn the man of the fact. The student was broken hearted about it. To add to the tragedy his wife took ill and died that winter. James was all broken up over it. He kept busy going back and forth, comforting the husband and children and raising money for their support. No one took the misfortune more to heart than he, yet in all his sympathy it never occurred to him to let down his standard of quality.

The scholarships for encouraging poor graduate students in their work were very inadequate. James and his friend, Professor Palmer (and in a quiet way, Josiah Royce), were kept busy raising money from their Boston friends, as well as taking it out of their own pockets, to tide over the hardships of some promising student. I remember one year the scholarships had been awarded and a somewhat bashful, though able student had failed to get on the list. He had been invited home by James and had spent the evening talking philosophy with him. James discovered the mistake that had been made and was very much excited about it. He insisted that the student simply mustn't be allowed to leave Harvard. The result was that a special fellowship was raised for him for the next year.

Nothing could exceed James's tender interest in the prospective birth of an original idea in one of his students. As a fond mother watches over her daughter during the period of expectancy with fear and fondness, so James watched over the development of a promising idea—overjoyed at its prospect and anxious lest it should fail of expression. I remember so well his interest in me when he began to suspect that I had a new idea. He seemed to feel it somehow before I did. I was working at the problem of time and trying to state it in my own way. But my statement was very obscure in my first paper to his seminar. Still he scented something. He talked to my friends about it. When I presented a second draft to Royce's seminar, he listened with great attentiveness both to my own statement of my theory and to Royce's skillful dialectical way of leading me out in the discussion. He said nothing that night, but he met a friend of mine the next day and told him triumphantly: 'Boodin has come out at last.' He wanted, however, to get at me in still closer quarters to question me, and so when I met him a few days later, he invited me to dinner and spent the whole evening, talking the subject over with me. He led me on so as to do most of the talking. He came back with question after question. I tried to answer as best I could. He had been very serious and noncommittal all the evening. Finally late in the evening he arose and walked up to me with enthusiasm and said: 'Boodin, you have earned your degree. Any man with one original idea deserves a degree.'

And I suppose there never was any doubt in his mind after that. I learned the fact, however, only after I had worried through some sixteen examinations. I had malarial fever in the spring when I was finishing my thesis; and James worried for fear I would not get it in. Then it was that he told one of my friends that if I could only get my thesis in, it did not really matter about my examinations, as I had earned my degree. My friend considerately did not tell me until it was all over. When I read my final paper which was to be defended before the whole department, James paid no attention to the discussion, but took down some words which I mispronounced and in which he drilled me afterwards. He said he thought he would do me more good that way. It was all a foregone conclusion and a bore with him.

II

It was at his New Hampshire summer home at Lake Chocorua in 1903, after three years in the West, that I learned to know him best of all—boating on the lake, taking long walks through the woods, haying with him and his brother-in-law, driving long distances through that beautiful country and listening to his interested discussion with his native neighbors as regards roads and other improvements. It was a wonderful experience. We didn't talk much philosophy, but we talked about everything, as he was interested in everything.

James with his keen human intuition had realized both my fondness and my extreme timidity of the fairer human half and in the kindness of his heart had prepared a beautiful surprise for me. So he thought. This was why he gave a generous, though half humorous scolding for my being obliged to come a day later than his rather sudden invitation suggested. It came out finally: 'I invited such a fine girl for you to meet. She can only stay two days and now one day has already gone and you will hardly be able to see her.' It was his favorite girl student, and James like all genuine, true hearted men was fond of girls. It was hard to realize on the instant what a great treat a man could miss with William James himself there and his lovely family about him. But she was a splendid girl—a philosophic nature tempered with all that is finest and frankest in womanhood. It was true that there was but little time left—a morning in a boat on Lake Chocorua amidst the water lilies, exchanging mutual admiration of William James; but it is a beautiful memory nevertheless and not the least beautiful part of it is James' thoughtfulness. Sometimes these little things of love endear our friends to us more than even the biggest services they can render.

On one of our walks we had with us a Harvard senior who was visiting the family. James was very interested in him. He found out all about the undergraduate's point of view, how there were only two 'snaps' left among the Harvard courses and how they were in danger of being stiffened up, who the athletic and other heroes were. Then the talk changed to poetry. The undergraduate was a 'shark' at English literature and talked about his favorites. He was surprised to learn that James had read all of Wordsworth, and said that was regarded as a great 'stunt.' James laughed and told him he read Wordsworth because he enjoyed Wordsworth's purity of style and intimacy with nature. The undergraduate grew eloquent about Browning whom he regarded as 'hot stuff.' It was there that James dissented from him. He couldn't tolerate Browning.

> O, yes, the lyrics of Browning, they are exquisite. But no man has any business putting philosophy into poetry. He just muddled it. Prose was made for such things.

And so the afternoon went, James showing us all the time his favorite nooks of nature—the glens in the birchwoods and the glimpses in the distance of the mountains and lakes.

Few know how genuinely James' love for his family figured in his creative work. He used to say, 'I must write this book so as to leave it for my family.' It was this thought, he told me, which spurred him on to write his *Varieties of Religious Experience* during his long illness in Europe, propped up on pillows in his bed. This love together with his anxiety to further the movement which with him had a religious significance led him to work so hard his last years 'to save something from the Destroyer' as he put it, and to bequeath to the world those last noble volumes, *Pragmatism, A Pluralistic Universe, The Meaning of Truth, Some Problems in Philosophy.*

As he told me, though it was evident without his saying it, his wife possessed just the characteristics which were needed to supplement his own brilliant life. 'I am nervous,' he said, 'but my wife has the calm and poise to balance the family.' She loved his frailties and took the responsibility of the home. James' family was a mutual admiration society and without this restful companionship of home and children, to which he lent himself with such absolute abandon, it is hard to see how his intense nature, on the point of breaking for so long, could have sustained itself for the noble work of his later years, not to mention the incentive which this home appreciation always furnished.

Perhaps I may be allowed to inject in this connection one item of mythology: William James and that crabbed, warm hearted and able Scotchman, Thomas Davidson, were friends for years. It was in Davidson's philosophic retreat in the Adirondacks that James often sought rest and recreation. It was there in hours of relaxation that James acquired his large knowledge of biography from Davidson's splendid library. The story is that Davidson always claimed the credit for James's marrige. James was getting up into his middle thirties; and Davidson, match-making bachelor that he was, thought James ought to get married. A beautiful and attractive Boston belle also came up to the Adirondacks; and Davidson had made up his mind that she was just the woman for James. So one day he said to James: 'James, I have picked out a wife for you and I am going to introduce you to her.' James took Davidson's judgment and married the Boston belle. Well, that was Davidson's side of the story. James never told me his; and somebody else knows better than either. But whether Davidson's forethought was as good as he supposed, his afterthought was true to the facts.

I have spoken of this family affection because it shows that more than one great passion must be taken into account in understanding a great life. And James' life can only be understood through these profoundly human relations. Those who think that philosophers are necessarily queer and lonesome people or who bewail the absence, in our American University life, of the stimulus of German beer or French champagne, may take notice that these are not indispensable conditions of science.

James was most delightful and informal at the table. It was here he showed his exquisite, genial sense of humor. Sometimes as a parody on the professional and academic, he would beg me, with great dignity, to be seated, giving me all the titles to which I was entitled according to the manner of the Germans: Esteemed Reverend Mr. Doctor Professor will you kindly be seated. And then he would laugh his contagious, hearty laugh. Again he would take off the frailties of the philosophic profession, their weakness for being mentioned and their love of professional gossip, always including himself, and ended up by saying:

> Now I have discovered a new definition of a philosopher. Philosophers are people who like to get together and gossip about each other and hear themselves complimented.

But there was no bitterness in his raillery. Later, when he had suffered so much from stupid and even wilful misunderstanding by the pedants of his profession, he would sometimes betray some impatience. But beneath was the kindly flow of human nature just the same. We would gossip too. Everybody likes to gossip—not the women only. He used to be surprised at my wide acquaintance with the profession and their characteristics. Again he would be genuinely amused at the take-offs on the social tendencies of the day, such as Barrett Wendell's statement that the Boston girl's language had degenerated into two adjectives, 'charming and rotten' and would get his young daughter's advice and found that she used 'perfect' for every other word, thus adding a third adjective. He would comment with equal ease on serious topics—national peculiarities and jealousies and the folly of war, etc. But in the levity, as well as serious moods, he would betray his keen psychological interest in facts, first hand individual facts, as well as his love for human nature.

One day the mail brought him the news that he had been elected to the distinguished old society in Rome—the Society of Lynxes. But it brought sadness rather than joy, it seemed to me. He said:

> When I was a boy I remember reading about this society with a great deal of interest and wondering if I could ever belong to a society like that. Now it only reminds me that I am getting old. And it means more annual dues.

After my visit at Chocorua he insisted on driving me himself across the mountains, some thirty miles to Sandwich where I was to pay a visit to my good friend and colleague, Jesse Macy of Grinnell. It rained all day—a soothing, pattering mountain rain, through New Hampshire's turning autumnal foliage. We sat quiet a good deal of the time in sympathetic meditation. Sometimes the native's estimate of distances would add a bit of humor to the drive. It was across a strange country to both of us and we kept inquiring the distances. Some one would tell us that it was fifteen miles more; and then we would drive another half hour and ask again and get the same reply. He would brighten up for a moment and laugh and remark: 'We are at least holding our own.' But on the whole it was a solemn trip. It was the last visit we had together, and somehow we both felt it. I was impressed with the way in which he spoke to his horse, relieving the silence of the mountain fog. There was an instinctive companionship between the horse and his master. The horse felt, too, the sympathy of a great soul. James was unusually serious about my future. He wanted to see me launched. He had been reading my time-manuscript and wanted to see it announced in the important periodicals. He would write some of the editors about me and did so. . . .

Again, after a silent interval, he would speak of his own plans for creative work, how slowly he made progress on his metaphysics and that he had rewritten the first part several times; and still there seemed to be nothing he could use. The fragment of it has only appeared after his death under the modest heading: 'An Introduction to an Introduction to Philosophy.' But even then it was left in three manuscripts. He would speak with feeling about his desire to rescue as much as he could 'from the Destroyer.' For the shadow of death lay across his path in the uncertainty which organic heart trouble always involves. His friends would regard this fear as one of his amiable weaknesses. But here too he proved pragmatically right, for it was his noble heart that finally refused to work. But there was no bitterness in the thought of death. It was only the thought of sharing in the life of the world and his family to the utmost, as long and as much as he could. For he felt the mission of a great movement, however modestly he looked upon his own part.

I naturally felt overwhelmed with gratitude for all his kind thoughts of me, and towards the end of the journey I asked him: 'Isn't there anything I can do for you in return?' He was much touched and put his arm round my shoulders for a moment and said with feeling:

> My dear boy, I can't think of anything you can do for me unless you could give me your youth. (And then he added after a pause:) No, I only want you to be a great metaphysician.

We finally arrived at Sandwich and had a cold lunch, as it was late for dinner. He was much taken with the genuineness and simplicity of Professor Macy; and they went out of doors into the rain for quite a while and talked over my life in Grinnell. Macy made him promise, because I was so useful, Harvard would not take me away; and James consented that I should stay in Grinnell a long time with Macy. He saw what splendid friends I had in that little college. Towards evening he returned in solitude in the rain and the fog; after having given me his last fond blessing and left me with the sweetest of all memories.

James told me he loved to be out in the mist and the mountain fog. Its mystery, its silent challenge to risk and exploration, its atmosphere of wrapped up immediacy appealed to him. It makes friends feel so close together. Mystic he was to a very much greater extent than he gave himself credit for being, just because of his vivid sense of first hand values, of the living reality of the flow of life and its fluent transitions. It was the movement, the flow, which he felt to be real; the substantives were but the perching places; the concepts were but instruments to the definition and control of this flow. This is what made James seem often, though only momentarily, a pure empiricist rather than a pragmatist—an advocate of the self-sufficiency of the immediate moment with its flash of luminous insight and conviction unspoiled by theory, while pragmatism must find truth as an outcome of expectancy and patient trial. It runs through his work, over and over again, this feeling for first experience, even unusual and outlandish experience. Better suspend theory, even pragmatic social testing, for the time being, rather than that experience should fail to have its say, for truth may be a gift, for the time being at least, to the private moment with God.

He was an idealist for he believed in supreme risk and creative strenuousity as regards the future. The finally real things for him were the eternal and supreme things. But even this religious idealism could not remain abstract for James. Religion was never a thing of the bare future for him. So near was God to man. The invisible presence backed him from the mysterious depths of the subconscious. The ideal power was one of friendly companionship, of expansiveness and sympathy, never of barren contraction.

This was beautifully illustrated by a little incident. Some of us had been listening to a noted preacher. I think it was Lyman Abbott. We were profoundly impressed by his appeal that worthiness of immortality was the important thing rather than the fact of immortality. We walked home with William James, and he invited us into his study. He asked questions and one of us grew very eloquent in defense of this abstract worthiness of immortality. James' reply was characteristic. He fastened upon us his benignant smile and said: 'Which would you rather: to be worthy of a fine beautiful wife or have one?' It silenced the argument, for it came right home to us. We admitted we would rather have the 'fine beautiful wife,' unworthy though we might be. It was brought home to us that the best things in life are not abstractions. They come as gifts and raise us by their coming.

The kindliness of James' own nature made it impossible for him to understand the abstract sacrifices demanded by the ancient gods of the Semites. Rather did he find religion realized in the communion of the saints—the immediate sense of companionship which he found sublimated in some great personalities, however inadequate he felt his own truly human experience.

I have before me a beautiful, cheery Christmas letter of December 21, '03, encouraging me and offering detailed advice about publications, rejoicing over Dewey's *Studies on Logical Theory*—'a genuinely new school of thought.' Yet while doing all this, he was ill in bed. In his own graphic language:

> My own Christmas doesn't promise to be very merry. I am in my eleventh day of confinement to bed or sofa, first with influenza of a virulent sort, and now with the catarrh still on me, with acute rheumatic inflammation of one foot. This latter may confine me for weeks—a somewhat unpleasant prospect.

It was. Most people wouldn't have been in a humor to write 'merry' Christmas letters to other people and share their trouble under the circumstances.

The encouragement I got from James that summer at Chocorua led me to take up my creative work, which had been buried beneath the cares and duties of life in a small western college. In the year 1903–04, I brought out my monograph, *Time and Reality,* in Baldwin's Psychological Review series. The book, except for the hearty appreciation by William James, would have seemed a dead failure to me. I quote James' letter about it in full, not because I feel worthy of its sentiment, but to give a sample of James' friendly help extended so often to lonely workers at a distance, as well as to those near:

> Chocorua, N. H., June 24, 1904
>
> Dear Boodin:
>
> I have just read your essay, having been obliged, by fatigue and by 'duties' to postpone the business until now.
>
> It is a masterly piece of work, both in thought and in style, and represents a synthesis vast enough, and original enough to give you an admitted mas-

ter's place. Of course I am in fullest sympathy with the doctrine you profess, and I am astonished at the agreement of your chapters on Truth with the doctrines of the Chicago and Oxford School. Certainly Dewey and Schiller will hail you as a great ally. Certainly I do. When you sent me the first part of the *MS.* long ago, I complained of the technicality of the style. Somehow that appearance has entirely vanished. Although the whole discussion is a highly technical one, the style is admirably simple, straightforward and clear. It is a pity that a doctrine which makes itself the champion of primitive irreflective life against the arrogations of the intellect should after all have to conduct its warfare with such highly intellectual weapons. Empiricism, but '*critical*' empiricism! Of course the intellectualists will seize upon the antinomy here, and try to make capital out of it, and will doubtless to the end of time have that tactical advantage over more concrete thinkers.

I have done no writing (or rather thirty-two pages of it only!) this year, but propose now to get at it. I haven't your letter with me and forget what it was you asked me to do about the MS.—whether to return it to you or to Baldwin, and whether to write an endorsement of it or not. Pray let me know . . . Pray write soon—O great Metaphysician, to yours truly,

Wm. James.

How extravagant, you say. I know it. But who does not like to have some friend who exaggerates one's merits and possibilities. And such appreciation, extended so genuinely and freely to the young philosophers of his generation, has done a good deal to stimulate creative activity and sometimes to make his generous estimate come true, thus verifying his own creative theory of reality. He was wrong, however, in supposing that I would be welcomed with open arms by the leaders of the movement. Both the severity of the logical demands of the book and the strictures it implies as regards the vagaries of the movement were distasteful to the impressionistic type with which the movement was both embraced and queered for a while. The personal commendation of James and his 'bragging' of it to his friends and students was most of the encouragement which I received. . .

Chocorua, Sept. 26, '06

Dear Boodin:

Your welcome letter of July 26th lies again before me—not answered with undue haste, indeed, but with the deliberation suitable to philosophic interchanges. I shall read your paper on Space with avidity, and hope it may be one-half as good as that on Time. Direction as a fundamental attribute of reality is an exciting idea to me, and to have it admitted once for all might greatly simplify our formulations. You needn't fret at having to teach the elements exclusively. It consumes one's energy, 'tis true, and forces idleness in higher things. But your brain is essentially dialectic and constructive, and is bound to do original work and 'get there' in the end, under *any* conditions, perhaps all the more effectively for having its results mature more slowly and naturally and inevitably. So don't worry!

As I live longer I acquire more and more confidence in the pragmatic *method* as a master key to solving problems. I sometimes believe that we are on the verge of a big secular revolution in thought, after which the whole Kantian or neo-Kantian, Bradleian, Roycean atmosphere of thought with its abstractions, a priorisms and 'necessities,' will appear paleontological. I cease teaching after this year, and only wish I hadn't postponed it so long. My vital energy is lowering, and if I wish to save anything from the Destroyer's hand, I must not waste time. I have next year a big elementary course in Paulsen, during which I shall hardly have strength to write, but I want to write an *Introduction to Philosophy* similar in some ways to his (partly as a market venture) partly to popularize the pragmatic method; and after that to write some more essays on difficult points in radical empiricism and collect the lot into a volume.

Good bye and good luck to you, dear Boodin. My wife joins me in regards.

Yours every truly,

Wm. James.

III

Even James' buoyant and lovable nature sometimes shows signs of discouragement which makes him more akin to the rest of us mortals. These discouragements were owing partly to the continued handicap of ill health of his later years and partly to the thickening misunderstandings which gathered round the pragmatic movement. Friendship meant so much to James that it hurt him deeply that many of his old associates and admirers contributed to the misunderstanding. Could he have realized it, however, he would have seen that it was not so much the friends who criticised him as those who romantically espoused the movement that hurt his cause the most. The following letter shows some of the sadness and irritation James felt, though his playful humor did not forsake him. I ought to explain, perhaps, that I had sportively remarked in a previous letter that I would like to win second place in the movement. The reply shows James' generous modesty. I should not have burdened him with my own work, I see now. But was he not my teacher and master, even though distant? And what other reward did I have except his approval?

95 Irving St., Cambridge, Mass., Oct. 28, '06

Dear Boodin:

I am very much indeed in the sere and yellow leaf this autumn, and may have any day to stop lecturing altogether. In the mass of printed and *MS.* matter that flows in, I naturally can't come up to time. I am trying to prepare some Lowell lectures advertised to begin November 14. They may not be given; but meanwhile I can't get at your MS. on the Ought. Shall I send it back unread or keep it a month at least longer?

I read your two articles on Space and Reality in the proof you sent me long ago, but I haven't re-read then in the *Journal.* I had some strictures to make, after admiring the clear and straight style of them, but I can't remember now just what they were and am unable to re-read for the purpose. My reaction must be postponed, like so many of my other functions.

I wish you would be the second pragmatist. Schiller and Dewey, between them, halve the first place, with Schiller, I think, a little ahead. I am willing to be fourth.

My Lowell lectures are on 'Pragmatism.' What asses all our critics are making of themselves on the subject of pragmatism and truth. (e.g. the excellent Russell in Woodbridge's last number.) It is time for a little 'imagination' in philosophy to begin—we have long heard it praised in 'Science'—imagination of what your opponent can reasonably mean by what he says. I do think that the misinterpretation of Schiller and Dewey is discreditable in the extreme.

Yours as ever, dear B. W. J.

All this has been brought to a brilliant focus and expression in *Pragmatism.* It seems strange to us now how there should have been all these misunderstandings about the doctrine. How simple and clear it all seems that truth must be tested by its consequences, as the tree is known by its fruit.

Who can doubt, too, that this human nature of ours must be reckoned with? Temperament plays its part in our seeking for truth. His striking statement of the fundamental divisions of mental constitution—'the tender minded,' those who have a strong feeling for principles, for unities;

and 'the tough minded,' those whose emphasis is on facts, on differences and cleavages in our world—has become classic. James' own temperament is a singular blending of the two. And how revolutionary this pragmatic method would become, old though it is, if it ever got into our blood. What a vast increase in the economy and efficiency of our conduct if we could learn to drop superfluous theories, mere technicalities that make no difference to the merits of the case, if we could learn to follow the leading of the hypothesis only as we realize its 'cash value' in the way of facts, in increased efficiency of conduct. At length this pragmatic consciousness is percolating into our science, our law and our religion; and the effects are as revolutionary as James dreamed they would be.

Cambridge, June 25, 1905.

Dear Boodin:—

I was very glad to get news of your having had another prosperous year, and I am glad you give so good an account of S. I am only a fortnight back from a three months' trip away to Europe, which I found mentally refreshing but physically fatiguing. 'I'm not the man I once was.' I had meant to take your 'Time' article with me to re-read, but somehow it was left out of my trunk, but I shall soon get at it now. I found a vigorous 'pragmatic' movement in Italy, and I found that Bergson could in most vital respects be counted on as an ally. I hear from a student that Royce has converted back a good many men from my teaching in his second half of the course. The more honor to him! But I can't write letters—and this is only to waft you a word of good will and affection.

Yours ever truly,

Wm. James.

An interesting experiment at Harvard during James' last years of teaching was the practice of dividing the course in metaphysics so as to give the students the benefit of two great teachers of diverging views—James and Royce. James took the students the first semester and used all his human convincingness, his genial irony and humor to impress the students with pragmatism. Royce followed the second semester. This letter shows the chivalrous spirit between the two friends who were fighting for the supremacy of the human mind. It also shows that James was beginning to feel the encouragement from Europe, especially from Italy and France. It was a sincere tribute when some years later at James' death all the great French papers came out in black borders. A bond of sympathy was beginning to spring up between James and Bergson, his much younger contemporary, who had himself been vitally influenced by the older master.

Bergson, however, did not seem to figure in James' imagination until the former's publication of his *Creative Evolution*. The former books of Bergson are subtle and metaphysical and had not appealed to James. He was evidently ignorant before this of Bergson's theory of time which has been extensively expounded in *Time and Free Will*. In all my talks with James upon the subject of time from 1897 to the publication of my essay in 1904, James never spoke of Bergson. And in the letter which follows where he is wildly enthusiastic about *Creative Evolution* he evidently regards this as Bergson's first statement of his time theory. Then, too, while there is some similarity in the results of Bergson's theory and mine, the method of approach is practically opposite—Bergson's method is intuitional, while my method is pragmatic. It was the concrete wealth of material and brilliancy of style of *Creative Evolution* which attracted James and which led him in his generous extravagance to speak of Bergson as master. How impossible that parentage is one can realize when one recalls that *The Will to Believe and Other Essays* had been out as a book (not to mention the dates of the chapters) since 1899. James' philosophy was already fairly before the world. Their point of view of truth, too, differed all the way from Bergson's mysticism to James' 'logical realism.' But though James' sense of time is confused, there can be no doubt of his genuine appreciation of *Creative Evolution* and the encouragement it brought him. It came to him as a sort of new revelation and as usual his generosity blurred the differences between his own view and that of the man with whom he sympathized. I quote his brief letter in full:

95 Irving St., Cambridge, July 7, 1907

Dear Boodin:

I have your welcome letter about my book and thank you for it. I have read all your own recent writings carefully, and I applaud their force and originality. In essential things you and I are side by side, and I am sure that our movement will prevail. But my brain won't allow me to write letters about details, so I spare you specific comments.

Have you seen Bergson's *L'Evolution Créatrice*—a perfectly divine production, in which intellectualism receives its definitive death wound and in which

your view of time (tho he seems ignorant of you) is vindicated for eternity! Read it. The wife sends her warm regards, and I am ever faithfully yours.
Wm. James.

I had kept out of the pragmatic controversy as my interest was rather in the application of the method to the larger problems of reality than in the misunderstandings that clouded the statement of the doctrine itself. I had even, now and then, taken occasion to satirize the excesses of pragmatism with characteristic philosophic irony. James did not resent this, but assured me that we were on the same road and that he followed with interest everything I wrote.

I realize, in looking back, that it might have been some comfort to him had I formally identified myself with the movement, though I did not deem myself important enough so that it could matter. To him, however, it was a propaganda. It came to appear as a life mission. I find the following in a letter written in 1905:

> . . . It would please me amazingly, dear Boodin, if you could conscientiously prove an ally. I don't see why our systems won't work splendidly together. The opponents are nowhere, and absolutism seems to me, particularly in view of their incapacity (even Royce's) at this present juncture, more and more a poor feeble old ghost.

But the fact that the ambiguous alliances of pragmatism made it impossible for me to join formally the ranks did not lessen the interest for me. While I was not appealed to by the coming glory of pragmatism, which James was anxious that I should share, I felt the call later, when disappointing misunderstandings and ill health had saddened James' life and when he himself felt the need of 'sloughing' off some of the associations.

I felt at length that filial loyalty required of me that I should get into the fight and bear some small share of the misunderstanding and odium which had been heaped upon the movement. And so I wrote the paper, 'What Pragmatism Is and Is Not,' which I submitted to James. For pragmatism as regards its central doctrine or method was then historic; and neither wild-eyed and long-haired enthusiasts nor malevolent critics could make it what they chose. Like Boston it is primarily a state of mind. But it is a very definite attitude; and while capable of indefinite development it presents a central core of method and temper. As James himself had developed and restricted pragmatism in his own mind during a number of years, his endorsement of my exposition acquires a certain historic significance. It also silences those who say, as some friends of mine have said, that they believe in my statement of truth, but that it should not be called pragmatism. There are many indications that James felt the need of definition and restrictions, as shown both in his own last writings and in a paper, prepared more or less with his collaboration, by his friend and pupil, Dr. H. M. Kallen, entitled, 'The Affiliations of Pragmatism' and published shortly after mine, the last year of James' life. My own paper has since been included in a volume, *Truth and Reality,* in which I have tried to interpret and build out further the pragmatic attitude to truth. I give James' letter here in full, as it throws light upon his state of mind at the time, apart from its approval of my statement.

95 Irving St., Cambridge, Oct. 20, '09.

Dear Boodin:

I am overjoyed at your paper—I keep the MS as you don't say you want it back. You are one of a very few men who have grasped our account of knowledge, simple as it is. I don't know what's the matter with the rest but you have rung the changes on it perfectly, and I hope your article will do some good. The tone of the others is changing fast, however—*vide* Montague and Lovejoy.

You ought to have got my *Meaning of Truth* before sending your letter. It was ordered to be sent you in advance. Read Knox's Review of Pratt's book on pragmatism in the October *Mind.* It puts the dots on the i's very neatly.

Yours as ever with affectionate regards,

Wm. James.

The MS on Metaphysics was James' hoodoo. He was keeping it with him for years, writing and rewriting—at the rate of thirty-two pages in one year. He had been worrying about it and came to a standstill in 1903; and it was on his mind to the end. Of course he wrote articles and books on pragmatism and other topics between times, which he didn't count. When James was diverted from his worry over abstract problems and let himself go in the direction of more concrete and psychological interests, his style flowed as smoothly as ever, and his creative genius seemed unabated to the end. The Lowell Lectures, on Pragmatism, which he dreaded so much, took shape with little effort and with tremendous consequences so far as the movement was concerned, when they were shortly launched. *The Meaning of Truth* and *A Pluralistic Universe,* with numerous papers followed. But all the while, through this after-bloom of creative genius, the metaphysics remained a fragment.

The fragmentary character of this particular piece of work which he had set himself to do, in a systematic and formal way, led James to feel that his life's work was peculiarly unfinished; he puts it pathetically in his note left with the manuscript:

> Say it is fragmentary and unrevised. Call it 'A Beginning of an Introduction to Philosophy.' Say I hoped by it to round out my system, which now is too much like an arch built up on one side.

Yet, interesting as the fragment is, it is doubtful whether it adds much, or would have added much even could it have been formally completed, to the concrete, human presentations in which he has expressed his far-reaching and comprehensive *Weltanschauung*—a philosophy built out suggestively and brilliantly on all sides. It is evident that he required the inspiration of living, human situations to do his work. Every important book, excepting in a sense the *Principles of Psychology,* was produced to meet a special human occasion. And the above-named work was the result of his vital relation to his students during years of teaching.

His *Briefer Course,* which was prepared cold-bloodedly for the market, was put together with so much impatience that it bears unmistakable evidence of its method of production—the scissors. In this connection a story is told by Dr. Dickenson [*sic*] Miller. James was in the Adirondacks for his favorite rest, when the publishers pressed him for the text book. He had no copy of the larger work with him. So he borrowed Dr. Miller's copy. He proceeded to cut the copy to pieces and to prepare his manuscript. With the naiveté of genius, he afterwards cut to pieces a new book and pasted the pieces into Dr. Miller's copy so as to make it complete. It is needless to say that this pasted copy is now a valued souvenir. A friend of James in telling the story remarked that inasmuch as James had only one copy from which to prepare his MS, it is plain to see that he was right in stating that the abbreviated work was in part rewritten. In spite of its having been an uncongenial task, the book has been the most successful, because the most human of psychological text books.

As I look over James' writings and communications during the last years of his life, I am struck with his freshness and brilliancy to the end, a little short of sixty-nine. In literary charm and breadth of sympathy nothing that he has done surpasses *A Pluralistic Universe,* and, in dialectical and severely logical thinking, *The Meaning of Truth* is his crowning achievement. Both these books came out in 1909, the year before his death. *Pragmatism,* which furnishes the program of the movement, was struck off for the Lowell Lectures and published in 1907. I have already spoken of *An Introduction to an Introduction*[1] which had been revised up to the time of his death. James illustrates strikingly that genius carries with it a perpetual youth and knows nothing of Osler's law, that men become stereotyped by forty, however true this is for the imitative average type of mind.

To be sure, there is a core of germinal insight, which runs through all James' creative work. But each production is nevertheless unique and strikingly new. His life was a series of surprises. And they were surprises to himself, as well as to others. Unlike Spencer, he had no early preconceived scheme to write so many books. He told me once, 'Each time I write a book it seems as though I was going to say all I had to say and as though this were my last. But something new always opens up.' Except for the mechanical accident of his heart's stopping, new and untapped insights would still have opened up to the world, though few, if any, have left more in quality and inspiration than he. To all ages he is a reporter of good tidings, that the human heart in its strivings may dare to be true to itself and that we cannot go wrong if we trust the leading of human experience.

I had hoped to get a glimpse of James again the summer of 1910. He had been in Europe to look after his brother in his illness and had just returned. I had written him at Chocorua from Salem Willows where I had spent the summer, when unexpectedly my eyes fell upon the announcement through the brutal headlines of a newspaper that William James was dead. I retired to my room and wept as I only had wept at the death of my own father when I was a boy. A light and a love had gone out of my life which could not be replaced. To relieve my sorrow I wrote a little tribute and with it made a solemn vow to try to help the cause which my master had loved so much. This tribute I wish to save as the memory of a sacred grief from the wreckage of the years by placing it here.

WM. JAMES—AN APPRECIATION. AUGUST 28, 1910. We feel like orphans in our bereavement. Who like him will follow our feeble efforts? Who like him will cheer us on to do our best? Who like him will have the generosity to praise the little service we have done? He was a

1. Published as *Some Problems of Philosophy.*

Superman, not of the brutal, selfish type of Nietzsche, but a Superman in his sanity, in the breadth of his sympathy, in the nobility of his kindness—a Superman, because he outstripped ordinary human nature so vastly in all that is best. His kindly leading shall divinely urge us on to still greater conquests. Why so precious a bit of mind-stuff should be bound up with such fragile clay, we cannot understand. But the mind itself remains. It warms, it inspires, it creates. The noble heart that stopped from over-work, still continues to throb in his immortal pages and in the still more real lives that survive to inherit as well as mourn. Unworthy though I am, I place this flower on his grave.

ROSWELL PARKER ANGIER

(1874–1946)

In the spring semester of 1917, when Harvard's Philosophy Department needed an emergency replacement for Hugo Münsterberg, who had recently died, they turned to Roswell Angier, a former undergraduate and graduate student at Harvard who earned a doctorate in 1903. At the time, Angier was a member of the Yale faculty, where he had begun as an instructor in 1906 and risen to full professor in 1917.

After he completed his doctorate, Angier served as assistant in the Physiological Laboratory at the University of Berlin, and from there applied for a position at the University of California at Berkeley. James deemed Angier one of Harvard's best 'laboratory Ph.D.s—not, I fancy a "philosopher," but a sterling good man.' James reported that even his colleague Edwin Bissell Holt, who could be harshly critical of graduate students, 'swears that Angier is the ablest man we've graduated in Psychology since we've been here.'[1] Instead of accepting the position at Berkeley, though, Angier began his career at Yale. In 1909 he became acting director of the Yale Psychology Laboratory; in 1920, he was appointed Dean of Freshmen; in 1937, Associate Dean of the Graduate School. During World War I, Angier was stationed at Mineola, New York, in charge of psychological testing for aviators.

Angier was an editorial director of *The Psychological Bulletin,* where he edited a special issue on the physiology of the central nervous system, and a member of the council of the American Psychological Association.

NOTES

1. WJ to Charles Bakewell. Scott, 384–85 (22 September 1905).

Another Student's Impressions of James at the Turn of the Century

In these personal impressions of William James, I shall confine myself to my student days at Harvard—1893 to 1897 (undergraduate) and 1900 to 1903 (graduate, in psychology). They were the most vivid and enduring impressions.

As a sophomore, philosophically *tabula rasa,* I took the eye-opening introductory course—logic by Palmer, history of modern philosophy by Santayana, and psychology by James. Compared with the others James made hard going of ordered lecturing. Certainly it could not have been said of him, as someone said of Royce, that lecturing was his natural form of breathing. 'You have read today's chapter,' he remarked from his favorite perch on a corner of the platform desk, holding up to the large class a copy of his *Briefer course;* 'I wrote the book, and what *I* think is all there—but perhaps there is a question.' In such sparrings for openings some debatable issue, perhaps self-initiated, usually bobbed up. He would then become animated and fluent, with rising assertiveness, and throw off with apparent unconcern the verbal picturesquenesses to which his writings have accustomed us. These clarifying interludes were our joy, and James' forte. Positive, even vehement in expression, he none the less impressed us as undogmatic and open-minded, as if science and philosophy were a never-ending but serious game. 'The best thing I can say for it,' he wrote in concluding his first exposition of his theory of the emotions, 'is, that in writing it, I have almost persuaded *myself* [his italics] that it may be true.'[1] We undergraduates had not read that sentence—but it would have clicked.

In the laboratory it was plain that James had neither flair nor patience for experimental work, and that he didn't care who knew it; he was a flat

1. W. James, What is an emotion? *Mind,* 1884, 9, 188–205.

failure at pretense. One day he was energetically soaping his hands over the hopper in the cluttered laboratory room while a woman graduate student was telling him that she did not know what to do next, suggesting that she might dissect a sheep's brain. 'Yes, yes,' James hastily agreed, as if also washing his hands of her and her problem, 'that's perhaps the best thing you *could* do.' But it is a grave mistake—one long persistent—to assume that James had small use, if not actual contempt, for experiment.[2] After all, it was not a fortuitous circumstance that he set up perhaps the first going psychology laboratory in America, and pioneered in exploiting the findings of experimentalists (several hundred pages in the *Principles*). James' biting gibes—'brass instrument psychology' and 'the elaboration of the obvious'—were aimed at contemporary experimentalists, not at experiment. 'The man who throws out most new ideas and immediately seeks to subject them to experimental control,' he wrote, 'is the most useful psychologist.' Helmholtz was one of his idols. What he missed in his experimenting contemporaries was the ideas.

It was when fighting for fair play to human and moral values as standards of truth that James became most vehemently eloquent, and impressed most deeply his student audiences. Neither the fine-spun logic of the absolutists nor science itself could be permitted to lord it over the cogent evidence of the 'brute datum' of experience. The relational *ad infinitums* of Bradley (*Appearance and Reality*) James dubbed 'sheer intellectual perversity,' and 'Bah! what silly quibbling' he pencilled in the margin of his own copy of Royce's *The world and the individual.* In science, if the law of the conservation of energy interfered with the concept of interactionism, 'what's the law of the conservation of energy among friends?'—he might have said. I particularly remember his impassioned battling, on experimental grounds, for the freedom of the will in an address on *The Dilemma of Determinism,* and another—most moving of all—on *Is Life Worth Living,* delivered on a hot June evening in tiny, crowded Holden Chapel. As James stood there in the cramped space, close in front of his audience, reading with a sort of tumultous rush from his nervous manuscript, perspiration streaming from his forehead, one felt almost palpably the tense absorption of the student group as he bared his own fighting faith in life's worthwhileness—closing, as his admonition to the faint-hearted, with Henry IV's greeting

2. For a recent expression of this notion, see D. B. Klein, Psychology's progress and the armchair taboo, Psychol. Rev., 1942, 49, 229.

to the tardy Crillon, after a great victory: 'Hang yourself, brave Crillon! We fought at Arques, and you were not there.'

Brilliant, high-strung, dynamic, vivacious, resilient, unexpected, unconventional, picturesque—these are some of the terms that at once recur in recalling James. Among many incidents, I remember his fetching embarrassment when baffled while figuring on the blackboard; his remark in the college Yard when congratulating me on securing my Ph.D.: '*but,* you've probably read what bosh I think it all is'; the startled turning of heads toward him in crowded Sanders Theatre as he conspicuously beat the audience to its applause of General Booth at the close of a moving address on the work of the Salvation Army among the poor; his fidgeting at a department symposium in Royce's house, and his silent exit, in carpet slippers, when Münsterberg was in full teutonic swing; his entrance, with elaborate stealth, clad in brown Norfolk jacket, striped trousers, *and* silk hat, into Royce's morning metaphysics class already under way, his attentive listening to Royce on The Absolute—and the departure of the two from the room. We left them on the steps of Sever Hall as we slowly trailed away, still arguing, as they so often did—James animated and Royce quiet, with his whimsical, tolerant smile.

HORACE MEYER KALLEN

(1882–1974)

In the summer of 1907, James wrote to his friend F. C. S. Schiller to introduce a Harvard graduate student who was coming to Oxford on a Sheldon fellowship:[1]

> He is a Russian Jew by birth,[2] very intense in character, very able and with high potentialities of all round cultivation, an enthusiastic and aggressive 'pragmatist,' an active political worker, a *decidedly* original mind, neurotic disposition, but sails indefinitely long close to the wind without losing headway, a man with a positive future and possibly a great one and in good directions: *Revers de la médaille: sticky,* conceited, censorious of all institutions. Nevertheless faithful, candid, goodlooking and in favor of all good things.[3]

James's enthusiastic and neurotic young student was Horace Kallen, then twenty-five, who had studied at Harvard for a Bachelor of Arts degree and returned in 1905 after teaching English at Princeton for two years.

Kallen arrived as an undergraduate disturbed by the disjunction between his secular and religious education and his daily experiences. His father, a rabbi, raised his son according to strict Orthodox Jewish tradition. Kallen felt that he was supposed to believe in the transcendent existence of 'One—One God, One Universe, One Humanity, One World, One Law of Nature, One Rule of Life for All Mankind.'[4] But on the streets of Boston he saw diversity and conflict. 'Non-Jews were troubling my days and nights,' he wrote, 'because, through no fault of my own, I happened to be different from them. My difference diminished me, shackled me, deprived me of my liberty and subjected me to injustice.'[5] He felt he could solve his problem only by repudiating Judaism.

But two Harvard professors helped him change his mind: Barrett Wendell presented the Old Testament in an historical and political context; William James, Kallen explained, taught an empiricism that 'acknowledges the reality of the multiple ways the singulars join together and move apart, no less identifiable than the presences they relate.'[6] James proved to be one of the most important influences of Kallen's life: 'the liberator whose being and whose teaching set me free from superstition.'[7]

James helped Kallen to define his role as a philosopher who also could do the work of the world. 'My earliest interests were as literary as philosophical,' Kallen wrote, 'and were soon crossed by direct participation in political and economic movements of the land, especially those aiming at the protection and growth of freedom, including the labor movement, the civil liberties union and the consumers' cooperative movement.'[8] He resigned from the University of Wisconsin after seven years of teaching in protest over a free speech issue. In *The Structure of Lasting Peace: An Inquiry in the Motives of War and Peace* (1918), he promoted his idealistic vision of a united world of nations that celebrated cultural, ethnic, and religious differences.

Kallen focused his thinking about the implications of diversity during his year at Oxford, when he became friends with Alain Locke, the first black American Rhodes scholar. He and Locke talked at length about 'my Jewish and his Negro difference'[9] and considered the implications of 'cultural pluralism,' a concept that Kallen hoped would counter the well-intentioned efforts of many social reformers to work toward rapid assimilation of immigrants. In articles in the *Nation* in 1915, in his *Culture and Democracy in the United States* (1924), and later in *Cultural Pluralism and the American Idea* (1956), Kallen argued for a national identity that incorporated a harmony of many voices.

This harmony seemed remote as society engaged in the first world war, and Kallen looked for an active role to promote peace and freedom. In 1919, together with a group of other concerned intellectuals, Kallen founded the New School for Social Research, a facility devoted to adult education that has attracted to its faculty some of the world's most respected philosophers, historians, and social scientists.

Like many of James's students, Kallen became a friend of the family—but unlike some, he established independent friendships with Alice and James's son William as well. A week after James's death, Alice wrote to Kallen to thank him for his condolences and assure him that she would depend on his help to edit James's work-in-progress, *Some Problems of Philosophy*.[10] There is evidence, however, that Kallen was unhappy with the editing decisions made by James's son Henry, who supervised the project, and Ralph Barton Perry, who acted as consultant.[11] In this essay, Kallen's criticism of Perry's biography no doubt reflects his feeling of rivalry with another of James's prized students.

NOTES

1. James personally supplemented Kallen's funds by a few hundred dollars.

2. Kallen was born in Silesia, which in 1882 was part of Germany, and emigrated to America with his family in 1887. He was raised in Boston.

3. WJ to F. C. S. Schiller. Scott, 443 (15 July 1907).

4. Horace Kallen, *What I Believe and Why—Maybe* (New York: Horizon, 1970), 167.

5. Kallen, *What I Believe and Why*, 169.

6. Kallen, *What I Believe and Why*, 169.

7. Horace Kallen, 'Remembering William James,' *In Commemoration of William James 1842–1942* (New York: Columbia University Press, 1942) 12.

8. Quoted in Milton Konvitz, 'In Praise of Hyphenation and Orchestration,' *The Legacy of Horace Kallen*, ed. Konvitz (Rutherford NJ: Fairleigh Dickinson University Press, 1987), 19.

9. Konvitz, 'In Praise of Hyphenation and Orchestration,' 173.

10. Alice James to Horace Kallen, 3 September 1910. American Jewish Archives. James had indicated that he wanted Kallen to edit this manuscript.

11. Myers, *William James* (New Haven: Yale University Press, 1986) 508 n.14.

Remarks on R. B. Perry's Portrait of William James

In 1920 Henry James, the eldest son of William James, brought out two volumes of his father's letters. Unless I am much mistaken, the publication of this selection from the countless letters of William James gave a new turn to biographical writing. Although the choice and ordering of the letters expressed, as perforce they had to, the temperament and preferences of the filial editor, the letters themselves made the effect of an authentic, if unintended, autobiography. The editorial additions were of the slightest and most objective. They consisted only of statements of fact indispensable for binding the letters together and sustaining the biographical continuity where the letters did not altogether of themselves do so. One had met this literary form before in fiction, but never in biography. The consequences in the writing world were swift and noticeable. The new biographical manner was at once quietly but extensively taken up and some of the biographies done in this style were awarded Pulitzer prizes. Mr. Perry's magisterial two-volume handling of William James's *Nachlass* has also received the Pulitzer crown, but it is a successful example neither of the new biographical form, nor of the old. Mr. Perry himself exposes the reason why. The work was 'originally undertaken,' he says in his preface, 'for the purpose of giving to the public selections from the great mass of correspondence, lecture notes, diaries, marginaria and other manuscripts left by William James and deposited by his family in the Harvard College Library. Although it seemed desirable to weave this material into a systematic account of James's devel-

The Thought and Character of William James as Revealed in Unpublished Correspondence and Notes, together with his Published Writings. By Ralph Barton Perry. 2 Vols. with illustrations. Volume I—Inheritance and Vocation. Volume II—Philosophy and Psychology. Boston, Little, Brown & Company, 1935. Pp. xxxviii, 826; xxiv, 786.

opment, there has been no abandonment of the original aim which was to provide a vehicle for James himself.' But somehow, 'James himself,' and his biographer's 'systematic account of James's development,' do not seem to have gotten harmoniously knit together. The master's *Nachlass* is neither permitted to tell its own story, nor yet directly employed as stones of the biographer's mosaic, building up his pattern. As biography the work falls between the two stools of the old biographical form and the new. The parts—'James himself' and the 'systematic account of James's development'—do not strike me as supporting one another. In the main they run parallel, and where they touch do so only at the edges, without combining into an organic composition.

Thus Mr. Perry has distributed some 500 letters of William James's not formerly published, upward of 50 of his father's, 30 of his brother Henry's, 17 of Emerson's, besides a variety of letters to William James from philosophical and literary correspondents, under six general headings: I. His Father's Son. II. Education and Career. III. Early Philosophical Orientation. IV. Psychology. V. Ethics and Religion. VI. The Ultimate Philosophical System. But one is not led to feel, as one reads, that his distribution is logically well-ordered or psychologically natural; alternative distributions suggest themselves, with different emphases. The letters from Emerson—however great their intrinsic interest—seem an irrelevancy. Curious reticences and reserves obtrude themselves. Well-known matter of central importance seems slurred over or ignored; topics of prime interest are disposed of in a paragraph. Nor does the terminal *Zerlegung* of the character and thought of William James, in a catalog of 'morbid' and 'benign' traits, present itself as growing out of what had gone before. The concluding chapter on the 'four Jameses' into whom Mr. Perry separates the one and only William leaves this reader, at least, with a feeling of a pattern fabricated rather than found, an analysis forced and artificial.

Much of this, I do not doubt, is a consequence, not only of the fact that the book attempts to fuse two unfusable biographical methods, but also, in part, of a deference for the sentiments and opinions of the living, and in part of the fact that Perry's was not the only judgment which entered into the selection and allocation of the material, though it was the decisive one. Perry says that his debt is so great to Henry James and Elizabeth Perkins Aldrich that he 'would name them as joint authors were it not that, having made the ultimate decisions myself, I must, for better or for worse, assume the responsibility.'

One soon recognizes that Mr. Perry has discharged his responsibility with a warmth of feeling, a personal piety for the living William James he knew and remembers, which imparts a certain glow to the four-visaged figure of words his so patiently and industriously assembled 'systematic account' adds up to, and to some degree overcomes his own distorting dissent from pragmatism. Ever and anon the feel of the living man breaks through and translumines also the 'systematic account.' But for the most part, the 'systematic account' beclouds the living man, and in the end, distorts him. 'Abounding and unbounded,' Perry calls him, in a moment of unconscious personal reminiscence. 'James,' he declares, 'transcended his own classifications in the act of creating them. They cannot be used to define his limits but only to prove his manysidedness,' and follows the declaration with a set of classifications of his own which should define the limits that James's cannot. Conceiving his subject as a temperament giving rise to philosophy, the biographer breaks the temperament up into 'benign' traits such as sensibility, vivacity, humanity, sociability; and 'morbid' ones such as hypochondria, hallucination, oscillations of mood, 'pathological repugnance to the processes of exact thought,' and then puts them together again in the four persons of James 'neurasthenic,' James 'radiant,' James simultaneously neurasthenic and radiant, and James the man of the world, experience, discipline, worldly wisdom, taste, breeding, patriotism and moralism, who though 'he wore bright neckties,' nevertheless 'knew his way around.'

That the record is susceptible to such treatment cannot be disputed; everybody's record is. But that the treatment uncovers its subject's inwardness or can lead to a realization of the living man 'in his very figure as he walked' I regard more than doubtful. Of course James had 'oscillations of mood'; of course he was acutely introspective and given to mulling over inner pains and pangs, as well as other 'benignities' and 'morbidities'—those were among the qualities which made him the very great psychologist he was, and allied him to the artists and poets rather than the businessmen and professors. But on the whole and in the long run, to whom, among the philosophical great, would these qualifications not apply? In James's disposition the power of using words at once precisely and suggestively combined with extraordinary delicacy of feeling and perception. He could and did give utterance to what most of us less articulate ones but dumbly suffer. Mr. Perry, I suspect, was, like James's mother, misled by William's unique capacity for precise expression, into a sort of psychological anatomizing that is more pertinent to a Nietzsche than to James. James may have been a neurasthenic with a fondness for bright neckties, but he *did* 'know his way around.' This was because he was so essentially integrated a personality. His traits, 'morbid' and 'benign,' were simply contrasted trends of a self-coherent temperament sharply disciplined to reality even during its 'hypochondriacal' and suicidal youth; in its maturity it certainly communicated nothing so much as the feel of self-possession and balance in its depressed as well as its optimistic moods. James called himself a 'motor' type, and his inner tempo was very noticeably swifter than that of those about him. If he was 'easily bored,' it was because he could bite off and assimilate the entire inwardness of a theme while others were still laboriously chewing at its integuments, because he could 'skip intermediaries' and nevertheless enfold their content. The rapid tempo was nevertheless compatible with indefinitely prolonged interest and effort in chosen fields, and Mr. Perry records how through nearly a score of years this easily bored mind returned again and again to a single problem such as the One and Many until it had solved it to its own satisfaction. Paradoxes of this sort are plentiful in James's record, and to temperaments of a much slower habit they may readily enough lead to inferences of 'morbidity' and the like. The swift mood and method being intrinsically incommensurable with ours, we slower temperaments see its outer polarizations while its inner coherence and stability escapes us.

Our comment, consequently, may impress others as self-contradictory. A major instance of this effect is Mr. Perry's assertion in one place that James 'prefers explanation and achievement to contemplation and imagination,' and in another, that it was a 'metaphysics of vision and insight rather than either activism and positivism which sprang from the ancient root of his thought.' This sort of contradiction can follow readily enough from an unheeding metaphysical assumption that a philosophy of flux must be incompatible with a contemplative attitude and that a rapid inner tempo must be active and practical rather than intuitive and purposeless. Yet the whole Bergsonian philosophy is an example of the contrary, and James's entire disposition and record—his aversion to administration, to laboratories, his indignant rejection of 'the bitch goddess Success,' his preoccupation with matters of the mind and spirit—define him as a scholar in the Aristotelian sense of that term. His whole life was a *skolé,* a life of leisure, a bookish life, contemplative and unbusinesslike, with nothing in it of the administrator, dictator, or manipulator. Mr. Perry's notion that James preferred explanation and achievement to contemplation and imagination is a more or less conscious logical deduction from a confusion of action with tempo; of purposefulness with dramatic *aperçu* of purpose as a development of consequences, of will as effort taken against resistance, and of belief as a selection from alternatives against odds. A less rationalist and somewhat more imaginative and intuitive appreciation of the Jamesian tempo might have made impossible this misreading of his character and disposition. It would be news indeed if it were true, news sensational and strange. It pulls the major features of James's thought and relationships out of drawing. Space does not permit their detailed examination; I will touch only on James's relationship to his father, to Bergson, and to C. S. Peirce, and on his imputed 'alogism.'

A naïve reader, finishing the section entitled 'His Father's Son,' would conclude that except in the vague and subtle ways in which two persons influence each other when they live together, William James took over nothing positive from his father's philosophy except his interest in religion. William himself was unaware of any connection in 1903, and wrote: 'I wish I could see that my philosophy came from my father.' And in 1903 its connections had not yet become apparent. That happened with the formulation of the central thesis of *A Pluralistic Universe.* On the record, there was a very high degree of emotional resemblance and intellectual interdependence of son and father. Both had had to struggle against felt physical disability. That of William James's father turned on the consequences of the loss of a leg as a young boy, and (I have already suggested this in my introductory essay to *The Philosophy of William James,* in the Modern Library Series) the intellectual life of Henry James the Elder became a research after a formula which should compensate for this physical inferiority and overcome its nervous and emotional consequences. In the youthful William James the physical disability took the form of backaches, failures of vision, and other symptoms belonging to a single syndrome. Henry James the Elder was living in a crippled and painful body to which he felt insuperably bound: philosophically this feeling expressed itself in the idea of an indestructible personal identity whose very being was evil; the Calvinist notion of original sin could be its adequate symbol. In 'Society, the Redeemed Form of Man' which in *The Literary Remains of Henry James* William quotes from, Henry tells how he fell into a terror that his horrible identity must continue from everlasting unto everlasting; how he keeps a hold on sanity by repeating psalms to himself; how in the course of time he wins relief from this terror of the sense of selfhood by adapting the teachings of Swedenborg to his own necessities. His adaptation takes the form of a system of philosophy which nullifies the separate personal identity without destroying it, and perfects the imperfections of personal diversity by taking them up into the homogeneity of God, in whom souls remain different but no longer separate, who is the unitary interpenetration of all the differents—a One in whom the Many are dissolved without being abolished. God thus is 'society, the perfected form of man,' realized by a sort of ascent of man from the evil of his separate existence to the perfection of his compenetrated companionship with all men in the unity of God. That the One reabsorbs the Many without abolishing the manyness, is Divine Creation, which thus overcomes evil and establishes good. The symbols with which the father of William James formulated his philosophy are those he had learned from the Princeton theologians and from Swedenborg. Told in that language, the cosmic process consists in the division of the concentrated unity of the Divine Creator into the diversity of his creatures. This diversification Henry James calls 'formation.' The reintegration of the creatures into the Creator without any total loss of their created identities he calls 'creation' or 'redemption.' Evil is individuality, separation, and the distinct, exclusive, or as Bergson would say 'closed,' moral judgments it implies. Good is the recovery of harmony and identity, the attainment of what would be the Bergsonian 'open society' which judges not. Its historical terminus is a free society of liberty, equality, and fraternity of the sort that Proudhon proposed. In sum, the doctrine by which Henry James the Elder accomplished his peace and salvation is one that assimilated the separate identities of this world of appearances into the compenetrated identity of the real world which is God. It removed the curse of remaining forever that deficient and inadequate self whose possible perduration had horrified him.

William James also left a personal record of an experience of terror about his own existence and destiny.[1] At the time a determinist in the sense in which most scientific naturalists were determinists, William's terror of his selfhood was associated with the idea that the laws of nature predestined it to an utter degeneration. To save himself from breaking under the stress of his fear, he repeated Scripture texts as his father had repeated psalms. To the father, the idea of suicide does not seem to have occurred. It did to the son. William reports it to the elder Henry in a letter from Berlin in 1867, and it remains a theme in his thought from then on. He refers to

1. *The Letters of William James.* Edited by his son Henry James. I 145–148.

it in subsequent letters to other correspondents and in his notebook. It is so obviously a component in his basic struggle to save himself that in 1925 I felt constrained to stress it as a force contributing to his philosophy.[2] In Perry's discussion it is conspicuous by its absence. Yet it illumines and clarifies the self-liberation and self-assertion by which James accomplished his inner integration. As that of Henry James the Elder had come *via* an adaptation of Swedenborg, that of William James was attained through an adaptation of Renouvier. By means of Swedenborg Henry James moved from metaphysical pluralism to a metaphysical monism not unlike that of Bergson. Through Renouvier William James moved from a metaphysic of naturalism and determinism to a metaphysic of pluralism and free will, quite unlike that of Bergson. Henry James laid the rule of salvation in acquiescence and self-negation because what he most wanted was to displace that mutilated self of his. William James laid the rule of salvation in self-assertion and struggle because what he most wanted was to affirm and defend his suffering self against the pressure of the world that made him suffer. St. Paul and St. Augustine, with whose experiences Mr. Perry compares James's, offer little in common when one looks at the older Henry's. Moods and events here echo each other for father and son in a startling way.

On the other hand, toward his father's ideas—certainly during his father's lifetime—the young William found himself essentially unsympathetic. The philosophical correspondence between the two printed in the appendix, especially the memorandum, contains William's complete logical refutation of the father's position.

But, significantly, the William of a quarter of a century later apprehends in Bergson's formulation of substantially similar metaphysics in the language not of Christian theology, but biologized philosophy, a release from the very logical difficulties of reconciling the One with the Many that made him reject this philosophy when he knew it as his father's. That which William testifies in *A Pluralistic Universe* to have drawn from Bergson is freedom to believe in the logically self-contradictory idea of a Many that are nevertheless One—though William gave this Oneness a meaning all his own, quite other than Bergson's traditional meaning. For Bergson, as for William's father, absolute separateness, plurality, is the *terminus ad quem* of a self-diversification of God who *is* Creative Evolution; creation is

2. *The Philosophy of William James Drawn from His Own Works.* With an Introduction by Horace M. Kallen. The Modern Library, 23 ff.

in many ways tantamount to a fall of which intellect is the expression and symbol; and from which intuition and insight into the real unity of the apparently diversified life is a redemption. With this metaphysics goes anti-intellectualism, Bergson's 'necessity of transcending concepts or mere logic,' so as to make it possible to accept the idea that the One can be Many and the Many One at one and the same time. And this James was now glad to accept. In most other respects—as any reader of the correspondence between James and Bergson, which Mr. Perry prints, can observe—there are very definite differences, in fact antagonisms, between the systems of the two men. These were muted during the controversy against the traditional absolutisms and rationalisms which dominated the philosophic scene. It is, however, quite clear from Bergson's introduction to *Pragmatism* that he was far from being unaware of them, and from James's frequently repeated statement that there was much in Bergson he did not understand, that he felt incompatibilities which there was no occasion to express. Bergson, like Henry James the Elder, stems from Plotinus and the Christian fathers through Schelling; he also draws much from the Cartesians. James stems from the English empiricists and Renouvier. I have shown in my *William James and Henri Bergson* how profound and inwardly irreconcilable the consequences of these different origins are, and say no more about them here. Not only the father's religious hopes consciously vindicated but also the unconscious survival in James's mind of his father's attitudes and insights and judgments enabled his acceptance of those items of Bergsonism that he did accept.

Always surer of science and of the methods and deliverances of science than to his last day he could be of the revelations and dogmas of religious faith, a measurable proportion of James's philosophic effort went toward equalizing the differences, and securing for belief an equal hearing in the court of free thought. His disputations regarding the will-to-believe, his survey of religious experience, his elaboration of the pragmatic theory of knowledge, all had this interest as a component of their wide-ranging import. But this interest took form as a more or less articulate purpose (*cf.* Perry, I 162–166) only after Henry James the Elder had died, and William had reviewed and restated his father's philosophy in his Introduction to the *Literary Remains of Henry James.* In that Introduction may be observed the seeds of the ideological reconciliation—reconciliation, not identification—as completed as might be, of *A Pluralistic Universe.* The stuff of the philosophic tradition, redirected by perspectives due to the father's philosophy, penetrated without essentially modifying the *aperçus* and the methods drawn from the new evolutionary sciences of life, and on the whole James remained personally undecided between them. All his positive insights are on the side of the sciences and their methods—including those in the field of religion. The genuine religionists—those that hold such compensatory dogmas as the immortality of the soul or the spirituality of the universe to be correct accounts of souls and the universe—depended on James's negations: his arguments upon the limitations of science and the like. In these compensatory dogmas, James himself said many times, he had no *personal* interest. Perry says he came to *believe* in immortality as he grew older (356); but, natural though this is, the evidence is far from convincing. James's innermost emotion and most abiding insight was in the reality of alternatives[3] and thence the fallacy of all foregone conclusions: 'The Pragmatism or pluralism I defend has to fall back on a certain ultimate hardihood, a certain willingness to live without assurances or guarantees.' In the summer of 1910, sick and faced with monitions of the end—James died August 23rd of that year—he ended the last work of his pen, his tribute to Paul Blood, with the words: 'Let *my* last word, then, speaking in the name of intellectual philosophy, be *his* word: "There is no conclusion. What has concluded, that we might conclude in regard to it? There are no fortunes to be told, and there is no advice to be given—Farewell!" '

In the end this meant, morally, a warfare of goods with one another as well as with evil; intellectually, scepticism and that exaltation of direct experience over its 'logical' manipulation which Mr. Perry deprecates as 'alogism' or 'a pathological repugnance to the processes of exact thought.' He declares that 'While James was thus perpetually driven to the processes of exact thought by his desire for clearness and cogency, he was at the same time repelled by a temperamental aversion and distrust; and these feelings, combined with a natural impulse to find metaphysical justification for them, led him to sweeping and extravagant assertions of the irrationality of being.' This assertion impresses me as itself sweeping and irrational. It is true that James was not interested in mathematics. Neither were the medievals who, models of 'exact thought' from the days of Peter the Lombard on, seem to

3. Although *A Pluralistic Universe* states or implies a spiritistic and theological metaphysic, akin to panpsychism, *Some Problems in Philosophy,* as it stands, affirms the 'logical realism' which is the formal or dialectical restatement of radical empiricism, to which panpsychism is a superfluous 'overbelief.' James died without having time to resolve the issue which is representative of his life's debate from the day his father died.

be coming into fashion again. There are exactitudes and exactitudes. Bergson, who was in his day a distinguished mathematician, Bertrand Russell, who is one of the agonists of 'exact thought' in modern dress, F. H. Bradley, who is a paragon among the exact thinkers of the last generation, all make 'sweeping and extravagant assertions of the irrationality of being' which could give James's a handicap. I have myself had a not altogether comfortable experience with James's dislike of 'exact thought' when he flayed me for using it in my doctor's thesis. In the perspective of years I have come entirely to agree with him. What Mr. Perry calls 'exact thought' is a certain technique of handling some form of language where interest in the symbols or the formulae and their manipulation displaces concern about the realities they stand for. James, being a great master of language, found that form of manipulating it a device either for concealing intellectual poverty or for obscuring reality. If he 'renounced logic' and insisted on the irrationality of being, it was on the basis of tens of years of painstaking study both of exact thinkers and their rationalistic systems. His controversy with his father, his arguments during the entire debate over pragmatism, his handling of the One and the Many, show a spontaneous and joyous skill in the logical art which sufficiently refutes Mr. Perry's charge. His *Pragmatism* is itself the essence of a concern to make thought livingly exact. And his exactitude was sufficient in the end to influence exact thinkers like Bertrand Russell and to force Bradley to compromise. After all, it is James's metaphysical insights that the contemporary sciences, with their stress on relativity, uncertainty, contingency, freedom, operational technique, come closest to. It would indicate, as I have shown elsewhere, that James was not against intellect but against intellectualism, that he was concerned to protect the living reason against hypostatic rationalism[4] and empirically-discerned reality against metaphysical rationalization. He was a realist about reason. On Mr. Perry's unuttered premise, Hegel would be an exact thinker, because he invented and employed a barbarous language, and every specialist in the manipulation of logistics would be an exponent of exact thought. So would every chess player and bridge-expert. But what has that to do with reality and our knowledge of it?

I suspect that Mr. Perry is here misled somewhat by his own rationalistic metaphysics. Of course he can invoke C. S. Peirce to back him—though Peirce had no illusions about mathematicians—but it is to be remembered

4. Cf. *The Meaning of Truth* and *The Philosophy of William James,* Chs. II and IV.

that Peirce's relations to James are of a character having certain analogies to James's own relations to his father. I began myself by taking Peirce at James's valuation, but I found as the years passed, and especially with the publication of Peirce's *Nachlass,* that it was partly the authority of William James that imposed this rather over-estimated man, who was an innovator in the extremely limited field of symbolic logic and a traditionalist in metaphysics, on people's minds, and largely the fact that by 'the methods of rigorous thinking' he was able to obscure the obvious and give the simple an effect of profundity. Unhappily, in his personal relations more or less a beneficiary of James's, he could hardly help chafing under this dependence and trying in every possible way to vindicate his personal autonomy. The distinction that he made between 'pragmatism' and 'pragmaticism,' the needless Greek constructions in which he restated the Schelling-like metaphysic of which he was an exponent, his approval of Henry James the Elder's solution of the problem of evil, his epistolary scolding of James, all seem to me parts of the effort of a man down on his luck and somewhat embittered to compensate for his dependency. Here is not the place, nor is this the occasion, to show that James's 'misunderstanding of Peirce' was no misunderstanding at the time it occurred, and that it was made into one as Peirce quite naturally, quite automatically, tried to separate himself from the practically paternal James. Peirce felt that he shone only by James's light and rightly enough wanted to shine by his own. His efforts to do so failed while he was alive, and now that he is dead they succeed only because James's light was first cast upon him. Mr. Perry's tendency to favor Peirce today coheres with the growing formalism of the philosophic *Zeitgeist* here. James would be the last to grudge it, but a somewhat more realistic perspective in this connection is obviously desirable.

There is another topic of some importance, on which I find myself at considerable variance from Mr. Perry. This is the relation of James's thought to Communism and Fascism. I can't help feeling that the discussion of a possible connection between Lenin and pragmatism could well have been omitted. It seems to turn on the references to Mach in Lenin's *Materialism and Empirio-Criticism.* Sidney Hook's brilliant effort to assimilate Marxism to pragmatism is more pertinent. But the whole matter seems rather forced. The case is different with regard to Mussolini and Fascism. Mussolini has invoked James on more than one occasion since he made himself *duce,* and thus started off a not inextensive literature, in some of which Mussolini's possible or actual connection with Sorel and with Papini's Lionardo group and afterwards with *Voce* is a theme of much research and dialectic. Perry draws a speculative structure of relationships upon this and declares that 'there can be no doubt of the broad fact that pragmatism and fascism, as well as bolshevism, hold some ground in common, and that Mussolini had a right to cite James.' To me it is far less doubtful that he had a right to cite Plato, the Bible, Dante, Hammurabi, Marx, Nietzsche, Hearst, and the Perry who wrote the piece on theories and beliefs in the *Harvard Theological Review.* Fascism has more in common with these than it has with the pragmatism of James. The fact that Mussolini 'cited' James did not follow from any knowledge he had of James; it followed from his desire to court American favor. In point of fact he had not read anything whatsoever of James, at least up to the time that he was speaking his name to American journalists. In 1926, when I asked him which of James's works he had read, he showed temper but had no answer.

I must make one more comment before I have done, and that is to regret that Mr. Perry felt it necessary to limit his remarks on the rôle of Mrs. James in the development of William's character and thought to one complimentary paragraph. She was not only the exemplary wife and mother that Perry properly appreciates (Chapter XXI, 375–76); she exercised a very positive intellectual influence in her husband's life. I am inclined to believe that the unconscious redirection of William's thought toward that of Henry the Elder's would scarcely have gone as far as it did without the conscious as well as continuous reaction upon it of Alice James; that her rôle in the mutations of William's thought was far greater than that of many correspondents to whom Perry gives chapters.

With this, I stop. I must not close without again signifying my appreciation of the fine workmanship, the spirit of affection and reverence, and, often, the eloquence, of Mr. Perry's 'systematic account' of the thought and character of William James. A philosophy, he himself recognizes, is something that grows from a temperament; a systematic biography, it may be added, is one temperament reshaped through the qualities, the perspectives, and the prejudices, of another. To mine, the documents, the ideas, the images, and the memories, which are now William James, fall into another pattern. There will be, with time, many such patterns, all different, and all recompositions of practically the same literary material. In their formation Perry's cannot fail to stand as a source and a guide second only in interest and meaning to Henry James's arrangement of the *Letters of William James.*

WALTER LIPPMANN

(1889–1974)

Walter Lippmann entered Harvard in the fall of 1906, with a class whose members included T. S. Eliot, Heywood Broun, and John Reed. Like Reed, Lippmann was an eager young reformer yearning for solutions to the political and social problems of his time. In the spring of 1908, with the help of another freshman who shared his enthusiasm for the international socialist movement, Lippmann established the Harvard Socialist Club and was unanimously elected its president. The members met twice a month to listen to the reading of papers and engage in arguments that frequently continued long into the night. The club, Lippmann asserted, 'represents a new spirit in Harvard student politics. Standing as it does for serious discussion of economic and social problems by undergraduates held together by no other bond than a real interest in the problems, it is a living example of what Harvard most lacks,—voluntary intellectual interest.'[1]

From a core of nine students, the club expanded to fifty members by the fall of 1909 and proved to be an active force on campus, protesting against the exploitation of workers, lobbying for women speakers, and demanding a credit course in socialism. Buoyed by their success at the college, the members became active in local politics as well.

Lippmann's extracurricular activities were not limited to the Socialist Club, however; he also helped found the Social Politics Club, was a member of the Debating Club and the Philosophical Club, and published articles in the *Harvard Illustrated,* which his classmate Hans von Kaltenborn edited.[2] Among his many readers was William James, who praised Lippmann's attack on Barrett Wendell's *The Privileged Classes,* which appeared in *Harvard Illustrated* in 1908. Lippmann was deeply offended at Wendell's assertion that the real privileged class in America was the working poor: 'It is the laboring class which is asserting privilege in its most dangerous form to-day, and its aggressions are symbolized to Mr. Wendell by the laborer in an electric car, who, returning from work, spreads his knees apart, and usurps more than his share of the seat.'[3] Wendell was afraid of socialism and preferred, Lippmann said, 'to regalvanize eighteenth-century ideals.'[4] Lippmann himself saw socialism as the great hope of the twentieth century.

Beginning in 1908, Lippmann and James met weekly for morning tea at James's home. Their first conversation, Lippmann wrote to his mother, was 'the greatest thing that has happened to me in my college life.'[5] He found James's philosophical pragmatism congruent with his own conviction that individuals could make large and lasting changes in society; and, like so many other students, he was flattered by James's earnest attention to his ideas. Not only James, but Münsterberg, Edwin Holt, and especially George Santayana caused Lippmann to shift his concentration to philosophy. When Lippmann decided to continue his studies to earn a master's degree, he served as Santayana's teaching assistant and sometimes as his companion, accompanying him to dinners with colleagues and friends. Lippmann found himself drawn to Santayana's philosophy, even though Santayana's idealism seemed irreconcilable with James's pluralism. 'I love James more than any very great man I ever saw,' Lippmann wrote to Bernard Berenson years after he had left Harvard, 'but increasingly I find Santayana inescapable.'[6]

Nevertheless, Lippmann's affection for James is clearly evident in this brief memoir, published in *Everybody's Magazine* a few months after James died. Lippmann had been writing for *Everybody's* at the request of his friend Lincoln Steffens, who had joined its editorial staff in 1909. In fact, Steffens submitted Lippmann's memoir under his own name, revealing the true authorship only after the piece was typeset.[7]

Lippmann's articles for *Everybody's* were the beginning of a prolific career as a journalist. In the fall of 1913 he joined the staff of the *New Republic*, whose first issue appeared on November 7, 1914. Also in 1913 he published his first book, *A Preface to Politics*. Among his other works are *The Stakes of Diplomacy* (1915), *Public Opinion* (1922), *A Preface to Morals* (1929), *The Good Society* (1937), and *Essays in the Public Philosophy* (1955).

NOTES

1. Walter Lippmann, 'Socialism at Harvard,' *Harvard Illustrated Magazine* March 1909: 139.

2. Ronald Steel, *Walter Lippmann and the American Century* (Boston: Little, Brown, 1980), 25.

3. Walter Lippmann, 'The Privileged Classes: A Reply,' *Harvard Illustrated Magazine* November 1908: 54.

4. Lippmann, 'The Privileged Classes,' 56.

5. Quoted in Steel, *Walter Lippmann*, 17.

6. Quoted in Steel, *Walter Lippmann*, 21.

7. Steel, *Walter Lippmann*, 38–39.

An Open Mind: William James

Within a week of the death of Professor William James of Harvard University, the newspapers had it that Mr. M. S. Ayer of Boston had received a message from his spirit. This news item provoked the ridicule of the people who don't believe in ghosts, but the joke was on Mr. Ayer of Boston. When, however, it was reported that Professor James himself had agreed to communicate with this world, if he could, and, in order to test the reports, had left a sealed message to be opened at a certain definite time after his death, the incredulous gasped at the professor's amazing 'credulity.'

William James wasn't 'credulous.' He was simply open-minded. Maybe the soul of man *is* immortal. The professors couldn't prove it wasn't, so James was willing to open his mind to evidence. He was willing to hunt for evidence, and to be convinced by it.

And in that he was simply keeping America's promise: he was actually doing what we, as a nation, proclaimed that we would do. He was tolerant; he was willing to listen to what seems preposterous, and to consider what might, though queer, be true. And he showed that this democratic attitude of mind is every bit as fruitful as the aristocratic determination to ignore new and strange-looking ideas. James was a democrat. He gave all men and all creeds, any idea, any theory, any superstition, a respectful hearing.

His interest in spiritualism is merely one illustration in a thousand. The hard scientists knew it was a hoax because they couldn't explain it, and the sentimentalists knew it was the truth because they wished it to be: but James wanted to know the facts. So he went to Mrs. Piper, and heard her out. Nay, he listened to Palladino and to Münsterberg. They pretended to know, and maybe they did.

And last year, when Frank Harris published his book on Shakespeare, to show that the 'unknown' life and character of the poet could be drawn from his works, the other professors laughed the theory out of court. James went to Shakespeare and read the plays all over again to test the Harris theory. Maybe the poet *could* be known by his works. The fact that the theory was revolutionary did not alter the possibility that it might be true.

So with religion. A scientist, living in an age when science is dogmatically irreligious, he turned from its cocksure reasoning to ask for the facts. He went to the lives of the saints! Not to Herbert Spencer, you see. When he wanted to study the religious experience he went to the people who had had it, to Santa Theresa and Mrs. Eddy. They might know something the professors didn't know.

And again: at the age of sixty-five with the whole of New England's individualism behind him, he asked about socialism. When he met H. G. Wells, he listened to the socialist, and, as it happens, was converted. So he said so. James was no more afraid of a new political theory than he was of ghosts, and he was no more afraid of proclaiming a new theory, or an old one, than he was of being a ghost. I think he would have listened with an open mind to the devil's account of heaven, and I'm sure he would have heard him out on hell.

James knew that he didn't know. He never acted upon the notion that the truth was his store of wisdom. Perhaps that is why he kept on rummaging about in other people's stores, and commending their goods. He seemed to take a delight in writing introductions, and appreciations of new books, and in going out of his way to listen to a young doctor of philosophy, or an undergraduate discussion of pragmatism, or the poetry of an obscure mystic. And, optimist that he was, by virtue of his unceasing freshness of interest, there is nothing more open-minded in our literature than his chivalrous respect for the pessimism of Francis Thompson.

> 'Speak not of comfort where no comfort is,
> Speak not at all: can words make foul things fair?
> Our life's a cheat, our death a black abyss:
> Hush and be mute, envisaging despair.'

He felt with all sorts of men. He understood their demand for immediate answers to the great speculative questions of life. God, freedom, immortality, nature as moral or non-moral—these were for him not matters of idle scientific wonder, but of urgent need. The scientific demand that men should wait 'till doomsday, or till such time as our senses and intellect working together may have raked in evidence enough' for answers to these questions, is, says James, 'the queerest idol ever manufactured in the philosophic cave.' We cannot wait for a final solution. Our daily life is full of choices that we cannot dodge, and some guide we simply must have. There can be no loitering at the crossroads. We are busy. We must choose, whether we will it or not, and where all is doubt, who shall refuse us the right to believe what seems most adapted to our needs? Not know, you understand, but believe.

That is the famous position taken in 'The Will to Believe.' As James has since pointed out, its real title should have been 'The Right to Believe.' No doctrine in James's thinking has been more persistently misunderstood. Yet it rests on the simplest of insights: that atheism and theism are both dogmas, for there is scientific evidence for neither; that to withhold judgment is really to make a judgment, and act as if God didn't exist; that until the evidence is complete men have a right to believe what they most need.

James has acted upon that right. He has made a picture compounded of the insights of feeling, the elaborations of reason, and the daily requirements of men. It is a huge guess, if you like, to be verified only at the end of the world. But it has made many men at home in the universe. And this democrat understood the need of feeling at home in the world, and he understood also that the aristocrats are not at home here. (Perhaps that's why they are aristocrats.) 'The luxurious classes,' he says, 'are blind to man's real relation to the globe he lives on, and to the permanently hard and solid foundations of his higher life.' And he prescribed for them—for their culture, I mean—this treatment: 'To coal and iron mines, to freight trains, to fishing fleets in December, to dishwashing, clotheswashing and windowwashing, to road-building and tunnel-making, to foundries and stoke-holes, and to the frames of skyscrapers, would our gilded youths be drafted off according to their choice, to get the childishness knocked out of them, and to come back into society with healthier sympathies and soberer ideas.'

This, and thoughts like this, and kindnesses like this, put James not alone among the democrats of this uncertain world, but among the poets also; among the poetic philosophers who, like Goethe, Schopenhauer, and Whitman, have a sense of the pace of things. Sunlight and stormcloud, the subdued busyness of outdoors, the rumble of cities, the mud of life's beginning and the heaven of its hopes, stain his pages with the glad, sweaty sense of life itself.

It is an encouraging thought that America should have produced perhaps the most tolerant man of our generation. It is a stimulating thought that he was a man whose tolerance never meant the kind of timidity which refuses to take a stand 'because there is so much to be said on both sides.' As every one knows, he fought hard for his ideas, because he believed in them, and because he wanted others to believe in them. The propagandist was strong in William James. He wished to give as well as receive. And he listened for truth from anybody, and from anywhere, and in any form. He listened for it from Emma Goldman, the pope, or a sophomore; preached from a pulpit, a throne, or a soap-box; in the language of science, in slang, in fine rhetoric, or in the talk of a ward boss.

And he told his conclusions. He told them, too, without the expert's arrogance toward the man in the street, and without the dainty and finicky horror of being popular and journalistic. He would quote Mr. Dooley on God to make himself understood among men. He would have heard God gladly in the overalls of a carpenter, even though He came to preach that the soul of man is immortal. So open-minded was he; so very much of a democrat.

GILBERT KEITH CHESTERTON

(1874–1936)

During his trip to Stanford University early in 1906, James read G. K. Chesterton's latest book, *Heretics,* and was much impressed. He immediately recommended the book to his friend Canning Schiller.[1] And he quickly sent a note of praise to Chesterton himself: 'I have just read your Heretics and cannot withhold my word of applause. You certainly do know how to hit truth in the pit of the stomach and bring it down. And what straight writing! Only beware of letting flat contradiction become a "mannerism" in your old age. You, of all men, can afford to speak classically and without exaggeration. Keep it up.'[2]

Heretics was an important work for Chesterton, a declaration of the political and social criticism to which he would devote much energy for the rest of his life. When he was twenty-one Chesterton left Slade Art School to begin a career as a writer. His first works, however, reflect the ambiguity of his professional identity: at the same time that he published book reviews, poems (*Greybeards at Play* and *The Wild Knight* were two early poetry collections), and literary criticism (*Robert Browning*), he also contributed articles to the London *Daily News* and, in 1905, began a weekly column for the *Illustrated London News,* where his memoir of James appeared.

In *Heretics,* Chesterton combined his interests in literary and social criticism to set out some important premises. He believed, he said, that a writer's underlying philosophy must be taken into account when we read his works. 'We have a general view of existence, whether we like it or not,' he wrote; 'it alters, or, to speak more accurately, it creates and involves everything we say or do, whether we like it or not. If we regard the Cosmos as a dream, we regard the Fiscal Question as a dream. . . . Every man in the street must hold a metaphysical system, and hold it firmly.'[3] Chesterton's acknowledgement of subjectivity and his democratic affirmation of wide access to a 'metaphysical system' echoed James's own thinking. In fact, James alluded to *Heretics* in the opening paragraphs of his first lecture on *Pragmatism*, citing Chesterton's remark that 'the most practical and important thing about a man is still his view of the universe.' James acknowledged that each of his listeners had a particular perspective on the world 'only partly got from books; it is our individual way of just seeing and feeling the total push and pressure of the cosmos.'[4] Both men agreed that anyone who constructs a system to explain and portray reality—whether that system is expressed in fiction or philosophy or simply in street-corner conversation—necessarily reflects personal needs, past experiences, and, in general, psychological disposition.

Despite James's enthusiasm for Chesterton, the two men did not continue to correspond. They met once, when Chesterton was living in Rye, England, where Henry James also lived. In his autobiography, Chesterton characterized Henry James as speaking 'with an air which I can only call gracefully groping; that is not so much groping in the dark in blindness as groping in the light in bewilderment, through seeing too many avenues and obstacles.'[5] When William visited Henry, the two men called on Chesterton, who noticed a 'fantastic contrast' between them: 'Henry James talked about toast and teacups with the impressiveness of a family ghost; while William James talked about the metabolism and involution of values with the air of a man recounting his flirtations on the steamer.'[6]

Chesterton believed that James had managed to construct a philosophical scheme 'out of fine shades and doubtful cases,' and he felt that pragmatism failed as a philosophy precisely because 'it is a cosmos made out of odds and ends,' rather than a system that could claim to be universal.[7] By the time Chesterton reached this conclusion he had taken a far different direction than James had expected in 1906.

Reacting against what he saw as a breakdown of moral values in the modern world, Chesterton increasingly was drawn to the tenets of Catholicism. The man who had disparaged systems became someone who declared that 'there are only two things that really progress; and they both accept accumulations of authority. . . . The first is strictly physical science. The second is the Catholic Church.'[8] In 1922 he became a convert to Roman Catholicism.

NOTES

1. WJ to F. C. S. Schiller. Scott, 395 (16 January 1906).
2. WJ to G. K. Chesterton. Scott, 396 (17 January 1906).
3. G. K. Chesterton, *Heretics* (New York: John Lane, 1905), 301.
4. William James, *Pragmatism* (Cambridge: Harvard University Press, 1975), 9.
5. G. K. Chesterton, *Autobiography* (London: Hutchinson, 1969 [1936]), 218.
6. G. K. Chesterton, *The Common Man* (New York: Sheed & Ward, 1950), 31.
7. Chesterton, *The Common Man*, 32.
8. Chesterton, *The Ball and the Cross* (Philadelphia: Dufour, 1963 [1910]), 96.

The Philosophy of William James
September 17, 1910

No one who met the late Professor William James even for a moment will fail to find some note of mourning for him of a personal as well as a public kind. He was full of those particular fine qualities that most people do actually find in Americans, though most people are surprised to find them. He was full of enthusiasm, of generous appreciation, of spirituality and simplicity. There are no men less prone than Americans to a mere materialism; indeed, their fault is quite the other way. In so far as America has really worshipped money, it has not been because money is tangible. Rather it has been because money is intangible; and Americans cultivate it always in its least tangible form—in the form of shares, trusts, promises, implicit understandings, and illegal powers. They worship the invisible strength of money; they adore it as a sort of airy magic; no men on the earth think less of the actual pleasures that it stands for. The Yankee millionaire likes adding more noughts on to a figure in his private books; it is a spiritual pride with him. Nothing can make him see that, in adding noughts, he is truly and indeed adding nothings. Thus, even when the American is avaricious, the American is not greedy. And when he is the reverse of avaricious, when he is, like Professor James, naturally magnanimous and idealistic, he is capable of being the most childishly unworldly and even saintly of all the white men of this world. William James was really a turning-point in the history of our time, and he had all that sincerity and intellectual innocence that is needed in such a pivot. For a turning-point, like any other point, must be simple and indivisible.

Like Bernard Shaw and others among the intelligences of our unrestful age, William James will probably be counted valuable rather for a revolution in the mode of teaching than for any of the actual things he taught.

Of course, he himself cared more for his dogmas than for his art of exposition, because he was a capable and healthy man. One cannot teach a truth clearly if one is actually thinking about the teaching and not about the truth. There, as elsewhere, the pure theory of art for art's sake must be abandoned; it is only because Rembrandt really tried to embody the old woman that the old woman has managed to embody Rembrandt. But whatever they were for James himself, James's doctrines are scarcely of so much value to the world as his spirited and satisfying style and temper. What Mr. Bernard Shaw did for the discussion of economics and politics Professor James did for the discussion of psychology and metaphysics. He forced them to join the undignified dance of common-sense; he insisted that the philosopher should have modesty enough to make a fool of himself, like the rest of mankind. Everyone is some sort of psychologist, since everyone has some sort of psychology. Just as real religion concerns everyone born with a heart, so real philosophy concerns everyone born with a head. According to Professor James, psychology was a kind of surgery in which each man must be content to be both the operator and the patient; every man must dig up his own soul like his own garden. But it was above all in his eyes a solid study. Economics is not really the study of tables and statistics which are more remote than money; it is the study of bread, which is more actual than money. So in the highest philosophy only the actual is important, and a truth is more of a fact than a phenomenon.

This practical plea of James for popularising philosophy is his finest achievement. It is always supposed that metaphysics must be full of technical and elaborate terms. Some would even argue that the word metaphysics itself is not one to be used playfully in the nearest pot-house. But, for all that, the ultimate study of thought and of the mind ought to be the simplest of all studies; not, I mean, simple in its task, but perfectly simple in its language. If we say something of universal scope we can obviously say it as easily of a plain or comic thing as of any other thing. Technical terms belong to the study of special physical facts—birds or beasts, or stars or stones, or weather. If somebody (with a turn for original observations) remarks that one swallow does not make a summer, that is a matter depending on special study of such seasons and birds. There are some seventeen swallows in the neighbourhood of my house, and some gloomy persons are of opinion that seventeen swallows have not succeeded in making a summer.

But merely the truth, whatever it is, is one only applicable to the particular bird and season. It could throw no light, for example, upon the fascinating problem of whether one Polar bear would make a winter. Natural History must be unnatural to the extent of using scientific and almost secret terms. So if the scientists choose to call the swallow *hirundo vulgaris*[1] (or whatever they do call it) and if they choose to call making a summer 'aestivation,' I think they are cheeky, but within their rights. But I object to their using this mysterious language when they are not talking about whether one swallow makes a summer, but only about whether one swallow makes two swallows. Abstract truths like logic and mathematics can obviously be illustrated as well by common examples as by abstruse ones. And I object to the man who gives the Latin name for the most recently discovered bean-plant when he is only engaged in proving how many beans make five. If two sides of a triangle are always greater than the third side (and all this I steadfastly believe) it can be proved from three-cornered hats or three-cornered tarts. I object to that fastidious mathematician who refuses to prove it except from the two secret triangles of the pentacle.

When full allowance has been made for his healthy and human reversal of the tone and methods of philosophy, it will appear even more regrettable that the actual system (or denial of system) with which Professor James later associated his name, was of the insufficient sort that it was. It was his glory that he popularised philosophy. It was his destruction that he popularised his own philosophy. 'Pragmatism is bosh,' said a man of unphilosophic training but good general brains to me the other day. Professor James appealed to the ordinary man; and the ordinary man condemned him. But let us remember that while this exhibits the rightness of the condemnation, it also exhibits the rightness of the appeal. Pragmatism *is* bosh; but the best test of this is the test of the great Pragmatist himself; the appeal to the nature and reason of the ordinary man. Pragmatism substantially means that the sun being useful is the same thing as the sun being there. The ordinary man in London in this present romantic summer would immediately reply that there is a considerable difference between the two ideas; that the sun is frequently not there when he would be particularly useful. The ordinary man in Arabia would probably add that he is often there when he is quite the reverse of useful. And it is not sufficient for the Pragmatist to reply that these are cheap and illiterate answers: they are. But the whole

1. The more frequently used term is *hirundo rusticae.*

point of Pragmatism (at least, of Professor James's Pragmatism, of Pragmatism at its best) is that it asks how ordinary people do actually use and feel ideas. Now ordinary people do actually feel the notion of truth and the notion of utility as utterly separate. The highest official figure of modern Europe happens to be a man of peasant origin; and his view of Pragmatism (other issues apart) would be echoed by all the peasants of the earth.

ANONYMOUS

This unsigned memoir appeared in *The Atlantic Monthly* in 1919, recalling a brief encounter between James and a little girl who happened to be vacationing at the same hotel. The friendship, if we may call it that, lasted about two weeks. Yet decades later, James's young friend remembered vividly 'the glow he left in my spirit. It lasted, that glow, a very long time. Indeed, it has never quite gone from me.'

She speaks for many of the writers in this collection, and for many more who never recorded their friendships with James. James, they testify, had a special quality that excited, energized, and buoyed the spirits of those who knew him. 'None of us will ever see a man like William James again,' John Jay Chapman wrote, 'there is no doubt about that. And yet it is hard to state what it was in him that gave him either his charm or his power, what it was that penetrated and influenced us, what it is that we lack and feel the need of' (p.53). From this memoir, and others in this collection, we can begin to understand the qualities that so endeared him to his friends. He was, said James Jackson Putnam, 'a manly and a radiant being. Loving and loved, he made all men think, and helped many a doubting soul to feel a man's glow of hope and courage, each for his own work. This was a noble task' (p.26).

William James: A Belated Acknowledgment

Long, oh, very long, ago,—as long ago as when I was eight years old,—my family betook itself for a part of the summer to a certain modest hotel on Cape Ann. (It was the only hotel which that stretch of the Cape then boasted, and it stood in the midst of a green and rocky wilderness. Ah, me!) I was the eldest child and, unlike my small brother and sister, I 'came to the table.' My instructions were, not to speak there unless I was spoken to—a really distressing prohibition for a little girl 'as sociable as Montaigne,' whose sociability was rarely suppressed at home. And alas! nobody did speak to me for days. We sat, my mother and I (my father came down only for the Sundays), at the side of the long board; beyond her, a line of people with some of whom she chatted pleasantly through breakfast, dinner, and supper; but beyond unlucky little me, only a line of empty chairs. Chairs empty, at least, until, one never-to-be-forgotten mid-day, there slipped into the one next me a being who, at my first glance, made upon me an indelible impression.

He looked like no one I had ever seen before; he looked, though I did n't know that was it, foreign. He was very slender, his clothes were of an entrancing, unfamiliar cut, he had a little pointed beard, he wore a soft, flowing, blue-and-green-plaid necktie, its bows and ends outside his waistcoat. He had—child as I was, I instantly felt it—an 'air.' Here indeed was excitement! Oh, if *he* would only speak to me!—But at first he only ate his dinner—I need hardly say that in that time and place the midday meal was dinner. Then, all at once, my attention was distracted even from him by a thrilling discovery. I was eating green corn and I had just finished my ear. 'Why!'—I lifted up my voice, rules and regulations thrown to the winds—'Why! I've found out something. *Every ear of corn has an even number of rows.*'

An admonitory glance from my mother. But I *could* not hold my peace.

'But it's *so!* It *must* be. *I always butter two at a time, and I never have any left over.*'

'Well, well, dear, never mind.' My mother was only half attending. 'We don't want to hear about it now.'

'But is n't it *so? Is n't* it?'

'Oh, I don't know, dear; I don't believe it is. At any rate, mother wants you to be quiet now. Wait till after dinner.'

Then—oh, then—a champion rode into the lists! Up spoke my wonderful neighbor.

'Excuse me, madam, but the little girl is right. Every ear of corn *has* an even number of rows.'

O joy, O rapture, O triumph beyond compare!

'Dear me!' My mother changed her tune. 'Has it really? How interesting!'

And thereupon ensued a conversation in which, thanks to my new friend,—a friend I felt him to be, even then,—I was not only included but 'featured.'

After dinner word went round that the new arrival was Mr. William James, recently returned from Paris and now an instructor at Harvard.

Mr. James and I established forthwith an intimacy—at least, it felt like intimacy to *me*—which lasted as long as he stayed. How long that was, I don't know. The period bulks so largely in my memory that it seems as if it might have been months; but I dare say it was no more than a fortnight or so. At all events, it 'made' my summer.

Not only at table did my friend and I converse. The beach, the cranberry marsh, a certain woodsy nook with a hammock in it: all these I remember as the scenes of confabulation with him. There must have been some understanding between him and my mother about it all. Otherwise I should never have been permitted so to 'tag' him. 'Don't let my little girl annoy you, Mr. James.'—'Oh, she does n't annoy me at all.' I like to think that that was the way of it. Possibly he went so far as to say, 'She interests me,' or even, 'I enjoy her.' At any rate, it does me good to think he did and so I am going to think so. That is pragmatism, is n't it?

It *was* at table, though, that the pragmatist-to-be most egged me on to chatter. (And, as will have been apparent, egging on was the last thing I required.) I suspect this was partly to tease my mother. Most likely the two were having their fun over my head. Anyhow, I was incited to some startling deliverances. Once, apropos of I forget what, Mr. James asked me, quite gravely, how many languages I spoke. My reply came without a moment's hesitation: 'Three.'

On which my mother told me not to talk nonsense. But Mr. James ignored her.

'Three, eh? Dear me, that's a good many for a little girl. What are they?'

'English, French, and hog-Latin.' Had I not had, that very spring, half-a-dozen French lessons out of a little yellow primer? And as for hog-Latin, the reader must surely remember 'what-gery that-gery was-gery.'

'Well,' said my friend, 'that certainly seems to be three. And so you speak French. Could you speak a little for me? Perhaps you know some French poetry.'

'I do.'

'Won't you say some?'

I promptly obliged with a recitation. How must my accent have struck upon the ear of the quondam dweller in Paris!

> Sois toujours comme la violette,
> Aussi modeste et aussi nette.
> Sois toujours pieuse, sois toujours bonne.
> C'est Dieu qui te voit, si tu n'es vu de personne.

I did not deem it necessary to mention that these lines comprised my entire *repertoire* of French 'poetry.'

Our best, our most penetrating talks, however, came off in *solitude à deux*. I recall one in particular. Mr. James is established in the hammock under the pines; I sit on the ground—at his feet literally as well as metaphorically. Across his knees lies a thin piece of board, and on it the gruesome remains of a frog. (He got the frog out of the cranberry-marsh. I was going along the path at the edge of the marsh, and I saw him—Mr. James, not the frog—springing from tuft to tuft over in the wet part. He had a tin pail and I called out, 'Are you going berrying?' But he shook his head.) He is doing things—deft, swift things—to the batrachian relics, with some bright little instruments, which he takes out of a small black-leather case. I look on, shrinking but fascinated. I have no faintest notion why anybody should want to kill a frog and cut it up; it seems cruel and horrid; but if Mr. James does it, it must be all right somehow.

Of the conversation there under the pine trees, no word remains with me, but its impress on my mind and spirit has proved permanent. In language suited to my understanding, the anatomist explained what he was doing and why he was doing it, and went on to tell and to show me things of absorbing interest, about frogs. And so I got—from William James!—my first glimpses into the wonder-worlds of physiology and psychology.

We presently passed to a discussion of my ambitions, of what I was going to be and do when I grew up. Of one thing I was certain: I was going to college. (Only a little while before, my imagination had been fired by hearing, for the first time, about girls going to college.) Mr. James said, well, I had better come to Harvard; they didn't let girls into Harvard now, but he thought they would by the time I wanted to come. Would *he* be there then? I asked. Yes, he guessed he would. And if I would let him know when I was ready, he would try to get me in. I straightway visualized an imposing edifice with a great door which my friend swung back while I, with head held high and his kind eyes upon me, passed through into the mysteries and glories of 'college.' And ever since that summer afternoon, this picture has risen before me oftener and more vividly than any of the scenes in which I actually beheld Mr. James.

Curiously enough, I remember nothing of the parting with my friend. I remember only the glow he left in my spirit. It lasted, that glow, a very long time. Indeed, it has never quite gone from me.

I never saw William James again. I was always expecting to encounter him

> . . . round some corner in the streets of life.

Once, after tarrying a week in a certain small hotel, I learned that for the first two days of my stay he had been under the same roof, had sat only a few yards away from me in the dining-room; and at the moment, I was inconsolable over having so narrowly missed him. But perhaps, after all, it was as well. Perhaps it is as well that we did not meet again at all; and that so there is no later impression to blur the image in my mind of the slender, upright figure, with the little pointed beard and the soft blue-and-green-plaid necktie, setting open for me, with a quick, free gesture, that massive, magic portal.

INDEX